72125170   15.75

7/8

WITHDRAWN

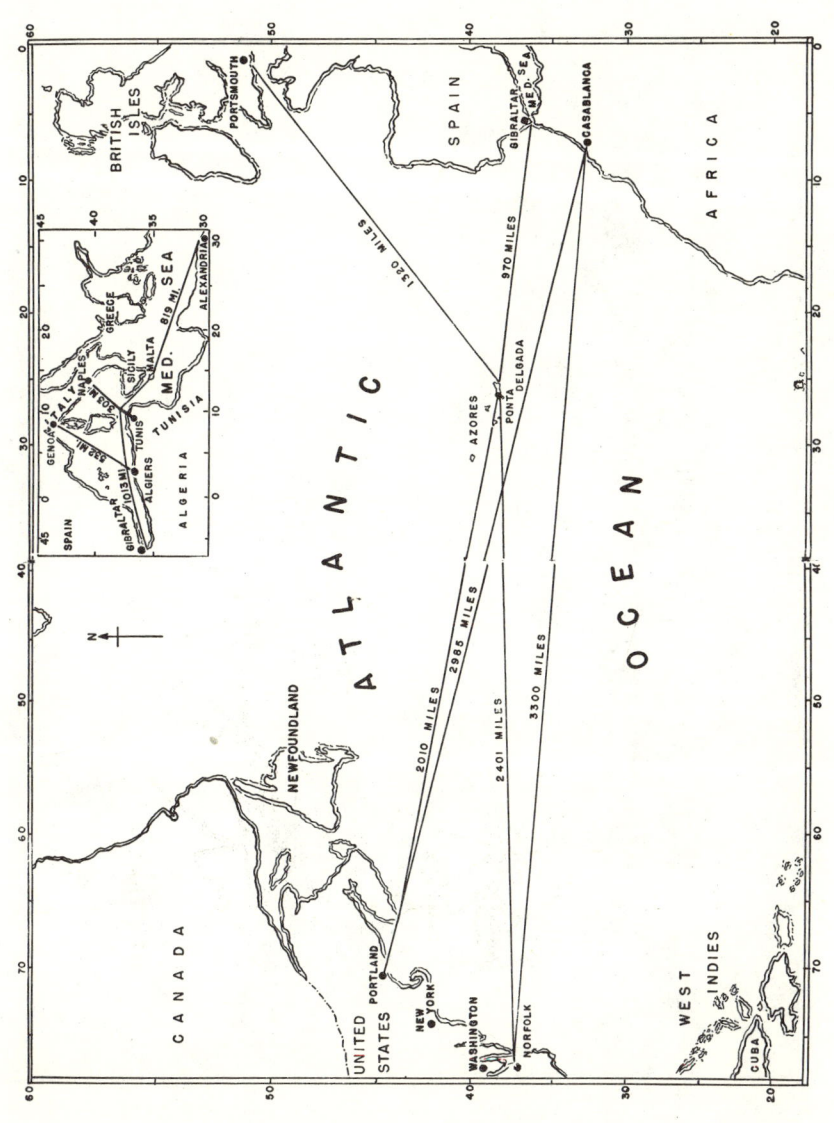

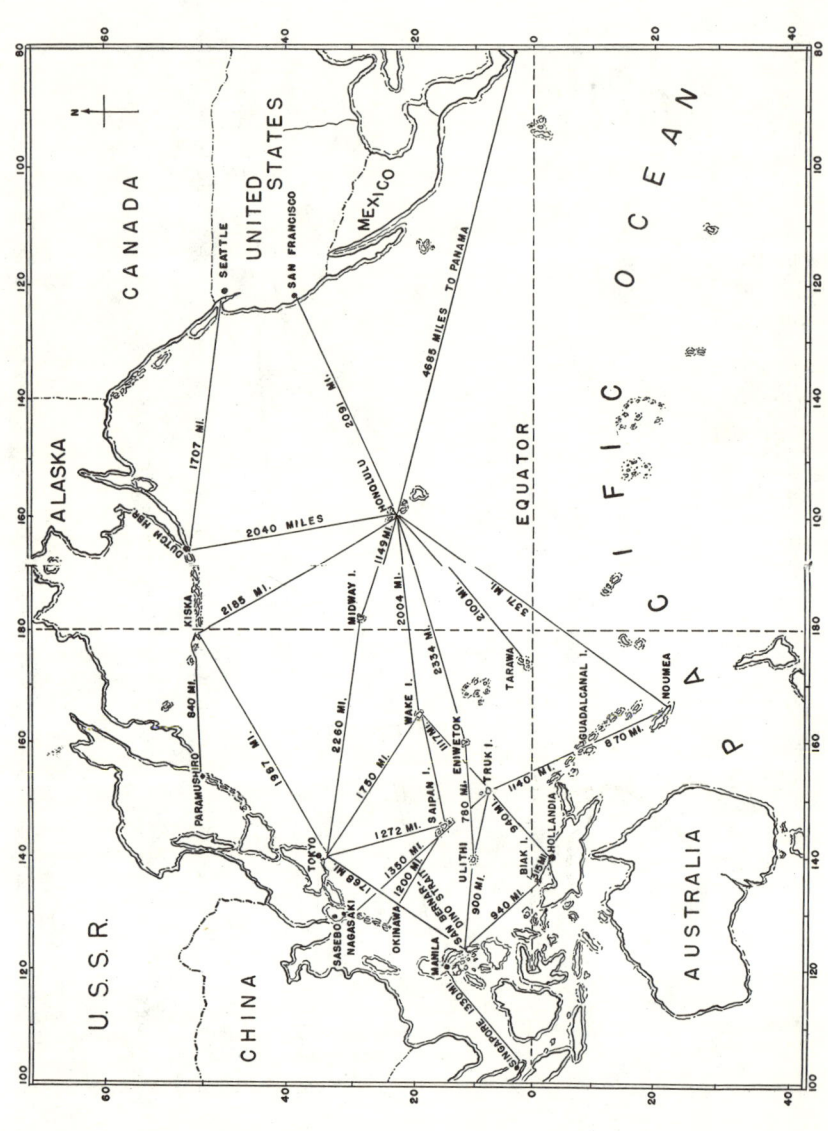

THE INFLUENCE OF SEA POWER IN WORLD WAR II

By

CAPTAIN W. D. PULESTON
U.S.N. (RETIRED)

GREENWOOD PRESS, PUBLISHERS
WESTPORT, CONNECTICUT

Copyright 1947 by W. D. Puleston

Originally published in 1947
by Yale University Press, New Haven and
Oxford University Press, London

Reprinted with the permission
of Yale University Press

First Greenwood Reprinting 1970

Library of Congress Catalogue Card Number 71-104248

SBN 8371-3997-X

Printed in the United States of America

To the workers who supplied and the regulars and reserves who manned the ships and planes of the United States Navy.

Preface

IN HIS books and essays Mahan[1] demonstrated the influence of sea power from 1660 up to the first World War. And before his death in December, 1914, he predicted that sea power would be the decisive factor in that war. The purpose of this book is to examine the influence of sea power on the second World War and the future of sea power in the atomic era. An earnest effort has been made to ascertain and give full weight to other factors influencing the course of the last World War, because only as sea power is viewed in its proper relationship to other attributes of great nations can it be properly evaluated and its true influence revealed. For example, there is no doubt that the Russian armies made an enormous contribution to victory; but it is also true that Great Britain and the United States, through their control of the seas, were able in 1942 to furnish Russia with arms and equipment essential to the maintenance of the Red armies, and that this same control of the sea simultaneously denied strategic supplies to the Axis Powers.

This is not a narrative history of the war, nor a critique of its naval operations. This work is primarily concerned with the objectives of the political leaders who headed the Axis and anti-Axis nations, and with the strategies used by their admirals, generals, and air marshals to attain these objectives by the use of land, sea, and air forces. The book endeavors to show the consequences of sea and land campaigns rather than the tactics of battles; it is particularly concerned with how the sea and land campaigns influenced and were influenced by control of the sea, and especially with how control of the sea was employed to gain control of the land and impose unconditional surrender upon the Axis nations.

1. Captain Alfred Thayer Mahan, U.S.N., author of *The Influence of Sea Power upon History, 1660–1783*; *The Influence of Sea Power upon the French Revolution and Empire, 1793–1812*; *Sea Power in Its Relation to the War of 1812*; and numerous essays.

PREFACE

In developing the subject, the writer has summarized Mahan's thesis in Chapter I and has assumed that it could be accepted up to 1914. The second and third chapters show the influence of sea power during World War I and how sea power influenced, and was influenced by, events between 1919 and 1939. The main task is then undertaken—to reveal the extent and limitations of sea power during the struggle which began in Poland and ended in Germany and Japan. If the task is completed successfully and convincingly, this book may be regarded as a postscript to the volumes of Mahan.

It is of course impossible to dogmatize about the future. However, there must be some effort to see ahead so that measures can be taken to safeguard the nation. Predictions based on past experience and the likely course of future scientific developments cannot be exact; but they are better than uninformed conjectures. A statesman who can see even a short distance into the future is better prepared than one who merely awaits events or consults a soothsayer. The last chapter of this book is written more in the hope of stimulating thought about American sea power in the coming atomic era than of precisely forecasting its development.

If it turns out that the atomic bomb has ended the influence of sea power, this volume will have described it at its zenith, when it saved one island empire, Great Britain, and destroyed another, Japan; when it succored one great land empire, Russia, and struck down another, Germany. If World War II marks the end of the influence of sea power, which the author does not believe, never has so persistent an influence on human history reached such transcendent power and then passed so swiftly into oblivion.

The data used in the text have been obtained wherever possible from official sources. Interrogations of German, Italian, and Japanese officials have furnished a mass of information about the strength, disposition, and plans of the armed forces of the enemy. Many of the direct and indirect quotations in the book are taken from the testimony of captured Japanese officials in interrogations conducted by the United States Strategic Bombing Survey [Pacific]

PREFACE ix

and published in two volumes entitled *Interrogations of Japanese Officials.* Testimony of prisoners, many of them in jeopardy of their lives, had to be weighed carefully; fortunately in practically every important respect it could be checked against documents written when the enemy plans were being drawn up. In addition many of the prominent participants have given their reasons for their actions; and throughout the war the enemy nations made regular broadcasts to their own people, shedding further light upon Axis plans and motives. It is certain that further information will be uncovered in the future, but it is extremely doubtful whether the main facts of the causes and conduct of the last war will be greatly changed.

Data on the British and Italian Navies have been taken from *Brassey's Naval Annual,* with the permission of its editor, Rear Admiral H. G. Thursfield, who also authorized the use of his *Calendar of the Naval War.* Use of information compiled in these authoritative publications was most helpful and is a pleasure to acknowledge. Data on the German Navy and its conduct of the U-boat war were taken in part from materials written by Grand Admiral Doenitz. These were supplemented by information from other sources, including a statement by Rear Admiral Weichold.

Ample information from Japanese sources exists concerning their naval and air forces and the various plans made by the Naval Staff and the Imperial General Staff to defeat the United States Army and Navy. Service journals of the United States Army and Navy, usually the *Naval Institute Proceedings, The Infantry Journal,* and *The Cavalry Journal,* have been used to supplement information on American plans. The main source for American naval plans and policies has been official accounts, notably those of Secretary Frank Knox and Secretary James Forrestal, and Fleet Admiral E. J. King's official reports to the President. I wish to express my appreciation of the encouragement which Secretary Forrestal, Fleet Admirals King and Nimitz, Admiral R. A. Spruance, Admiral F. J. Horne, General A. A. Vandergrift, United States Marines, and many others gave me in the preparation of this book.

PREFACE

I am indebted to the staff of the Yale University Press, and particularly to Eugene Davidson, for many helpful suggestions. The Office of Naval History of the Navy Department also lent aid, particularly Captains J. B. Heffernan and R. C. Parker, U.S.N., Captains A. D. Turnbull and S. E. Morison, U.S.N.R., and Professor Robert G. Albion. Professor J. A. Iseley of the History Department of Princeton University, who served as a lieutenant in the Navy during the war, not only checked the manuscript but made a great many useful suggestions. Lieutenant R. W. Schoolcraft, a participant in some of the campaigns, prepared the maps. Above all, I am grateful to Lieutenant Catherine C. Atwood, U.S.N.R., who has edited the manuscript with great care both as to style and content, and clarified many of the events in their relation to one another and to the larger thesis of the book. To all these good friends I am indebted; but none of them is responsible for the facts stated. The opinions expressed are my own, and under no circumstances should be attributed to the Navy Department.

W. D. P.

Lake Wales, Florida,
March 21, 1947.

Contents

Preface		vii
List of Maps		xiii
I.	Mahan's Concept of Sea Power	1
II.	Germany's Bid for Sea Power	6
III.	Sea Power between Two World Wars	14
IV.	September, 1939, to July, 1940	30
V.	Sea Power Saves Great Britain	49
VI.	The Opposing High Commands	77
VII.	Procurement and Personnel	84
VIII.	Japanese Sea Power in the Western Pacific	105
IX.	The Struggle for the Central Pacific	131
X.	The Battle of the Atlantic	159
XI.	The Campaign for the Solomons and Aleutians	180
XII.	Sea Power and Amphibious Warfare	214
XIII.	Reconquest of the Western Pacific	244
XIV.	Sea Power and Surrender	275
XV.	The Impact of New Weapons on Sea Power and World Relations	290
Index		301

Maps

The Atlantic Ocean	Frontispiece
Northwest Europe	29
The Mediterranean Area	58
The Pacific Ocean	102–103
Oahu	109
The Philippine Islands	114
Area of Japanese Conquest in the Western Pacific	121
The Coral Sea	133
Midway Islands	158
Northwest Africa	169
The Solomon Islands	179
Guadalcanal	186
The Aleutians	208
New Guinea	223
The Marianas	232
The Battle for Leyte Gulf	256
Iwo Jima	277
Okinawa	280
Japan	284
The Pacific Ocean	Frontispiece

THE INFLUENCE OF SEA POWER IN WORLD WAR II

I

Mahan's Concept of Sea Power

IT IS impossible to discuss sea power without reference to Captain A. T. Mahan, who in the first 89 pages of his book, *The Influence of Sea Power upon History, 1660–1783*, summarized, and in the remaining pages validated, his theory that control of the sea insured control of the land.

Not content with the corroboration of a century and a quarter of history, Mahan submitted his thesis to a more searching test in his second book, *The Influence of Sea Power upon the French Revolution and Empire*. Mahan points out that during the Napoleonic Wars which lasted, with one brief interval of peace, from 1793 to 1815, all the resources of Europe were eventually controlled directly or through his allies by Napoleon, who was not only one of the world's greatest generals but also a most efficient administrator. Nevertheless England, the power that controlled the sea, emerged victorious. Napoleon's Continental System did injure British commerce by prohibiting Russian exports to England, but it had a more distressing effect on the Russian than upon the British economy. Russian exports of ships' timber, hemp, and other commodities to the United Kingdom were stopped. The loss of income affected nobles and peasants alike and the Czar denounced the system although he knew Napoleon would declare war. Even if by some stroke of military genius Napoleon had won his last battle, he would only have delayed his doom; he had already consumed the manhood of France and antagonized not only Russia but the whole of Europe in his futile effort to avoid the consequences of British control of the sea.

Mahan's thesis was based on the results of battles, campaigns, and wars fought with sailing ships built of wood and armed with smooth-bore guns. His theory of the influence of sea power, formulated in 1890, was confirmed by the results of the Sino-Japanese War, 1894–95, the Spanish-American War, 1898, and the Russo-Japanese War of 1904–5. Thereafter the leading navies of the world based their strategy and for many years their tactics on the doctrines of Mahan, and the statesmen of Japan and of much of Europe accepted his evaluation of sea power.

There were naval dissenters in France during the 1890's who asserted that their fast torpedo boats, which were soon to evolve into destroyers, spelled the doom of the pre-dreadnoughts and the end of British dominion of the seas. But in 1904–5 the Japanese Navy proved that the torpedo boats, when properly integrated with battleships and cruisers, became the protectors rather than the enemy of capital ships and increased the influence of sea power.

The submarine was next hailed as the conqueror of the battleship, and again the end of sea power was predicted. In the first World War the failure of the Royal Navy to adopt vigorous defensive measures and the energetic use of U-boats by Germany did, it is true, threaten to starve out Great Britain. This fact obscured the employment by Britain's Grand Fleet of steam-propelled submarines with a surface speed of 20 knots as a fast wing of the fleet and the use of other submarines to assist in the blockade of Germany. It remained for American submarines during the second World War to demonstrate that subsurface ships reach their maximum effectiveness as an arm of the superior surface fleet.

After World War I, air enthusiasts in their turn hailed airplanes as the destroyer of surface ships and again eclipse of sea power was predicted. Naval officers more familiar with the failure of torpedo boats and submarines to annihilate the surface fleet demurred, and a few even suggested that airplanes properly integrated with a fleet would add to the fleet's strength and also increase their own offensive

MAHAN'S CONCEPT OF SEA POWER

powers by acquiring additional mobility when being operated from floating airfields.

Advocates of a completely integrated naval air arm had the historical evidence of the torpedo boat and submarine to sustain their conviction that airplanes, whose peculiar characteristic is speed, would add more to the strength of a fleet, whose characteristic is mobility, than to an army, whose characteristic is the ability to hold. These advocates of an integrated air force admitted that under certain conditions ships—even battleships—could be sunk by aerial bombs or torpedoes. But they maintained that with aircraft carriers to accompany the fleet, its own sea-borne planes could not only protect the fleet from enemy planes but add greatly to its offensive powers.

With this conviction, both the Japanese and American Navies constructed aircraft carriers and concentrated on naval aviation. In addition to aircraft on carriers, observation planes were carried on battleships and cruisers. The presence of planes on battleships immediately increased the battle range of the 16-inch guns, as their fire could then be controlled at the maximum range of 35,000 yards, which is beyond the vision of a fire control officer in the maintop.

American officers, and doubtless others, also realized that naval aviation integrated with the superior fleet would shorten naval wars. No longer could a weaker fleet, even the second best fleet, do as the German High Seas Fleet had done in the first World War and shelter itself behind powerful coastal defenses. Unless protected by a greatly superior air force, the weaker fleet must either come out in the open sea and fight or submit to being bombed or torpedoed in harbor.

The inability of a weaker fleet, in a future war, to shelter itself in harbor should permanently demolish what for over two centuries has masqueraded as a naval maxim. This myth, known as the "fleet in being," was created by Admiral Herbert, afterward Lord Torrington, to justify his precipitate retreat to the estuary of the Thames after the defeat off Beachy Head in 1690. Herbert claimed that by escaping from

Admiral Tourville's victorious fleet and keeping his fleet in being, its mere existence paralyzed the movements of the French Fleet and prevented a French invasion of England or Ireland. The failure of Admiral Tourville to exploit his victory was due to indecision in the French Court and his own lack of initiative. But his inactivity lent credence to the myth. Thus the conduct of two mediocre admirals laid the foundation for the maxim formally announced by Admiral Colomb over two centuries later, that an inferior, defeated British Fleet, protecting itself with the sand banks of the Thames, had the miraculous power of paralyzing the movement of a powerful, triumphant French Fleet.

This theory was demolished by Admiral Togo five years after it was announced by Colomb, when he blockaded the Russian Fleet "in being" at Port Arthur and simultaneously escorted and supported the landing of Japanese troops in Korea and Manchuria. In lectures at the Naval War College Mahan exposed the chimera. Yet it persisted until the last war during which the British, American, and Japanese Fleets repeatedly ignored weaker fleets "in being" and escorted troops and supplies overseas. It should now be decently interred.

Aviation was perhaps the most influential new weapon, but several others developed between the two World Wars facilitated landing an amphibious force on a hostile shore, among them amphibious landing craft, flame throwers, various devices for making smoke, and a whole battery of weapons based on electronics. These new weapons encouraged the Navy and particularly the Marine Corps to believe that the final test of sea power—overseas invasions—would be easier than in 1914–18. During the second World War American battleships bombarded heavy coastal guns in Normandy and Honshu, American carrier planes annihilated Japanese naval aviation, and the Navy landed amphibious forces almost at will in Europe, Africa, and the western Pacific.

It is believed that these events of the second World War have proved beyond any question that the whole galaxy of new weapons and craft including rockets, radar, controlled missiles, PT boats, supply and maintenance ships, improved submarines, aircraft carriers, and their planes has increased, not diminished, the striking power of the American Fleet; added to, not subtracted from, the value of control of the sea; strengthened, not weakened, the influence of sea power relative to land power.

In succeeding chapters the reasons for believing that the new weapons have increased the value of sea power are submitted. If these reasons are accepted by the reader it may perhaps be further inferred that future weapons, even the atomic bomb, will add to and not detract from the value of the American Fleet and its overseas bases, which together with American production constitute the essential elements of this country's sea power.

II

Germany's Bid for Sea Power

DURING most of the eighteenth century British statesmen maintained a navy at least as strong as the combined Navies of France and Spain. By 1815 the so-called "two-power standard" was generally accepted by the British people as well as by the Cabinet. And the system of Imperial defense was based upon an overwhelming navy and a small regular army, much of which was stationed in overseas garrisons to protect British naval bases.

During the last quarter of the nineteenth century there developed a minority group sometimes known as "Little Englanders" who thought that the Empire was large enough and that the two-power navy should not be maintained. Gladstone and Campbell-Bannerman, leaders of the Liberal party, became the spokesmen for the group, while Disraeli, Salisbury, and Balfour, Conservative leaders, supported the theory of continued expansion and a big navy.

The policy of the British Empire and the size of its navy, thereafter and until the first World War, depended upon the party in power. In 1888 a Conservative Cabinet formally announced its determination to maintain a two-power navy as protection against the Navies of France and Russia, Britain's contemporary rivals. In 1894 Gladstone resigned; among his reasons for doing so was his unwillingness to sponsor the increase in expenditures for the Royal Navy demanded by his own First Lord of the Admiralty.[1] The Cabinet, refusing to follow Gladstone, retained office and accepted Rosebery, a Liberal-Imperialist, as Prime Minister.

As early as 1902 the threat implied in the growth of rival

---

1. See Puleston, *Mahan. The Life and Work of Captain Alfred Thayer Mahan, U.S.N.*, pp. 146–147, and John Morley, *The Life of William E. Gladstone*, III, 506–510.

GERMANY'S BID FOR SEA POWER 7

European fleets was recognized by the Conservative government. In January of that year the Foreign Office concluded an alliance with Japan that allowed the Admiralty to strengthen naval forces in European waters by withdrawing the battleships of the Asiatic Squadron, which of course reduced Britain's naval strength in the Far East. The Liberals returned to power in 1905 under Campbell-Bannerman, who had opposed the Boer War, but the Cabinet included Asquith and Grey who, like Rosebery, were Liberal-Imperialists. Yet this Cabinet, as we shall see, did not maintain the traditional two-power standard.

In the course of many wars with Holland, France, and Spain during the seventeenth and eighteenth centuries, the British Navy had developed a systematic strategic deployment for its fleets. First it secured the waters surrounding the British Isles, particularly the English Channel and the North Sea. Next it extended its strength to the Bay of Biscay, the Straits of Gibraltar, and the western approaches to the British Isles. It would then dominate the Atlantic Ocean and the approaches to the western seaboard of Europe, securing its communications to the Western Hemisphere and, via the Cape of Good Hope, to the Far East. If circumstances permitted, it extended its control to the Baltic and Mediterranean Seas. However, at the beginning of the Seven Years' War, 1756–63, one of Britain's most successful, the navy was driven out of the Mediterranean and did not return until the peace.

The same fleets and squadrons that protected British (and friendly) ships denied enemy ships the use of the oceans. Simultaneously British squadrons based on ports in America and India gave local protection to overseas trade and possessions. Obviously, to maintain stronger fleets in all oceans, a British Navy greatly superior to possible rivals was required. In addition, soldiers to garrison the overseas bases and facilities to repair and refit sailing ships (later, to refuel steamships) were necessary because all fleets must return to port periodically for overhaul.

European fleets, particularly the German, continued to increase. In 1904 Britain accepted the overtures of France and, in 1907, those of Russia, both former rivals, and joined the Triple Entente as a counterpoise to the Triple Alliance of Austria, Germany, and Italy which, largely controlled by the Wilhelmstrasse, dominated the continent. These decisions indicated a complete change in British foreign policy and strategy. The growth of the American and Japanese Navies, as well as those of Germany, Russia, France, Austria, and Italy had made it impossible for the British to exercise their customary global control of the sea even with a two-power navy. But Japan was an ally and the United States had been increasingly friendly since the Spanish War. After 1902 Great Britain could have maintained a navy twice as strong as that of Germany, a navy that could have dominated the Atlantic and the Mediterranean without making commitments on the continent to secure the assistance of the French Fleet.

By 1912 the German Navy had grown so powerful that it became necessary for the British Admiralty to withdraw the Mediterranean Fleet to home waters to preserve the essential margin of naval superiority in the North Sea. The War Office inquired whether the navy could guarantee the communications of the garrisons in the Mediterranean with the British Isles; the negative answer compelled a consideration of the problem of Imperial defense by the entire Cabinet. At the critical meeting, with Prime Minister Asquith presiding, Sir Edward Grey, Foreign Minister, informed his colleagues of the commitments already made to provide a British Expeditionary Force to assist France in the event of war, and pointed out that England now had the choice of three courses of action: to settle British differences with Germany; to increase the size of the navy until it could provide an ample margin of superiority over the German High Seas Fleet in the North Sea, with sufficient ships remaining to secure the Mediterranean; or to strengthen the ties with France by increasing the size of the British Expeditionary Force and guaranteeing French interests in the Atlantic. If the latter course were taken the French Navy would in return concentrate in the Mediterranean and protect British possessions and communications in that area.

The Cabinet was unwilling to make the concessions necessary to reach an understanding with Germany. Lloyd George, Chancellor of the Exchequer, opposed any increase in the tax rate or any reduction in the expenditures for social reforms; the Cabinet agreed with Lloyd George and refused to authorize the expenditures necessary to increase the navy. That left only one course of action, namely, to entrust British interests in the Mediterranean to the French Navy and in exchange to place upon the Royal Navy the responsibility for French interests in the Atlantic. This the Cabinet tacitly accepted, but conditioned its approval by reserving the right to make the final decision whether and when to intervene on the continent. With this momentous decision Britain abandoned her traditional policy and naval strategy which together had created and maintained her sea empire.

In 1914 Field Marshal H. H. Kitchener became Secretary of State for War. On his recommendation the Cabinet authorized the raising of a huge British army which was expected to secure British interests when the treaty of peace was made at the war's end. Canning and Castlereagh had had no difficulty in securing British interests in 1815 with a pocket-size army and the world's greatest navy. Napoleon, who learned the value of sea power by opposing it, testified at St. Helena that British ambassadors would receive respectful attention in every capital in Europe as long as the Royal Navy controlled the sea. But the same Liberal Cabinet that in 1912 had refused to increase naval expenditures permitted Kitchener to build up the army until eventually it reached four million men.

In August, 1914, the British Expeditionary Force rapidly reënforced the French and together they won the battle of the Marne. Assisted by the Navies of Japan, France, and the Dominions, the Royal Navy in a few months secured complete control of the sea except in the Baltic and Black Seas. The North Sea was the critical area; the control of the five oceans and the connecting seas depended upon the ability of the British Grand Fleet based on Scotland to defeat or restrict to the eastern half of the North Sea the German High Seas Fleet based upon Heligoland Bight.

In the battle of Jutland, June, 1916, Admiral Jellicoe permitted Admiral Scheer to escape to his bases with a few ships sunk and many damaged but with the fleet practically intact and still requiring continuous surveillance by the Grand Fleet. Had Jellicoe destroyed the German Fleet, even with heavy British losses, the Grand Fleet would have been relieved of its ceaseless vigil; men and ships necessary to maintain its superiority over the German Fleet could have been diverted to meet the growing menace of the U-boats that in February, 1917, offered the final and most formidable challenge to the British exercise of sea power.

If the British Government had taken submarine warfare seriously when it was first launched early in 1915 and had diverted some of the men and material from Kitchener's army to the Royal Navy, there could have been an adequate defense against the increasing number and efficiency of the U-boats. Instead, the Cabinet steadily enlarged the army until in the winter of 1916–17 it approximated the size of the French, but the Royal Navy was unequal to protecting the merchant ships necessary to furnish food and raw materials to the United Kingdom, whose people were threatened with starvation. And the British armies, which were fighting in France, Greece, Palestine, and Mesopotamia, and which Kitchener had fondly imagined would dictate the terms of peace to Europe, were in danger of having their communications with the British Isles severed by German U-boats as completely as the communications of Japanese garrisons in the Pacific islands were to be severed by the United States Navy in the second World War.

The spectacular although temporary success of the U-boats in the capable hands of German commanders caused many superficial observers (including some naval officers, who should have been better informed) to conclude that submarines were the unconquerable weapon of a weaker navy, and that their development meant the end of surface fleets and of the exercise of sea power. Submarines, it is true, are the only ships that can operate independently in immediate proximity to greatly superior forces of surface ships. They were the most formidable challengers of surface ships in the first World War, and can at any time make controlling the sea a dangerous operation. Alone they can obstruct the use of the sea by a superior surface fleet, but alone they cannot safeguard their own merchant fleet. At most they can exercise only half the function of sea power. Like other types of ships, surface and air, they attain their maximum efficiency as a component of a superior fleet which also contains surface ships and aircraft. Submarines, it is plain now, are not necessarily the enemies of superior fleets. They should be, and in the United States Navy are, as useful as the air or surface ships to the fleet.

During the first World War the British Government did not suppress the steady flow of supplies from overseas to Germany by way of the adjacent neutral states of Holland, Denmark, and Sweden. In fact, the Ministry of Economic Warfare actually helped to replenish German stocks of foods and raw materials; it permitted the Dutch and Danish fishing fleets to obtain coal and fishing gear and other commodities needed by the fishing industry in the United Kingdom, in spite of the fact that most of the catch of the neutral fishermen went almost entirely to Germany, while the fish ration of the Danes and the Dutch was substantially reduced. It also allowed the Danes to obtain fodder for their herds and foodstuffs for the herdsmen, although it was known that most of the Danish butter, cheese, canned milk, and eggs exported also went to Germany. The same British Ministry, abetted by the Foreign Office, allowed Sweden to obtain food for her farmers, miners, and industrial workers, although it was known in London that the export of products from her mines and factories went almost entirely to Germany. Admiral Jellicoe and the Admiralty protested in vain. Not until the United States entered the war, and then only at the insistence of President Wilson, was trade with

Germany by way of the neutral neighbors gradually cut off; then for the first time Germany felt the effect of sea power in all its severity.[2]

The British and their allies did make full use of their control of the sea to obtain their own supplies and munitions. By January, 1917, numerous merchantmen carrying munitions of war enabled Anglo-French artillery on the western front to inflict such losses upon German troops that the High Command made the irreparable error of declaring unrestricted submarine warfare against all merchantmen. This fatal decision brought the United States into the war and eventually decided the outcome. Just as the pressure of British sea power in 1812 caused Napoleon to invade Russia, so the ability of France and England to obtain a comparatively unlimited supply of munitions from the United States caused Germany to resort to her submarines to halt the flow, and that action brought the United States into the war.

Sea power was the decisive factor in the first World War, but it was not British sea power alone, although the British Navy made by far the largest contribution of naval strength and the Grand Fleet was the essential link in the Allied chain. After April, 1917, the Japanese controlled the western Pacific, the Americans the eastern Pacific, the British, French, and Italians the Mediterranean, while the British with some assistance from the Americans controlled the North Sea and subdued the U-boats.

It is possible that the classical British naval strategy would not have been effective in 1914. The British Isles were threatened by Zeppelins and U-boats, the repulse of which was essential, and this defense absorbed men and material formerly available for the navy. The United Kingdom had always provided the bulk of the men and material necessary to sustain the Empire. It is possible that after 1900 Britain could not have supported a global navy along with the additional defenses needed against the new weapons, the submarines and aircraft. Whether under the new conditions the United Kingdom could have maintained the Empire with such a great navy and a small army ready to assist continen-

2. See Rear Admiral M. W. W. P. Consett, *The Triumph of Unarmed Forces*.

tal allies by landings in strategic positions must remain a conjecture. In any event the classical naval strategy was not used. In the decade before 1914 successive British ministries did not provide a navy large enough to defend the home base and the overseas communications of the Empire. But when they were involved in war they undertook to maintain simultaneously the world's largest navy and an army of four million men. American intervention saved the United Kingdom from starvation and the Empire from destruction, but the British people have never recovered from the strain of their enormous war effort on both land and sea.

III

Sea Power between Two World Wars

DURING the first World War neither the Zeppelins nor planes offered any serious threat to Allied control of the sea, and surface raiders were only a nuisance. The U-boats, because of British failure to take vigorous countermeasures in time, became a real menace, although Allied surface ships eventually succeeded in defeating them. It is important to realize, however, that even if U-boats had defeated the surface ships it would have signified only that submarines thereafter would be the essential type of ship to control the sea. No one would have denied the value of sea power because control of the sea had been gained and exercised by subsurface instead of surface ships.

Between the two World Wars aviation enthusiasts raised a very different issue. Convinced that the increasing efficiency of aircraft foreshadowed the doom of surface ships, they coined a new term, "air power," and argued that it would mean the end of sea power. Had they been more familiar with what Mahan meant by sea power they might have claimed that "heavier-than-air ships had displaced surface ships" as the essential instrument in gaining and maintaining control of the sea and thereby dominating the land.

Much unnecessary rancor would have been avoided if the proponents of air ships and surface ships could have agreed on common definitions. The difference of opinion might then have been reduced to the simple proposition: could air ships or surface ships alone control the sea? If either could dominate alone, obviously no administration should waste taxpayers' money on the other. If, on the other hand, both air and surface ships were still necessary, the United States would have to provide both, and the only technical problem remaining would be the proper proportion of each type. At the end of the first World War it was plain to many forward-looking American naval officers, like Admirals Moffett, Yarnell, and A. W. Johnson, that with the increasing efficiency of planes both air and surface ships would be required by the United States Navy. Thanks to the influence of these men, the opposition of ultraconservative officers who denied aviation its proper place in the fleet was overcome and the American Navy pioneered the development of aviation as an integral part of the fleet.

A wide difference of opinion, most of it honest, still exists among land, sea, and air officers concerning the relative importance of ground troops, ships, and aviation, and the relative values of control of the sea, the air, and the land. Much of this difference arose because there has never been a generally accepted definition of the terms "air power" and "sea power." It is very late, perhaps too late, to establish definitions acceptable to the various schools of thought. But until the terms are defined any serious attempt, no matter how objective, to estimate the relative value of sea power in the latest war or the current usefulness to the various nations of their land, sea, and air forces, is certain to excite hostile criticism. And so to reduce controversy to a minimum another attempt will be made herewith to clarify the terms "sea power," "land power," and "air power."

Partly because Mahan did not define "sea power" concisely, that term has often been used in the limited meaning of "naval strength." Similarly most contemporary writers use the term "air power" when they really mean "superior air strength" or "preponderant aviation." Historical examples will help to define "sea power" and "land power"; Great Britain exemplifies sea power; Russia, land power. To date no nation has achieved an empire primarily by "air power" or by a preponderant air' force; and, to add to the difficulty, air power does not yet exist in the comparable sense that Mahan used when he coined his now celebrated but elastic term "sea power."

"Air power" in the full and comparable sense of Mahan's term "sea power" will not exist until air-borne commerce is so extensive and essential to the economy of a nation that its existence can be threatened by the suppression of its airborne commerce. Furthermore, not until air tankers, air transports, and air cargo ships can maintain a steady flow of fuel, men, and munitions for combat planes can aviation become independent of land and sea transport and attain its full stature. Navies have always been dependent upon their shore bases for supplies; air ships are likewise dependent upon land bases and upon land or sea transport. Only when the bulk of the freight now carried by merchant ships is airborne can the term "air power" be used in a sense that compares to "sea power." Fortunately there are other terms such as "control of the air," "control of the sea," and "control of the land" sufficiently exact to contrast the powers and limitations of ships, troops, and planes, and of fleets, armies, and air forces; and there can be no misunderstanding the terms "air strength," "sea strength," and "land strength." It is possible that air commerce will become so essential to the economic life of nations that "air power" can be used to connote attributes comparable to land and sea power. When it does air power, like sea power, will be valuable only because its possessor is enabled to compel a superior land power to yield, and thus to control the land by means of the air. The sea and air are equally barren; they are only useful as highways; and the sole reason for maintaining surface, subsurface, and air fleets is to control and dominate land. At their zenith, sea and air power will only be a means to an end. They should be the objectives of sagacious statesmen in time of peace and, once obtained, the instruments to preserve the peace or win the war. Even when statesmen have provided the men, munitions, ships, and bases in time of peace, courageous crews drawn from the whole people, along with resolute captains and admirals, are necessary for control of the sea. Rome overthrew the numerically superior fleets of Carthage, and in more than one Anglo-French war the British Navy began hostilities with fewer ships in commission but emerged victorious.

To evaluate sea power, it is necessary to compare its relative value with that of air and land strength. It should be remembered, however, that these three elements are not fortifications of the naval bases in the western Pacific. This restriction handicapped the United States Navy and correspondingly increased the relative power of the Japanese Navy, whose astute representative, Admiral Baron Kato, sponsored the proposal. The combined effect of limiting capital ships and prohibiting the improvement of fortifications and facilities of naval bases in the strategic triangle between Formosa, Singapore, and the Philippines made it very difficult for the American Navy to operate in the western Pacific and reduced the influence of the United States in the Far East. This blunting of American sea power was doubly unfortunate, for British influence in the western Pacific had not recovered from the effects of the first World War. Consequently the ability of the two leading sea powers to curb Japan in the Far East was reduced just when it was most needed. They were delivered from this situation not by the wisdom of their statesmen but by the folly of the Japanese Government, which in 1934 denounced the naval limitation as of January 1, 1937.

The Naval Conference of 1922 and its successors succeeded fully in limiting the development of battleships and aircraft carriers; they eventually limited cruisers and destroyers and by fixing the tonnage and armament of cruisers created a hybrid type of ship. The League of Nations never succeeded in limiting land and air armaments. The ground troops and the air forces of Europe (except those of Germany and her former allies) and of Japan and the United States were at liberty to increase the efficiency of their weapons by new design and construction. While reduced appropriations hampered efforts of the American Army and Navy to improve antiaircraft batteries, the growth of commercial aviation rapidly improved the design and power of aircraft. Thus progress in the technical development of land planes and armies exceeded that of antiaircraft defenses and navies.

The vigorous use of U-boats by the Germans had convinced the French Government that submarines were an essential arm of a weaker navy. Since the army absorbed the bulk of French revenue, their navy could never equal the

British and if their Foreign Office needed to be able to check Downing Street the policy of building an underwater fleet was correct. But Japan also opposed the abolition of submarines under the mistaken assumption that they would be of more assistance to her than to the United States, although actually the Japanese Islands were more vulnerable than the British Isles to a submarine blockade and undersea war against merchantmen. Japanese submarines, on the other hand, never could be more than a nuisance to the United States, a continental nation that contained within its own territory all necessary foodstuffs and most essential strategic raw materials.

During the first World War aviation had taken an important part in the campaigns ashore. Fighter craft had intercepted enemy planes attempting to attack ground troops and installations; scouting planes had extended the range of reconnaissance activities; observation planes had controlled artillery fire; bomber groups had assisted in breaking through the enemy line or furthering the advance of attacking formations when they moved beyond support of their own artillery, and had also served for independent missions beyond the support of the other arms. Zeppelins, moreover, had raided the United Kingdom, alarming and exasperating the public. The reaction of the British people caused the Cabinet to create an independent air force with the primary duty of protecting the country from air attacks. This decision did not immediately affect the Royal Navy which had had little need for an air arm; it did handicap the Army at once by taking away control of the organization and training of air squadrons destined for service with the ground troops.

After the war numerous air advocates in Great Britain and the United States convinced many laymen and some military officers that the next conflict would be decided in the air by a huge blow or series of blows which would prevent mobilization, destroy arsenals and munition factories, and throw the citizens into a panic. At that time the American and British Governments were determined to reduce over-all expenditures on armaments; but the legislators of

SEA POWER BETWEEN WORLD WARS 19

both nations accepted the arguments of airmen, and air officers were able to get appropriations when other branches were not. In the United States neither the President nor Congress could be persuaded to add new ships or ground weapons. Not until 1930 could the Army get appropriations to develop antiaircraft guns and fire control equipment, and even by that date the Navy could not get money to enable it to improve its defense against aircraft. To add to the difficulty of developing antiaircraft armaments, professional opinion on the problem swung violently from one extreme to the other. Airmen were themselves divided, some asserting that only fighting planes could stop aircraft, while others were equally positive that it would take other means. The arguments were equally heated in Great Britain, where densely populated areas were close to continental air bases. Some British airmen were confident that they could stop bombers with fighters, while others were equally sure that the only defense against bombers was to retaliate with heavier attacks on enemy cities.

British air officers asserted that by providing suitably situated and equipped air bases throughout the Empire, Royal Air Squadrons could relieve both the navy and army of their responsibilities for maintaining the Empire. These officers were later given the opportunity to demonstrate their argument in the Middle East. But at this time the Royal Air Force, eager to show its own independent powers, neglected to find and train personnel for its place as a vital arm in the Imperial triphibious forces; and it required two years of war to teach British aviators that close association with ground troops and ships not only did not handicap their operations but actually increased the powers and reduced the limitations of their weapon.

By establishing an independent air force, the British Government removed from their battleships and cruisers the very officers who would have made their navy air conscious, and denied the fleet what it most needed, close cooperation between surface and air ships and a corps of aviators trained to fly over long ocean stretches and to work in harmony with the ships. The Japanese and American

Navies retained control of their naval aviation and maintained and trained air squadrons on carriers, aircraft tenders, battleships, and cruisers. Japanese and American naval aviation, in fact, had many similarities; the main difference in the sea-air organization and tactics developed in peace by the two countries was the employment by Japan of more shore-based planes to supplement the efforts of her carriers.

After 1918 the French Air Force adopted the policy of quantity production of planes. This decision standardized the design, and for a few years provided France with the world's most powerful air arm; but it stifled research and overstabilized French air factories.

Although the French Air Force was nominally independent, many aviators detailed to the navy were former naval officers and all were assigned permanently to the Coast Defenses and operated with the navy. The policy of the French Navy, like that of its Army, was defensive. In 1939 it had only one aircraft carrier built, the *Béarn,* which was interned in Martinique in 1940. Two others were under construction when the war started. The Italian Air Force, under Mussolini's sponsorship, designed some very superior planes and developed a few excellent pilots and squadron leaders. Generally speaking, however, neither men nor equipment equaled the French or British. Since Mussolini's objective was control of the Mediterranean, he did not construct aircraft carriers but depended upon land-based planes to give air cover to his surface ships and to attack enemy vessels. When Hitler determined to create the Luftwaffe, the German General Staff was still strong enough to assure that German aviation, nominally independent of the Wehrmacht, was permanently assigned to certain ground troop formations. To guarantee that integration would be complete ground and air troops wore the same uniform and corps insignia. Thus it happened that the Royal Air Force maintained a greater independence than any other; and it required the stern lessons of war and the order of the Prime Minister to compel gallant officers of that force to join their army-navy colleagues in a triphibious team.

Both the British and the American Governments had made determined efforts to reduce expenditures between the two World Wars. In 1935 Hitler had agreed not to build a navy more than one third the size of the British; subsequently he had informed the British that he would put no limit on his submarines. Meanwhile the British Government had determined to rebuild their fleet, and on the first day of 1937 had begun to work. The new construction program met many difficulties. The British overseas trade and shipbuilding industry had been ruined by the depression and foreign competition. British shipowners could and did have ships built more cheaply abroad. In order to keep as much of their capacity intact and as many of their skilled workers employed as possible, British shipbuilders, with the government's permission, had distributed the new construction among all shipyards, and reduced the hours of work. In spite of these determined efforts many of their skilled craftsmen had dispersed to other industries, and the national shipbuilding capacity of 3,000,000 tons had been reduced to 2,000,000. Production of ships in the British Isles, an essential element of British sea power, had been seriously reduced.

After the naval limitations treaty had been denounced (by Japan's announcement of termination as of December 31, 1936), the United States Navy contented itself at first with making blueprints. It could, in fact, do little more; the naval holiday had scattered the comparatively few highly skilled draftsmen and artisans who had been trained during the first World War. Not the least of the injuries done the country by the 1921–22 Conference was the near destruction of its shipbuilding industry. It took imagination, boldness, and industry to recreate the shipyards in time to serve the nation during the second World War.

The situation in the Far East between 1931 and 1941, created by the treaties of the 1921–22 Washington Conference and current European rivalry, was made to order for the Japanese expansionists then in control of the government. In 1931 their army marched into Manchuria, the first step toward dominating the coastal provinces of China. During President Hoover's administration, Secretary of State Stimson made persistent but ineffectual efforts to halt the invasion. President Roosevelt was absorbed with domestic problems during his first term, and the British Government were unwilling to act. When Hitler began to denounce the restrictions of the Versailles Treaty, Washington as well as London concentrated its attention upon Europe and left Japan with a free hand in China, except for futile diplomatic protests and some economic aid to that country. Thanks to their control of the western Pacific the Japanese Navy could land divisions, mixed brigades, or regiments of their large and efficient army anywhere along the coast of China or the banks of her navigable rivers. In 1937 their amphibious forces invaded Shanghai and gradually overcame all organized resistance in southeastern China. Chiang Kai-shek refused Japanese overtures for peace, and inspired a mass migration of Chinese, who moved their machines from their pitifully inadequate factories deep into the interior, preserving a Free China with Chungking as its capital.

The United States openly expressed its sympathy for China and urged Chiang to continue his resistance, but efforts to extend economic aid were almost nullified by Japanese control of the western Pacific. When the Japanese occupied Shanghai American exports were diverted to Canton or Hong Kong; the Japanese then occupied Canton and threatened Hong Kong, and cargoes from this country were rerouted to Indo-China for transshipment to Kunming. This continued until the collapse of France enabled the Japanese to intimidate the local French authorities and force them to embargo all goods destined for China. American ships were then sent to Rangoon, whence their cargoes were forwarded by the Burma Road to Lashio, thence via Kunming to Chungking. This road, a monument to the endurance of the Chinese peasants, was built almost wholly by hand labor, using picks and shovels. Its capacity was overrated by American officials; it was unusable in the rainy season and under the most favorable conditions could carry only a fraction of the supplies that were badly needed. But the traffic on it was a symbol of the determination of the

American Government to assist China. The fortitude of the Chinese was probably most severely tested in the summer of 1940 when under Japanese pressure Winston Churchill refused to allow goods destined for China to land at Rangoon. Secretary Hull protested, Stalin sent supplies overland through Sinkiang, and in the autumn Great Britain reopened Rangoon. The Chinese were always able to obtain some critical materials by bribing Japanese officials, but the goods received from all sources were a mere trickle, and only the willingness of the Chinese people to endure unspeakable hardships and the determination of Chiang to resist to the end enabled Free China to survive.

Army and navy officers dominated the Japanese Government, but they could not agree whether it would be wiser to expand into the continent of Asia or along the chain of islands extending southwestward through the Philippines to Indonesia. Whether they expanded into Asia or into the islands, the comparatively small capacity of their factories and their limited resources in men and material placed a definite limit upon their national exertions. Prudence would have suggested a gradual expansion in one direction or the other followed by long periods of consolidation and conciliation. It was manifestly impossible for the Japanese to maintain a navy that could resist the United States Fleet in the western Pacific if the American people ever decided to stop the expansion of Japan by force; and the most chauvinistic Nipponese naval officers realized that their overseas possessions were held on sufferance until they could secure permanent control of the western Pacific.

The Japanese High Command apparently never thoroughly considered the effect of the determined opposition of the United States to their aggressive designs. Certainly they did not make and carry through a well-thought-out plan of operation in China or the South Seas. After their invasion of Manchuria they allowed themselves to be drawn more and more deeply into China, and while fully involved in an uncertain and costly continental war felt it necessary to attack the United States in the hope of profiting by the temporary division of the United States Navy between the

Atlantic and Pacific and the preoccupation of the American Government with Europe. The reckless manner in which the Japanese added to their enemies and overextended their position in the western Pacific was in direct contrast with the conservative policy and strategy of their High Command in the successful war against Russia earlier in the century.

The armed forces of Japan did obtain one important advantage from their prolonged struggle with China. The army and navy learned how to integrate ground troops and ships with land and sea aviation, and the navy learned how to combine its ship-based and land-based planes with surface ships and submarines. Together the army and navy constructed specially designed landing craft for amphibious operations, and the High Command united land, sea and air forces in one highly efficient triphibious combat team. In the present humiliation of Japan it would be easy to forget that the Japanese High Command pioneered in modern amphibious warfare and was first to demonstrate that the development of aviation, far from diminishing the value of sea power, had increased its mobility, impact, and general effectiveness.

It is to be noted that the Japanese did not consolidate their Army and Navy Departments, or unify their command in Tokyo or the theater of operations. They knew it would be absurd to give a landlubber general command of an expeditionary force while at sea; he would be a figurehead at best and a genuine menace if he attempted to assert his authority. Similarly, the best admiral or air marshal in the world would lack the technical knowledge to direct a regiment ashore. The method of the Japanese was highly successful until they encountered a larger combined force, with more ships, planes, and men, whose High Command used the same simple, common-sense methods of directing amphibious landings.

Like Japan in the Pacific, Italy took advantage of her temporary control of the central Mediterranean to defy both France and Great Britain. Under Mussolini's direction the troops that conquered Abyssinia were transported and supplied by sea. Italian possessions, like those of Japan, proved

SEA POWER BETWEEN WORLD WARS 27

to be temporary; the High Commands in Rome and Tokyo both forgot that the possession of land beyond the sea depends on maintaining control of the sea or making terms with the nation enjoying sea power.

Until 1937 the sea power of Great Britain and the United States was shackled by the 1922 treaties which established an artificial balance, obstructing the natural development of their navies. The treaties assisted Japan and Italy, who used their temporary naval strength to further their programs of expansion. Their navies did enjoy temporary control of the adjacent seas, and for a brief period their expansion prospered. But both lacked essential elements of sea power. The productive capacity of their factories was insufficient, they were dependent on overseas markets for essential raw materials, and their shipping was always at the mercy of a superior sea power. It was a foregone conclusion that their overseas conquests would not endure.

German factories, on the other hand, could produce the necessary goods for a major war provided sufficient amounts of essential raw materials were imported. The High Command, profiting by the experience of 1914–18, stored reserves of strategic materials, German scientists explored all means of providing substitutes and their thoroughness and efficiency succeeded in reducing though not removing the country's dependence on imports. Germany could draw upon all eastern Europe but even in peace she could not produce sufficient goods to exchange. Only by using in addition gold and veiled threats did she succeed in obtaining sufficient products from the Balkans and Russia. And her constantly increasing needs compelled her to take an ever more threatening attitude toward her small neighbors.

Great Britain, more aware of the value of sea power than the United States, took steps as we have seen to rehabilitate her navy in 1937, and soon had 70 per cent of her shipbuilding capacity constructing combat ships. Her navy regained partial control of naval aviation a few years before the war, but was far behind the Japanese and American Navies with their own integrated air forces.

Between 1921 and 1941 the United States Navy was badly

handicapped by lack of appropriations for combat ships. Its position in the Pacific was weakened by the restrictions on fortifications in the Far East. But in spite of governmental neglect the American fleets carried out training programs unparalleled in naval annals. The main body of the United States Fleet was usually based on southern California, and year after year staged communications, gunnery, and engineering competitions to improve the efficiency of the entire fleet personnel. Monthly strategical exercises of surface, subsurface, and air ships were held, testing the professional abilities of fleet and squadron commanders. The program culminated in an annual movement either to the East Coast of the United States, or to Pearl Harbor. All ships of the Atlantic Fleet joined in these operations; amphibious exercises were carried out to insure the readiness of the Fleet Marines to land on a hostile shore, to test the defenses of the Panama Canal and Pearl Harbor, and to ascertain, as far as peace maneuvers can, the ability of American admirals to direct and command the fleet. The Navy wished during some of its maneuvers to move the fleet and its supply ships from Honolulu to Manila; but the State Department, fearful of irritating the Japanese, vetoed this exercise, and some of its more cautious officials wanted to prohibit operations of the United States Navy west of the 180th meridian. After 1940 for diplomatic reasons the Pacific Fleet was based on Pearl Harbor. Its ships trained and furnished nucleus crews for newly constructed vessels, which involved frequent changes in personnel, reducing the efficiency of individual ships. Despite these drawbacks the Navy succeeded in carrying out fleet maneuvers and maintaining, from the point of view of training, a fairly satisfactory state of readiness.

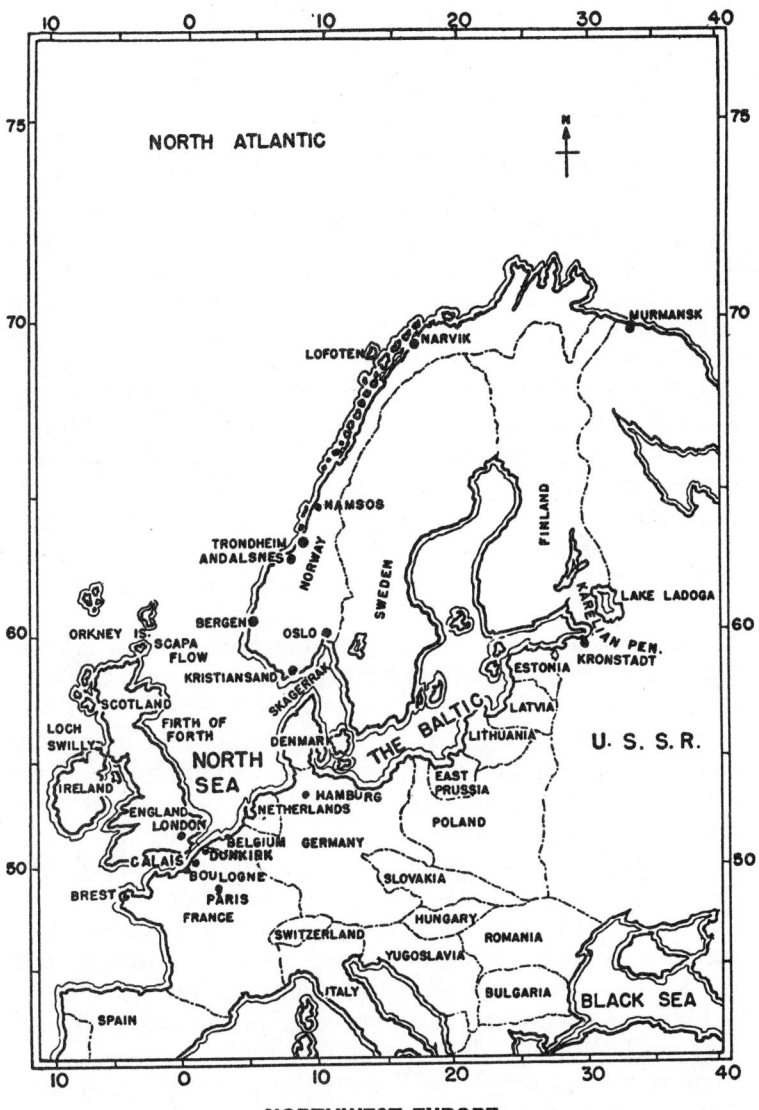

NORTHWEST EUROPE

IV

September, 1939, to July, 1940

LONDON and Paris were astonished when Russia signed a nonaggression pact with Germany in August, 1939. Hitler had other surprises in store for them. With his eastern frontier temporarily secure, he rapidly completed the preparatory movements of his air and ground troops, and on September 1, without formal declaration of war, launched the Nazi forces against the hapless Poles. His armored divisions, a tactical combination of tanks and motorized infantry and artillery, rolled like a myriad of juggernauts across the plains of Poland. Dive-bombing Stukas were prepared to assist the artillery in reducing any local strong points or, if the objective was beyond the range of artillery, to undertake the task alone.

Simultaneously German long-range bombers struck well behind the front, heavily damaging more than thirty of Poland's largest cities, crippling the supply of munitions, and rendering thousands of Poles homeless; long-range bombers also interrupted rail and road communications by destroying the marshaling yards of the railways and the important centers of motor traffic. The demolition of dwellings had far-reaching results; thousands of terrified civilians clogged the highways and added a formidable obstacle to the free movement of Polish troops. The German air attacks on Polish civilians were no more inhumane than those by the Japanese on Chinese cities, but the Western World, more concerned with Europe, was more horrified by this second wholesale destruction of populous areas.

Just as the agony of the Poles seemed complete, Russian armies marched across the eastern frontier without opposition. Within four weeks Poland was occupied and for the fourth time partitioned. The German-Soviet boundary coincided generally with the Polish-Russian frontier proposed by Curzon after the war of 1914–18, except that Russia obtained in addition certain valuable strategic positions, notably in south-central Poland where the Russian frontier was projected westward of the headwaters of the Pruth River, which in its middle and lower reaches was a barrier to a Soviet advance into Bessarabia, a former Russian province occupied by Rumania in November, 1918.

During the German invasion of Poland about twenty divisions were left behind to guard the West Wall, and they had no difficulty in blunting the minor holding attacks launched by the timid Gamelin.

At sea the war was equally savage, although fortunately fewer women and children were exposed to its impact. At the time Hitler ordered the German Army into Poland he had a small homogeneous fleet designed for a defensive naval war against Russia or France. The navy consisted of approximately 70 U-boats (50 of these were modern but small, designed to operate in the Baltic and North Seas and around the British Isles, while a few were of a larger class that could operate as far as Gibraltar); 22 destroyers; 5 light cruisers; 3 heavy cruisers of 10,000 tons, all over-armored for their displacement, and capable of making 26 knots (2 of them, the *Scheer* and the *Graf Spee,* carried 11-inch guns, the *Hipper* 8-inch guns, and all 3 were potential commerce destroyers); and 2 battle cruisers, *Scharnhorst* and *Gneisenau,* of 26,000 tons, carrying 11-inch guns and armor enough to fight in a line of battleships. Under construction were 4 heavy cruisers, *Bluecher, Luetzow, Prinz Eugen,* and *Seydlitz,* 3 battleships, the *Bismarck* and the *Tirpitz,* and 1 unnamed which was never completed, 8 destroyers, some torpedo boats, and some U-boats. There were 2 aircraft carriers, the *Graf Zeppelin,* which proved a failure, and the *Peter Strasser,* which was not finished.[1]

Hitler's navy had a few flying units, but these were placed under control of the Luftwaffe, and Grand Admiral Doenitz, who wished to use them as scouts for U-boats, discovered

---

1. Admiral Karl Doenitz, *The Conduct of the War at Sea.* The names of some of the German ships were subsequently changed, but the total number remained the same. Published by the Navy Department, January, 1947.

that the planes were designed for land instead of naval warfare. The pilots lacked experience in fighting and in navigating over the sea, could not identify the various types of ships, did not understand naval terminology, and could not direct U-boats to the convoys that they sighted.

To summarize, Hitler could oppose 2 26,000-ton battle cruisers and 3 10,000-ton pocket battleships to 14 British capital ships. He had no aircraft carriers, the British had 7. He had 2 battleships building, the British 7. In addition France had built or was building 10 battleships, 3 aircraft carriers, 18 cruisers, 64 destroyers, 12 torpedo boats, 28 large submarines, and 51 smaller ones.

Admiral Doenitz later complained that Hitler had not anticipated war with Great Britain and had neglected the navy. His views are supported by Vice-Admiral Weichold, who wrote in December, 1945, that the leading men in Hitler's government and armed forces were "all landsmen and soldiers accustomed to the land. As in the policy which led to the war, they attributed the decisive importance [of an entirely continental strategy] to conditions and forces on the continent [Europe] and underestimated the size and powers of the world, as they did everything which lay on the other side of the sea. Above all they failed to recognize the demands of the sea itself and the invisible strength of sea power." [2]

Whatever the cause, the German Navy in 1939 was utterly unable to seek a fleet engagement or dispute the Anglo-French control of the sea. Instead Grand Admiral Raeder proposed to employ its combat ships and planes in direct attacks on neutral and hostile merchantmen bringing essential foodstuffs and raw materials to enemy countries.

Raeder and the Navy General Staff knew, of course, that the British Isles were dependent upon overseas trade for food and raw material and, convinced that the U-boat was Germany's most effective weapon, immediately began to increase the building program from 2 to 4 U-boats per month

2. Vice-Admiral Eberhard Weichold, "The War at Sea in the Mediterranean." Published by the Navy Department, February, 1947.

toward an eventual 20 to 25 per month. The surface navy, obviously too small to defeat the British, was given the task of assisting in the destruction of British commerce, and fast merchantmen were converted into sea raiders to attack ships along the vital British line of communications.

When the occupation of Poland had been completed, the bulk of the German troops were returned to the western front. The war in Europe then in its larger aspects resembled the situation at the commencement of the long struggle between Napoleon and Pitt and his successors after the battles of Trafalgar and Austerlitz. Germany, with a nonaggression pact with Russia and a secret understanding with Italy, had a greatly superior army and superior land aviation. The Anglo-French alliance had much superior navies and oceanic air strength. Airplanes changed the tactics and strategy ashore, while submarines and naval aviation altered the character of warfare at sea. Planes and submarines were employed by both sides, complicating operations but not affecting the basic nature of the struggle. It was a contest between land and sea power, both assisted by aviation. German and British land-based planes projected their strength some distance over the seas. British carrier planes could have flown many miles over land, but were needed for duties at sea.

The British Navy dominated the war at sea. Winston Churchill, recalled as First Lord of the Admiralty, infused new vigor into naval operations. The few German merchant ships still at sea were either captured, compelled to scuttle themselves, or seek refuge in port. Within 24 hours German merchantmen ceased trading except in the Baltic, or by sneaking along the coasts of Denmark and Norway, ready to run for sanctuary into neutral waters. Imports from overseas could reach the Reich only by way of Belgium, Holland, Denmark, Norway, or Sweden.

The conquest of Poland gave Germany a long frontier with Russia that facilitated the exchange of goods guaranteed by the nonaggression pact. But both Russia and Germany were stockpiling the same strategic raw materials. The exchange of these goods never reached the expected volume and soon became a cause of irritation between the suspicious partners. The extreme need in Germany for rubber, tin, and similar essential goods created an exchange between Japan and Germany across the trans-Siberian railway, but the quantities available by this route were very limited. The immediate effect of the suppression of the Reich's sea-borne trade upon her ability to wage war is nowhere better shown than in the drastic measures taken to obtain the goods once carried in German ships, or to manufacture substitutes in Nazi factories.

The British and French Admiralties, anticipating that the German naval effort would be directed primarily at their merchant ships, took prompt measures to protect their seaborne trade. Merchantmen were assembled in convoys and individual ships were armed against planes as well as submarines. Transports, supply ships, trawlers, mine layers, and mine sweepers were requisitioned from the merchant marine and placed under the direction of the respective admiralties. The British Admiralty assumed all responsibility for routing and protecting merchant vessels and their cargoes. The Royal Navy had improved its means of combating U-boats, and had developed new methods of detecting them as they operated submerged. The antisubmarine section at the Admiralty established close liaison with the Coastal Command of the Royal Air Force and made extensive use of land-based and carrier planes to search for and attack U-boats.

In striking contrast to the first World War, when the bulk of both the British and the German Navies was concentrated into the Grand Fleet and the High Seas Fleet respectively, the Nazis repeatedly deployed battleships, battle cruisers, cruisers, and destroyers—their entire surface navy—reenforced by planes, in attacks against British sea communications. The British Navy, under no necessity of keeping a fleet ready to intercept a German fleet, also deployed its capital ships and aircraft carriers along with its cruisers and destroyers to protect its own shipping and to attack German ships and planes. The attack and defense of seaborne commerce brought on many minor engagements in the North Sea and along the coasts of Jutland and Norway.

Carrier-based planes were providing the most effective form of scouting for hostile surface, subsurface, and air ships. The planes taking off from the *Ark Royal* reconnoitered five million square miles of ocean in the first five months of the war. Simultaneously the British and the French Navies were employing their own submarines to scout for and report the approach of enemy planes and submarines. Anglo-French operations at sea emphasized that a tactical combination of surface, subsurface, and air ships in one task force or fleet adds to the powers and reduces the limitations of the various types of ships composing the formation. Arithmetically the strength of a task force equals the sum of the strength of its members; tactically the combat strength of a task force greatly exceeds the aggregate strength of its individual members. How effectively the task forces of the British Fleet coöperated is indicated, for example, by the promptness with which, early in the war, a task force, including an aircraft carrier, rescued a damaged submarine pursued by German planes. The engagement which ensued was the first concentrated air attack on surface ships, and the surface ships beat off the attack with their own planes and antiaircraft fire.

The Germans had enough submarines to attack men-of-war as well as merchantmen. On October 14 the Admiralty announced the loss of the battleship *Royal Oak,* sunk by Lieutenant Commander Gunther Prien while at anchor in Scapa Flow. The Admiralty accepted the reponsibility for this unnecessary disaster, which was caused by failure to provide proper obstructions at the harbor entrances.

The German Air Force followed this submarine attack with air assaults on ships at the Firth of Forth and Scapa Flow on October 16 and 17. The British admitted that the cruisers *Southampton* and *Edinburgh* were "slightly damaged" and the *Iron Duke,* a demilitarized battleship, was "damaged." The Germans extended their air attacks to the Orkney Islands, forcing capital ships of the British Fleet to retire to the west coast of Scotland and to Loch Swilly in north Ireland, adding about 100 miles to the distance German bombers had to fly before striking capital ships and compelling these planes to cross England where they were exposed to British fighters and antiaircraft fire.

British submarines, planes, and small surface ships scouted the North Sea giving warning when German raiders attempted to reach the Atlantic. Cruisers and smaller ships operated in the North Sea and the English Channel to intercept small German raiders trying to reach the Atlantic, while British capital ships based on northern Ireland and western Scotland were ready to intercept any German battle cruiser or pocket battleship venturing forth.

The airplane increased the strategic value of the British Isles, for they were as favorably placed for air as for naval operations. Unfortunately however the government had not constructed an integrated naval air force that could cooperate with the surface fleet and thus cope with the Luftwaffe. And Chamberlain, in reporting the results of the first serious air attacks on the fleet, stated that "it would be unwise to assume that we shall always be as successful as we have in these first exchanges."

The comparative failure of the submarines caused Hitler, late in November, to employ his first secret weapon, the magnetic mine, which could be planted by planes or submarines on or near the bottom of the shallow estuaries leading to England's largest harbors. These mines could not be removed by regular sweepers, and were activated and then detonated by an electric current generated by the iron or steel hull of a ship passing over them. For a brief period these mines inflicted severe losses on Allied and neutral ships; but British scientists quickly devised a "degaussing girdle" that demagnetized the hulls of ships and rendered the magnetic mines harmless. In addition, new mine sweepers, with wooden hulls, were equipped to tow specially constructed iron sweeps through the shallow waterways and thus harmlessly detonate the mine fields. In a few weeks the magnetic mine ceased to be a menace, but it continued to be a nuisance. This early contest between scientists was symbolic of the war to come. German scientists created a new weapon that British scientists countered; scientists of the opposing nations had been enrolled in the armed forces and their activities increased as the war progressed, reaching a climax in the atomic bomb.

During the middle of December the Germans began air attacks on merchant ships. Their first efforts were unsuccessful. To obtain a percentage of hits that would justify the effort expended and loss sustained, aircraft were obliged to fly at low altitudes over their mobile targets, bringing themselves within range of the small caliber guns and even of the machine guns carried on these steamers. The morale of the crews was greatly stimulated by their ability to strike back at the approaching aircraft. The meager results obtained by German air attacks against coastal shipping surprised naval officers as well as aviators, for it had been assumed that these comparatively slow ships operating in the narrow waters that restricted evasive tactics would be easy victims of airmen.

Sometime in September the Germans unloosed the *Graf Spee* in the Atlantic. For three months the *Spee* evaded pursuit, meanwhile sinking at least six merchantmen. On December 12 Commodore Henry Harwood, commanding the South American Squadron, including the *Exeter,* a heavy 8-inch cruiser, and two light 6-inch cruisers, the *Ajax* and the *Achilles,* concentrated his force in the estuary of the River Plate. The commodore explained to his captains the simple tactical plan he proposed to use against the *Spee,* which was expected to appear in those waters. The 8-inch flagship *Exeter* would attack from one side, while the two 6-inch cruisers approached from the other. All would close the range as rapidly as possible, to make their smaller guns effective against the heavier armor and armament of the *Spee.*

At daylight on December 13 the *Exeter* sighted and was sighted by the *Spee.* The *Spee* began the battle by opening fire simultaneously upon the *Exeter* with one turret while the other turret divided fire on the two smaller cruisers. As the three British cruisers closed range the *Exeter* was hit and, badly damaged, dropped astern. The *Ajax* and the *Achilles* closed to 8,000 yards. During their maneuver the *Ajax* had two turrets put out of action and the *Achilles* was also damaged. But the combined fire of the three cruisers had damaged the *Spee,* and she laid a smoke screen and steered a zigzag course, endeavoring to increase the range. The pace proved too hot for all combatants. After 80 minutes of fighting the *Achilles* and the *Ajax* opened range and contented themselves with following the *Spee* until she entered Montevideo Harbor. The *Exeter* proceeded to the Falklands for repairs but the heavy cruiser *Cumberland* joined the *Ajax* and the *Achilles* on the night of December 14, making it impossible for the *Spee* to get out to sea without a fight. Another engagement was unnecessary. Hitler ordered the captain of the *Spee,* who had been requested by the Uruguayan Government to leave after four days in port, to scuttle his ship. The *Spee* was sunk in the south Atlantic, like the squadron of the admiral for whom she was christened, and in a similarly hopeless struggle against a superior navy. The damage she had inflicted upon British shipping did not compensate Germany for her loss and the internment of her crew at Buenos Aires.

Seventeen months later, in May, 1941, the German Admiralty despatched another and more powerful commerce destroyer to the north Atlantic, the battleship *Bismarck,* whose career was even shorter than the *Spee's.* The same conclusions can be drawn from both episodes. Heavily armored and well compartmented, the *Bismarck* carried eight 15-inch guns and could steam at 28 knots. Certainly if any vessel could interrupt the steady flow of supplies to the United Kingdom, the *Bismarck* could. She flew the flag of Admiral Luetjens, who had distinguished himself in the Norwegian campaign and had commanded the *Scharnhorst* and the *Gneisenau* in a successful but brief raid on Atlantic shipping lanes before being driven into Brest. In company with the *Prinz Eugen,* an 8-inch gun cruiser with a speed of 32 knots, the *Bismarck* was sighted in Bergen Harbor on May 21, 1941, by an observation plane of the Coastal Command. The *Prinz Eugen* was a worthy companion of the *Bismarck,* and the British Admiralty had correctly surmised that these crack ships would make a dash for the Atlantic sea lanes. Two cruisers, the *Suffolk* and the *Norfolk,* were directed to proceed at once to Greenland Strait (sometimes called Denmark Strait), through which the *Bismarck* would have to pass to reach the Atlantic. On the evening of May 23 the two cruisers sighted and trailed the *Bismarck* and the *Prinz Eugen,* reporting their position, course, and speed. This information enabled the battle cruiser *Hood,* flying the flag of Rear Admiral Holland, and the newly commissioned battleship *Prince of Wales* to intercept them on the following day.

The British system of defense against surface raiders had worked perfectly. The trap had closed promptly on its victims, but the jaws were not strong enough to hold the powerful superdreadnought. One salvo of armor-piercing projectiles from the *Bismarck's* 15-inch guns sank the *Hood* as she attempted to close the range. The *Prince of Wales,* whose crew had scarcely shaken down, next felt the weight of German shells and dropped astern out of range. Soon after this first engagement the German ships steamed into a wide belt of fog and mist. While their movements were concealed the two vessels separated and operated independently.

So far the success of the *Bismarck* had exceeded all German anticipations. But every British man-of-war in the north Atlantic knew her whereabouts, and many were converging upon her reported position. The battleship *King George V,* from the Home Fleet, the *Renown,* the *Sheffield,* and the *Ark Royal* from Gibraltar, the *Rodney* and the *Ramillies,* on escort duty, all dropped their tasks and sped toward the scene of action bent on sinking the *Bismarck.*

About 10.30 A.M. on May 26, a flying boat of the Coastal Command sighted the *Bismarck* only 550 miles from Lands End; she had averaged 25 knots since last seen and unless slowed by air attacks bade fair to elude her pursuers and reach Brest. Within an hour aircraft from the *Ark Royal* sighted the hunted ship, and just before dark a squadron of torpedo planes made two hits, one of which struck on the quarter of the superdreadnought, disabling the rudder and severely damaging the propellers. Subsequently the *Bismarck* could only make 12 knots. During the night she was again hit by torpedoes from a destroyer squadron. At 9 the following morning the *George V* and the *Rodney* quickly made a shambles of her weather decks and silenced her batteries. To save ammunition the cruiser *Dorsetshire* was ordered to sink this tough Leviathan. It required two torpedoes in her starboard and one in her port side to send the mighty *Bismarck* to the bottom.

Hitler and Goering had taken direct charge of the efforts made to bring the *Bismarck* to port. The Luftwaffe had extended an air umbrella some 300 miles at sea, and destroyers, torpedo boats, and U-boats were hastily summoned to clear a path into Brest after she was hit. Admiral Luetjens had recently brought the *Scharnhorst* and the *Gneisenau* safely into that harbor after their raid on British supply lines, but he could not repeat this success with the *Bismarck*. After the *Bismarck* was attacked he had released the *Prinz Eugen,* which evaded the British cordon, reached Brest, and survived the war, only to be sunk at Bikini Atoll during the tests of the atomic bomb.

The fate of the *Bismarck* and the *Spee* and the comparative failure of the *Scharnhorst* and the *Gneisenau,* kept in Brest under air attack and surveillance for ten months before they were able to reach Norway, where they were again bottled up in port, proved the futility of commerce destroying alone as a means of winning a naval war.

In the autumn of 1939, while the Allied navies deployed to meet German attacks on sea-borne commerce, British and French industry faced serious production problems. Shipyards and factories were making frantic efforts to increase the production of ships, planes, tanks, and other munitions to meet the needs of their armies and navies. Simultaneously both governments sent purchasing missions to Washington to place contracts in the United States. The Neutrality Act prevented the purchase of munitions, and even after the administration had succeeded in getting parts of that act repealed, war materials in the United States were placed on a "cash-and-carry" basis, definitely limiting Anglo-French buying. Both nations needed additional dollar credits to finance the necessary transactions, and to obtain them requisitioned American securities owned by their citizens. In spite of these drastic measures during the first nine months of the war, purchases by the Western Allies were handicapped by lack of American exchange. President Roosevelt was able to get only part of the act modified by Congress by agreeing that American ships be kept out of the war zone and passports refused to Americans wishing to visit the combat area.

The unreadiness of Anglo-French industry was due in part to the belief prevailing in both countries that the defensive was the superior form of war. As late as 1935 the French High Command, depending on the Maginot Line, then nearing completion, and the numerical superiority of the French Army, had been confident that a German invasion could be resisted without help from the British Army. The subsequent increase in Hitler's army caused a revision of this estimate and the British War Office had agreed to land another expeditionary force. And by October 11, 1939, 158,000 British troops of all arms and services were in France, and were placed under the command of General Gamelin, who used them to extend the western flank of his army along the French-Belgian frontier. Allied confidence in the Maginot Line remained unshaken. Gamelin dictated Anglo-French land strategy, but it was strictly in accord with the spirit existing in both nations and armies and was essentially defensive.

As has been indicated, Gamelin had made no serious effort to relieve the pressure on Poland by attacking the Germans in their West Wall position. When the bulk of the German formations that had conquered Poland were returned to western Germany, Gamelin settled himself comfortably behind his concrete walls to await developments. French movements were limited to minor air and ground patrols in the no man's land that separated the two armies. By the middle of October the French troops had abandoned or been driven from the few advance positions occupied during the Polish campaign, and had destroyed the bridges across the Rhine except at Strassburg, where the bridgeheads on the

French side terminated within the Maginot Line. No further proof of Gamelin's determination to remain on the defensive was needed.

The British Army was as passive as the French. In fact the glorification of the defensive form of war had begun in England during 1917–18, when Lloyd George condemned all the offensives undertaken by Haig. Later Winston Churchill lent his great name to this doctrine by praising the defensive in his book, *World Crisis*. Liddell Hart, military correspondent for the *London Times* and leading exponent of the defensive between 1919 and 1939, stated that Hore-Belisha, Minister of War, had adopted many of his ideas, and it was Hore-Belisha who had selected Lord Gort to be Commander of the British Expeditionary Force. So it happened that not a trace of the fiery spirit of Ferdinand Foch or the imperturbable determination of "Papa" Joffre and Douglas Haig to take the offensive at every opportunity, which had inspired the Allied armies in the first World War, was to be found at the Anglo-French headquarters.

The Allied Army Command were content to entrust the safety of France and Britain to a few thousand tons of concrete, stretched along the French-German frontier, and in spite of the Blitzkrieg campaign in Poland persuaded themselves that the Germans stupidly would knock their armies to bits against the French entrenchments. From time to time the calm, almost bored, French general entertained press representatives in his comfortable field quarters. While they dined on viands prepared by the finest chefs in France, he emphasized the strength of the Allied position. The correspondents in turn convinced the American as well as British and French publics that all was well along the western front.

As the year 1939 drew to a close there was throughout the three great democracies an unjustified feeling of security that could be traced in part at least to Gamelin and Gort. This confidence was engendered at the very time German formations were being concentrated in such strength along the whole front from Holland to Switzerland that an attack in force could be launched at any point at any time.

SEPTEMBER, 1939, TO JULY, 1940

While the western front was static, the Soviets began absorbing Latvia, Esthonia, and Lithuania, all former Russian provinces that Lenin had made independent. Hitler, still under the necessity of placating Stalin, coöperated by repatriating Germans who had settled in these Baltic provinces. Beginning with a protectorate, Moscow soon established the Soviet system of industry and government among the inhabitants, many of whom fled westward to escape their conquerors.

Stalin next made demands on Finland, which conceded many of them. Nevertheless on November 30 Soviet armies marched across the Finnish frontiers. The action of the Kremlin caused some tension in the Reich itself, for German armies under Lieutenant General von der Goltz had assisted in the liberation of Finland in 1917, and there is no doubt that for many reasons large numbers of Germans resented the Russian invasion of Finland.

Anglo-French sea power could do no more to help Finland when the Russians invaded than it had done for Poland. With Germany dominating the Skagerrak, assistance could reach the Finns only through Murmansk, and then only if an expeditionary force could have established itself there. A wave of sympathy for the Finns swept Great Britain, France, and the United States but it possessed no strength of action. A combined Anglo-French Expeditionary Force was hastily assembled and held in readiness until Norway and Sweden, for fear of being involved in the war, refused to let the troops cross their territory. The need for these soldiers elsewhere was acute and very soon this force was dispersed. In light of the subsequent campaign in Norway it was well for both Sweden and Norway that they made the decision they did.

Some of the Russian demands upon Finland were justified, particularly the re-cession of the islands in the Gulf of Finland and positions on the Karelian Peninsula which dominated the entrance to Kronstadt and in the possession of a hostile power would block the approach to Leningrad. The Russian campaign was badly managed but the Finns were eventually defeated, in the middle of March, 1940, sued for peace, and obtained fairly moderate terms. The French and British Cabinets made futile offers of help at the last minute, though no one in authority knew where soldiers could be found in case Finland accepted their offer of assistance and attempted to prolong the war. Finland had learned that London and Paris could only extend their well-intentioned resolutions, and made her peace with Russia.

The Russo-Finnish War revealed diplomatic tensions between the Axis Powers and Russia. Italian papers did not conceal their sympathy for Finland and their suspicion of Russia. Mussolini permitted Italian planes to be bought for Finland, and Hitler was reported willing to allow these planes to pass through Germany. Hitler had difficulty in keeping his quasi partner Stalin and his ally Mussolini together. American feelings were all for Finland and were even to survive the time when Finland would join Germany.

It was seen in Russia that the military leaders had underestimated the resistance of the Finns and had mismanaged the war. After Finland had yielded, several drastic changes were made in the organization and high commanders of the Red Army. But the northern flank of the Soviet Republic had been strengthened by the strategic islands and territory taken. Relieved of the threat from the north, Stalin was in a position to make plans for extending the frontiers in the south. But the reverses suffered in Finland and the open indignation of important German elements caused by the Finnish War did not increase the Soviet trust in Hitler. Likewise, people in the Reich, particularly army officers who had served in the last war, had not failed to note the dangers to Germany of any further advance of Russia into Scandinavia. Hitler's determination to secure control of Norway was undoubtedly stimulated by Russian expansion to the northwest.

When the Anglo-French High Command determined in September, 1939, to remain on the defensive on land and were unable to influence events in eastern Europe, it was more necessary than ever to use their only weapon, control of the sea, to suppress German trade on the Atlantic Ocean.

And when the British Government announced that in retaliation for the illegal sowing of mines by Germany all German exports would be subject to seizure, it appeared that full use would be made of British sea power.

Under conditions existing in the autumn of 1939 the Royal Navy could not maintain an effective blockade that would satisfy the requirements of International Law. But the government could legally suppress practically all the trade to Germany, direct and indirect, by extending the list of contraband goods and invoking the doctrine of continuous voyage. Instead of employing the only method left of getting full value from their superior navy, however, the Foreign Office, advised by the Ministry of Economic Warfare, in December, 1939, negotiated a series of war trade agreements with European neutrals that sacrificed Great Britain's belligerent rights on the sea.

Two paragraphs of the agreement with Sweden will show how British civil servants ashore tied the hands of British sailors afloat. Paragraph I reads: "The Royal Swedish Government will endeavor to maintain at their normal level Swedish exports to and imports from the United Kingdom of commodities normally exported to or imported from that country, so far as such commodities are able to find a market in the United Kingdom and Sweden respectively, and will give all reasonable facilities to that end." Paragraph II reads: "The Government of the United Kingdom will endeavor to maintain at normal level British exports to and imports from Sweden of commodities normally exported to or imported from that country so far as such commodities are able to find a market in Sweden and the United Kingdom respectively, and will give all reasonable facilities to that end."

The War Trade Agreements negotiated by London enabled the neutral states to continue to trade with both Germany and Great Britain, and probably resulted in some exchange of British and German goods. Swedish iron ore was exported from Narvik to Germany and Great Britain. After loading ores, the British ships were met outside Norwegian

waters by men-of-war and escorted to the United Kingdom.
German ships crept along the coast, ready at all times to reenter a neutral harbor or roadstead to evade capture.

Neither Germany nor Great Britain was satisfied with the anomalous situation, and after Norway had refused the demand of the British and French Governments that she lay mine fields to deny German ships access to her coastal waters, the Anglo-French navies decided to mine certain strategic portions of the Norwegian waters and thus force the German ships to come beyond Norway's jurisdiction. On April 8 the two navies laid three mine fields off the Norwegian coast and within Norwegian territorial waters.

The Germans launched the first air-supported overseas invasion just as the Anglo-French forces were laying these mine fields. Under cover of its air squadrons the inferior German surface fleet was divided into two parts to support the troops who were embarked in camouflaged merchant vessels and who quickly overran Oslo, Kristiansand, Bergen, and Trondheim. Simultaneously transport planes and parachute jumpers seized the vital southern Norwegian air bases and the Germans quickly established their fighter planes ashore. Submarines were the only British and French ships that dared to enter the Kattegat, so that German transports protected by destroyers and torpedo boats had little opposition and did not suffer heavy losses. When the British Fleet appeared in the neighborhood of Bergen there were enough German aircraft established ashore to deliver air attacks on the surface ships and compel their withdrawal. Thereafter the operations of the Germans in southern Norway were opposed only by submarines, light craft, and a few mine fields laid by planes.

Meanwhile numerous naval encounters had occurred in and around Narvik in northern Norway. On April 9 the battle cruiser *Renown* engaged the *Scharnhorst* and the *Hipper* off Narvik in a passing encounter with little damage to either side. On the same day 11 German destroyers, each carrying about 300 troops in addition to its regular crew, entered Narvik. The captains of the two Norwegian coast defense ships *Norge* and *Eidsvold* refused to surrender;

their ships were torpedoed and the German force took possession of the town and port. At three the next morning a British flotilla of five destroyers entered the harbor. The British were outnumbered but pushed home two attacks. Both sides fought well and skillfully and losses were approximately equal. Surviving British destroyers kept watch over the entrance until three days later, April 13, when nine British destroyers supported by the battleship *Warspite* entered the fjord. In an all-day battle, which was almost without loss to themselves, the British sank or ran ashore nine German destroyers that had survived the previous action.

This naval victory drove the German troops who had disembarked the day before back into the hills, but the British had no troops to land. When the British naval force departed, the German soldiers took possession of Narvik Harbor and port facilities. Two days later a British force was landed at Harstad, in the Lofoten Islands. But not until May 28 did the British succeed in dislodging the small German force and capturing Narvik. British and French forces were also landed at Namsos on April 14 and at Aandalsnaes on April 17, but were too weak to effect a junction and had to withdraw shortly after. On June 9 the British evacuation of Narvik sealed the German conquest of Norway, which passed almost unnoticed amid the catastrophic downfall of France and the Low Countries.

In the two battles inside Narvik the British had sunk or run ashore eleven German destroyers, a good proportion of Nazi destroyer strength. The German Navy paid more heavily for Norway than the Army, and although it cost the British Navy several ships sunk and many more damaged, the greatly superior fleet could accept losses and still retain its superiority over the German Navy. But many British destroyers and cruisers were temporarily disabled just as the German storm was about to break over France and the Low Countries.

With the German occupation of western Europe to the Pyrenees, the neutral states, particularly Sweden and Switzerland, took advantage of England's extremity to wring further trade concessions from her. For a time the whole energy of the Royal Navy was absorbed in preventing the French Fleet from joining Hitler and in evacuating the expeditionary force. Concessions were required then, but after the situation at sea was restored the British Government still acquiesced in the actions of these neutrals.

When the United States entered the war, American economic experts investigated the situation resulting from the War Trade Agreements between Great Britain and Sweden. They found that Sweden was rendering great and diversified aid to Germany. Swedish iron ore furnished one fifth of the ore used in German steelmaking throughout the war, and steel is, of course, the basic metal for all munitions. In addition it was discovered that Sweden permitted her railways to be used by Germans to transport troops and equipment to Norway and north Finland and thus avoid exposure to British ships. And German merchantmen were allowed to sail in convoys in the Baltic Sea, escorted by Swedish men-of-war.

Sweden's help to Germany probably did more to prolong the war than that of any other neutral, but Switzerland had integrated her economy with the Reich's, Spain contributed regularly to Germany by way of the Vichy French Government, and Portugal, although she was nominally a British ally, did likewise. Turkey lay within the orbit of British sea power during the first nine months of the war but little use was made of the advantage. Clearly it can be said that Great Britain did not fully employ her control of the sea to put economic pressure on Germany.

V

Sea Power Saves Great Britain

ON MAY 10, 1940, before he had completed the conquest of Norway, Hitler launched simultaneous attacks against Holland, Belgium, and France. British destroyers, mine sweepers, and torpedo boats sailed immediately for various Dutch ports. The mine sweepers kept harbors open, while destroyers and PT boats evacuated refugees and gave some protection against German planes. Within a week Holland yielded, but in that short time British destroyers had evacuated Queen Wilhelmina, other members of the Royal Family, and the Cabinet. Practically all the Dutch Navy and merchant marine sailed for English ports and formed a valuable reënforcement. British men-of-war brought away Dutch demolition parties that had blown up oil tanks in Rotterdam and blocked canals and locks by sinking ships.

Weygand relieved Gamelin on May 19 but was unable to stop the German avalanche. Pétain succeeded Reynaud as Premier on June 17 and asked Hitler for an armistice the following day. Within 7 weeks the German armies had crushed France and the Low Countries. Nevertheless the British Navy with air cover from the Royal Air Force successfully evacuated the bulk of the expeditionary force and a substantial number of Belgian and French troops. More important still, the greater portion of the French Fleet and merchant marine escaped from France.

The political impact of the German success was more than doubled because before the invasion of Norway professional army opinion in Paris and London had been convinced, first, that a German frontal attack on the Maginot Line would collapse with heavy losses, and second, that if a march through Holland and Belgium were attempted, while the Dutch Army could not long resist, the Belgian first line of defense along the Albert Canal would hold until the Seventh, First, and Ninth French Field Armies plus the British Expeditionary Force could reach the main line of defense along the Dyle River from Namur on the Meuse through Louvain to Antwerp. Therefore it was presumed that the risk of defeat was sufficiently great to deter the Germans from attacking, and the French General Staff had not hesitated to despatch some of their most efficient divisions to Syria and deploy a large amount of their aviation along the Italian frontier.

The collapse of Norway and Denmark caused some British and French officials to reconsider their estimates of German strength. On the advice of Admiral of the Fleet Sir Dudley Pound, Winston Churchill, then First Lord of the Admiralty, resisted strong naval and parliamentary demands to commit the Home Fleet to the rescue of Norway; both Admiral Pound and his assistant, Vice-Admiral Tom Phillips, insisted that the navy and its air arm be kept ready for greater emergencies.

Many factors contributed to the unprecedented German success on land. The Governments of Holland and Belgium, hoping to remain neutral, had officially announced their intention to attack any force crossing their frontiers. They would not permit staff conversations with the Anglo-French High Command. Plans for concerted action had to be improvised on May 10 when they appealed to Paris and London for assistance. The Anglo-French High Command, in an effort to reënforce the Dutch and Belgians and halt Hitler's onrushing armies, promptly set the French Seventh Army, the British Expeditionary Force, and the French First and Ninth Armies in motion to the north, General Corap's Ninth pivoting on the French forces entrenched along the prolongation of the Maginot Line. Motorized elements of the French Seventh Army reached southwest Holland within 72 hours after the movement began, but not in sufficient force to be effective. The British Expeditionary Force and the French First Army were on the line of the Dyle by May 13, where they were joined by the Belgian Army falling back in good order from the outposts along

SEA POWER SAVES GREAT BRITAIN   51

the Albert Canal. The German movement through Holland and Belgium, powerful as it proved, was only the secondary blow. Hitler afterward called it a feint to draw the Anglo-French armies into Belgium. The main German thrust was through Luxembourg and southern Belgium.

Hitler's armies aggregated more than 200 divisions, including 12 armored divisions. They were supported by over 8,000 combat planes, trained both for strategic bombing and close tactical support of the ground troops. To this overwhelming superiority Hitler's plan of invasion added the advantage of surprise, which was fully exploited by officers of the Wehrmacht, still flushed with the victories over Poland and eager to avenge the German defeat in 1918. In pursuance of Hitler's orders, Kleist's army broke through the Ardennes Forest May 10 and 11, hurling back the partly mechanized French cavalry which vainly endeavored to cover the advance of General Corap's Ninth Army into Belgium. By May 14 Rommel's armored division had crossed the Meuse and driven a wedge between the French First and Ninth Armies.

To the astonishment of most military observers this small gap made by one armored division could not be closed by two entire French armies. Instead it was widened first by German tanks which crossed the Meuse at Sedan, then by motorized and mechanized infantry divisions following closely behind the armored divisions. When Weygand relieved Gamelin on May 19, he hoped by launching simultaneous counterattacks from Péronne on the south and Arras on the north not only to reunite his armies but to cut off the German divisions leading the advance. Instead, combat teams of the armored divisions, with Marshal von Rundstedt's army close behind, paced by air scouts and dive bombers, broke up all attempts by Weygand to mount counterattacks and began to reach the Channel by May 21. Until the 27th the Belgian Field Army, although suffering heavy losses, held the line north of the British. By this time it was evident to King Leopold that the British and French Armies in Belgium were hopelessly separated from the French divisions in northern France. The King of the Belgians surrendered his army on May 28. His action exposed the north flank of the British Army, hastening but not causing its inevitable evacuation, since it could not execute the orders of its government to join the French armies to the south. Lord Gort, British Commander in Chief, could extricate his army only by an immediate retreat to the Channel near Dunkirk where the Royal Air Force could afford some protection against the Luftwaffe and the Royal Navy could embark his beaten but unbroken battalions.

All the assistance rendered Gort's forces by the Royal Navy and Air Force would have been useless except for the indomitable courage of the rank and file and the resolute leadership of the British Command. With their northern flank entirely exposed and their southern flank almost enveloped by German armored divisions, the British rear guards, assisted by courageous remnants of the French and Belgian Armies, held back the triumphant Germans long enough to allow the main body and substantial numbers of the French and Belgian troops to make an orderly retreat. Two fresh battalions despatched in destroyers from England to Calais entrenched themselves and held up German armored forces advancing from Boulogne until the beachhead was secure. The willingness of some British formations to sacrifice themselves enabled the others to reach and establish the beachhead at Dunkirk. These infantrymen were annihilated, either killed or so severely wounded that when the Germans broke through they were captured. The destroyers that had ferried them across the Channel suffered heavily while furnishing sporadic artillery support and embarking wounded soldiers and civilian refugees to England.

During these perilous days Winston Churchill became Prime Minister. He embodied the determination of the Britons to die rather than yield, and he coördinated the resistance of British civilians with the armed forces. The British Admiralty now directed all small craft in south and east England to proceed to Dunkirk. Over 200 naval vessels from destroyers to armed yachts, assisted by almost 700 coasters, launches, ferryboats, and river rowboats returned

SEA POWER SAVES GREAT BRITAIN 53

to England her army and thousands of gallant Belgians and Frenchmen. These men-of-war, merchant ships, and private boats, and the hundreds of crews capable of manning them could have been mobilized only in a nation bred on the sea. The commander of this improvised regatta, Vice-Admiral Bertram Ramsay, was knighted for his service.

Overhead the Fighter and Bomber Commands of the Royal Air Force, assisted by the naval air arm, gave all the protection they could offer. Based on England, their limited radius of action prevented British fighters from intervening in Belgium, but over Dunkirk they could control the air as long as their personnel could fly. Only the Royal Air Force could not keep patrols aloft continuously; there were times when troops and ships suffered uninterrupted attacks from the Luftwaffe and German field guns. On the first day three destroyers and a number of smaller craft were sunk by German planes. But fortunately, during five dark nights, the usually choppy waters of the Channel were calm. Small British craft sped back and forth between May 29 and June 2. In round numbers 225,000 British and 113,000 Belgian and French soldiers were evacuated. The success of the operation can be measured by the British loss in the whole campaign, which approximated 30,000. On June 3 Captain Tennant, senior naval officer at Dunkirk, reported, "Embarkation completed."

The Royal Air Force was not able to assist in the evacuation of Norway, and its air arm could offer the navy only scant support. Losses in Norway were relatively greater than at Dunkirk, but although German dive bombers were given no air opposition, there was no panic. The King, the Government, and a nucleus of the Norwegian armed forces were brought to England. The coöperation and disciplined courage of the land, sea, and air forces and the unfaltering resolution of the people of the United Kingdom made possible the evacuations of Norway and Dunkirk in the face of the most powerful army and air force the world had yet seen, whose leaders had boasted that no British soldier would escape from either Norway or France.

The evacuation of Narvik on June 9 left Norway entirely

under German control and gave the German submarines and surface raiders easier access to the north Atlantic. The British strengthened their control on the northern route to the Atlantic by occupying first the Faroe Islands and on May 10 landing in Iceland. Bases on these islands facilitated the British task of protecting their own trade and suppressing the enemy's.

As the British Navy adjusted its naval forces to the new situation, the German armies wheeled southward across the Somme to complete the destruction of the French armies. Premier Reynaud appealed to President Roosevelt for armed intervention, which only Congress could authorize. Fully aware of the immediate effect of the collapse of France on Great Britain and the possible effect on the United States of a British defeat, Roosevelt increased the supplies he was sending to Britain. It was American field pieces, machine guns, and rifles that reëquipped the British Expeditionary Force. The President even sent substantial quantities of new guns and planes being manufactured for American forces. Franklin Roosevelt contributed as much as any individual, with the possible exception of Winston Churchill, to the rehabilitation and rearming of the British Army.

President Roosevelt did an even greater service to Britain when he officially informed the French Government that if the French Navy were turned over to Hitler the people of the United States would never forgive the people of France. British naval liaison officers in French ports had been urging all naval and merchant ships to sail promptly for British ports when the President's message was delivered to Pétain. However, the ancient rivalry between the French and British Navies had been revived at the Washington Naval Conference, and the most influential French officer between the two wars had been Vice-Admiral Jean Darlan, a violent Anglophobe, who became the French Commander in Chief during the war. His antipathy to the British persisted and because of his professional prestige and popularity many French officers and men were influenced to refuse the gen-

SEA POWER SAVES GREAT BRITAIN 55

erous terms offered by Churchill to those who would continue to serve against Germany.

To prevent the possible absorption of the French Fleet by the German Navy, the British Government determined on July 3 to take a number of decisive measures. All French personnel on ships in British ports were given the option of serving on their own ships, under their own flag, in British squadrons with the same pay and allowances as those of the British personnel, or of being repatriated at British expense and their ships taken over by British sailors. Many French officers and men continued to serve in the Free French Navy under Vice-Admiral E. H. D. Muselier, who became Commander in Chief of the Fleet under General de Gaulle. Two old battleships, 2 light cruisers, 8 destroyers, and numerous French submarines joined the Free French Fleet in the British Isles.

In Alexandria the French Squadron of one battleship, several cruisers, destroyers, and smaller craft was immobilized by its admiral. Only skeleton crews were kept aboard, the majority of the men living ashore at British expense. Ammunition, breech blocks of the guns, torpedo war heads, and all fuel except that needed for port consumption were landed.

At Oran, Algeria, 2 superdreadnoughts, the *Dunkerque* and the *Strasbourg,* 2 old dreadnoughts, the *Provence* and the *Bretagne,* 3 cruisers, and a number of destroyers and submarines were under the command of Admiral Gensoul. On July 3 Gensoul was invited to bring his ships to British ports, where the personnel would be given the option of joining the Free French Navy or of being repatriated after turning the men-of-war over to British crews. If these terms were not accepted within six hours, Vice-Admiral Sir James Somerville informed his former colleague, it would be his painful duty to sink the French ships. The French admiral refused the terms. British surface ships first bombarded the vessels as they crowded Oran Harbor, and then dive bombers from British carriers sank the *Bretagne* and forced the *Dunkerque,* the *Provence,* and a destroyer to run aground.

The *Strasbourg* and several destroyers escaped under a smoke screen, making their way to Toulon, where they remained until the Nazis took possession of that port in 1942. On July 8 the captain of the *Richelieu* at Dakar refused a similar demand. British depth bombs and aerial torpedoes first disabled and then sank this newest French superdreadnought in the shallow harbor.

The French Government retaliated on July 5, 6, and 7 with air attacks on Gibraltar. The relations between Paris and London were badly strained during these operations but in spite of its resentment at the British action and its helplessness, the French Government did not turn over the remainder of the navy or the African colonies to the Germans. American opinion generally approved the stern British measures and the administration continued to impress upon Pétain that any unnecessary collaboration with Hitler would be viewed with grave concern. On July 12 the British Government informed Pétain that no further action would be taken against French men-of-war unless they attempted to return to France. And the last action against French ships was caused by the departure from Toulon for Dakar of three cruisers and as many destroyers on September 11, 1940.

It was essential for the British Navy to prevent Hitler from obtaining possession of French combat ships. No duty of the Royal Navy or of the British Government was more important. And no assistance given to Britain by President Roosevelt was more valuable than the pressure he maintained upon Vichy to limit its collaboration with Hitler during the second half of 1940. General Pershing was President Roosevelt's first choice for Ambassador to Pétain's government, but when the health of the general prevented his accepting the task, the Chief Executive chose astute Admiral W. D. Leahy, former Chief of Naval Operations. Leahy represented his government ably in one of the most difficult diplomatic assignments of the war.

Disarming the French Navy added an almost insuperable burden to the Royal Navy. The invasion of Norway had already increased the tempo of British naval operations. Support of ground forces in Norway, France, and the Low Countries, and the evacuations of Norway and Dunkirk had entailed severe naval losses. In addition, many warships, particularly destroyers and smaller craft, had been severely damaged and were out of action for weeks or months.

The German Navy suffered proportionately and never seriously threatened the British control of the sea except in the Baltic. German convoys, escorted by destroyers or torpedo boats and often provided with air cover, crept along the coast between North Cape and the Pyrenees, along the Mediterranean coast between southern France and Genoa, and from the Dardanelles to the Adriatic. During the campaigns in Africa, German and Italian convoys from southern Italy and Sicily to Libya were repeatedly attacked by British naval and air ships, while British convoys between Gibraltar and Alexandria were assaulted by Axis ships and planes. Neither side could transfer troops any distance without the fact being discovered, and strikes by air or sea were the usual sequel. Under these conditions the coördination of British land, sea, and air forces developed rapidly.

When Italy declared war upon Great Britain and France she possessed, built or building, 8 battleships, 17 cruisers, 100 destroyers, and 110 submarines. As we have seen, Mussolini had constructed no aircraft carriers, since his fleet had been created to operate in the Mediterranean and he had expected his land-based planes to provide air cover for the surface ships and to attack enemy ships. On paper Italy had a more balanced and formidable fleet than Germany but its personnel was not as efficient. However, this navy entered the war in the Mediterranean at the moment when British naval resources were taxed to the utmost, and in addition in the restricted waters of this sea British ships, with Italy's coming into the war, were continuously exposed to attacks from the air.

The diplomatic situation appeared equally cheerless. Hitler's prestige was at a new peak. Spain was openly hostile to Britain. In the Middle East, Syria was garrisoned by Vichy troops whose commanders were ready to assist German tourists to penetrate into Iraq and Iran. The

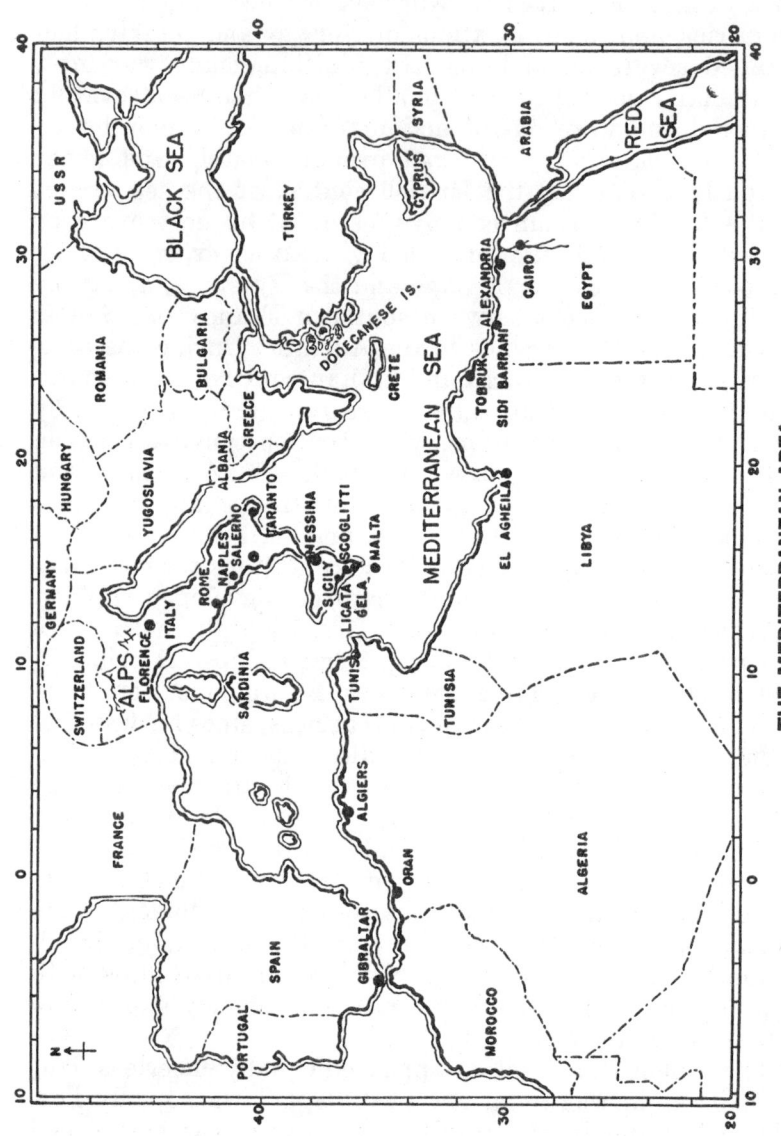

quasi alliance between Russia and Germany still existed. Bulgaria and Rumania had been absorbed by Germany. Bessarabia and northern Bukovina had been seized by Russia. However, the situation was not as dark as it seemed. In the Balkans, Yugoslavia and Greece continued to resist Hitler's blend of blandishments and threats. Turkey, pulled in opposite directions by the opportunistic associates, Hitler and Stalin, remained neutral but pro-Ally. The repeated seizures of territory in eastern Europe by the Nazi and Soviet troops suggested that the deeply rooted rivalry between the dictators could not remain concealed much longer. Stalin, amazed at the strength displayed by the Wehrmacht in its conquests of western Europe, made General G. K. Zhukov, one of his ablest officers, Commander in Chief and devoted the energies and resources of the Soviet Government to preparations for war. This policy immediately reduced the amount of Russian exports available for Germany. Maneuvers of the Red Army near East Prussia further annoyed Hitler, nor was he softened by Molotov's visit to Berlin in November. Outwardly, German-Soviet relations remained unimpaired; actually, the cleavage was increasing.

Churchill did not propose to sacrifice the Empire to insure the safety of the United Kingdom. He was playing for all or nothing. Before the defenses of Britain were secured he despatched two divisions to Egypt. This contingent was small compared with the troops available to the Axis in the Mediterranean, but with this initial reënforcement the British ground forces in close coöperation with their naval and air arms undertook the desperate struggle to control the Mediterranean and hold the Middle East.

On June 11, 1940, the Italian Air Force bombed Malta for the first time. This tiny island served equally well as an air and naval base. From its airfields British fighting planes could protect the garrison and dockyards and increase the air cover given the Royal Navy by its own carrier-based planes in the most dangerous stretch of the long line of communications, and could simultaneously attack Axis vessels. Malta's fortress and antiaircraft guns gave it protection from enemy ships or planes; its naval dockyards supported the light cruisers, destroyers, and submarines that continually harassed the Axis line of communications to Libya, and made temporary repairs on capital ships and carriers, enabling them to proceed to Gibraltar or Alexandria.

Malta's extensive and well-equipped air shelters afforded security for its armed forces and for the civilian population, furnishing the labor that repaired and refitted ships and planes. Despite heavy air and frequent submarine attacks the two British naval squadrons, one based on Alexandria and the other on Gibraltar, provided a steady flow of supplies, food, munitions, planes, and personnel replacements from the British Isles or Egypt to Malta, which became not only a symbol but a vital link of the British sea power that controlled the Mediterranean. Indeed, Malta became such a formidable obstacle to Axis operations that first the Italian and then the German Air Force, operating from well-equipped and well-supplied airfields in near-by Sicily, vowed they would annihilate the island. Instead, continually replenishing its strength from the sea, Malta absorbed air blows that would otherwise have fallen upon British ships or planes; its fighting squadrons and antiaircraft batteries continually reënforced by naval convoys made it the graveyard of the Axis air forces in the Mediterranean.

An example of the part taken by Malta and the close coöperation of British sea, air, and land forces occurred early in July. Admiral Somerville's squadron from Gibraltar escorted a convoy of troops and supplies to the vicinity of Sicily where it was passed to the protection of Admiral Sir Andrew Cunningham's squadron, which had steamed from Alexandria to receive the reënforcements. These men, munitions, and other material were destined for General Wavell's Army of the Nile. An Italian naval force including two battleships endeavored to intervene, but the Italian admiral promptly withdrew when he reached extreme gun range. The Italians then launched air attacks, damaging the cruiser *Gloucester*. During the next two days the British ships were severely bombed on several occasions by Italian planes. Only near hits that caused superficial injury were made; the *Gloucester* continued with the squadron.

SEA POWER SAVES GREAT BRITAIN   61

The efficiency of the Fleet Air Arm continued to increase after it had been returned to control of the Admiralty. Naval airmen bombed Sidi Barrani, and in company with Royal Air Force planes blasted enemy installations on the Dodecanese Islands and the supply columns of Marshal Rudolfo Graziani's army when it began its first invasion of Egypt. The Fleet Air Arm promptly avenged the attack on London by an Italian air squadron on November 11, for on the same night Fairey Swordfish planes from the *Illustrious* and the *Eagle* delivered a torpedo attack upon the Italian Fleet at Taranto. Despite the protection of captive balloons and antiaircraft guns, one *Littorio* class and two *Conte di Cavour* class battleships were put out of action, greatly improving the relative position of the British Navy in the Mediterranean. It was the first successful employment of carrier-based torpedo planes against capital ships and emphasized a point often forgotten, that aviation can assist the superior as well as the inferior fleet, and is an aid, not a threat, to the exercise of sea power.

Experience in the western approaches to the British Isles demonstrated the need for even closer coördination between the Coastal Command of the Air Force and the Admiralty, which was responsible for the routing and protection of seagoing convoys. The action of the air arm at Taranto convinced Churchill that the navy should be given operational control over the Coastal Command and that was done. Events in the Atlantic and the Mediterranean combined to show that closely integrated aviation was necessary to the Royal Navy if it was going to control the sea.

Much of Italy's naval strength lay in submarines, but the undersea boats were not effective against British surface ships, and suffered severe losses. Likewise British submarines operating in the Mediterranean suffered numerous casualties, for the summer weather is usually fine and the water clear. Submerged submarines can frequently be seen from the air, and, once sighted, can be pursued and repeatedly attacked.

Mussolini ordered the invasion of Greece from Albania on October 28, 1940. Churchill immediately sent liaison officers to arrange assistance for Greece as pledged in 1939. On

November 5 the British established a naval and air base on Crete. There were not enough ground troops to garrison this large island adequately and to meet other demands, such as reënforcing the Greek Army in Greece and operating with the Free French to eject Vichy troops from Syria.

Among the British land, sea, and air forces there was cordial and efficient coöperation. After gaining control of the Mediterranean, the British combined their arms to destroy Graziani's army that had invaded Egypt in September and had carefully accumulated stores in Sidi Barrani for an advance on Cairo.

On December 8 the Mediterranean Fleet bombarded this Italian base. The next day Wavell began his advance; three days later Sidi Barrani and the equipment and supplies so painfully accumulated were in British hands. Battleships, carriers, cruisers, destroyers, and smaller craft steamed parallel to the coast, giving direct air and naval support to Wavell's troops as they marched westward. Transports and merchantmen supplied water, munitions, and food to the ground troops, and embarked Italian prisoners, damaged tanks and trucks, thus leaving Wavell free to pursue Graziani's beaten soldiers. The Italians were soon crushed between British ships at sea and British troops operating along the fringe of the desert. Approximately 135,000 Italians surrendered, and by February 8, 1941, Wavell's army was in possession of the eastern half of Libya and established at El Agheila. The continued necessity of helping Greece eventually compelled Churchill to rob Wavell's army in Libya and facilitated the subsequent advance of Rommel, but Wavell's destruction of the Italian Army showed that the British High Command had learned to operate land, sea, and air forces as one military unit. On the whole, the British Government had cause to be satisfied with its position in the Mediterranean as 1940 drew to a close.

The complete failure of the Italian armed forces to break British control of the Mediterranean was due more to the great superiority of British personnel than to the merit of any particular arm of the services. A few Italian officers dis-

SEA POWER SAVES GREAT BRITAIN 63

played rare personal skill and heroism, notably in the operation of their midget submarines and their efforts to attach mines to the hulls of British ships in protected harbors. But for the most part neither the officers nor men of the sea, land, and air forces showed any desire for close combat with the British forces.

Control of the Mediterranean by the British Navy was important but control of the Atlantic was vital; supplies from North America were essential to the people and industry of the British Isles, and the sea lanes in the north Atlantic that terminated in the western ports of the United Kingdom and north Ireland were the life lines of the Empire. The Germans began their air and submarine attacks on British shipping in 1939; the following spring the air attacks were greatly increased and continued during the invasion of Norway. This was a natural development, for although Hitler and the General Staff were essentially continental strategists they did know that it would not be necessary to invade Great Britain if the merchant shipping that supplied the British Isles could be destroyed. But their efforts to cut the sea communications failed.

In 1938, after dismissing von Blomberg, von Fritsch, and Beck, Hitler had completely dominated the General Staff; the campaigns in Poland, Norway, the Low Countries, and France had been planned by him and their phenomenal success had increased his prestige and convinced many orthodox German strategists that he was an untutored but genuine military genius. According to Colonel General Alfred Jodl, Hitler ordered the invasion of western Europe because he believed Great Britain would yield if France were conquered. According to Admiral Doenitz, when the British Cabinet refused to make peace, Hitler ordered the navy to make preparations to invade England.[1]

When this order was given the triumphant German armies were within 22 miles of Dover and there was no army in England that could have resisted the Wehrmacht. If the

---

1. At that time Admiral Doenitz was Commander of the U-boats. He succeeded Grand Admiral Raeder as Supreme Commander of the Navy in January, 1943.

United Kingdom had been on a peninsula connected with France by a neck of land 10 to 20 miles wide, Hitler's standard would soon have floated over Buckingham Palace. All the British air and land forces in the country would not have even delayed Hitler's divisions. This fundamental fact should not be forgotten in considering how Britain's insular position and her control of the sea helped her to repulse the successive attacks of the Wehrmacht and the Luftwaffe.

While the Wehrmacht practiced embarking and disembarking, the navy and air force redoubled the attacks on shipping. The German conquest of western Europe ringed the British Isles with air and sea bases that were quickly utilized. In July of 1940 U-boats were based in France. At the same time a large number of British destroyers and escort vessels were under repair, and others were taken from escort duty to be ready to strike at the expected German invaders. From July through September more German U-boats were operating and fewer British escort ships were available to protect the convoys. Losses of British merchantmen increased rapidly. German planes scouted for and operated with submarines and surface raiders against British and neutral shipping, while the British countered with closer coördination between the Air Force Coastal Command and the Admiralty.

The Luftwaffe soon found that horizontal bombing did little damage to British ships. Resort was had to dive bombing that inflicted greater loss; however the dive bombers also suffered proportionately. Next, a combination air attack was developed; horizontal bombers would initiate an engagement in the hope of diverting all antiaircraft fire, and dive bombers would then swoop down for the kill.

In July and August German aircraft increased their attacks on shipping. On August 8 large squadrons of horizontal and dive bombers made three heavy raids, inflicting and incurring severe losses; 66 aircraft were shot down in the battle area. The assaults were resumed on the 11th and the 13th, when the last heavy attack over the Channel occurred with still greater German losses. The Luftwaffe began to attack the estuary of the Thames, Portsmouth, and

SEA POWER SAVES GREAT BRITAIN 65

Dover in an attempt to cut the shipping routes and destroy port facilities as well as ships.

Informed of the British losses in tankers, President Roosevelt in the late summer facilitated the transfer of American tankers to the British flag. And in September the two governments announced that 50 overage American destroyers, still effective for escort duty, were to be exchanged for British bases in the Atlantic at Newfoundland, Bermuda, the Bahamas, Jamaica, Antigua, St. Lucia, British Guiana, and Trinidad, an exchange that benefited both nations. On September 28 the first detachment of American destroyers arrived, completely equipped, at an English port. The first in port was rechristened the *Churchill*. The British meanwhile had received an equally valuable addition to their tonnage from the merchantmen of Norway, Holland, France, and Poland; consequently on September 3, 1940, after a year of war involving heavy losses of merchant ships, the Ministry of Shipping controlled slightly more merchant tonnage than when the war began.

Air Marshal Hermann Goering, eventually realizing that the Luftwaffe must defeat the British fighting squadrons before attempting to establish an air blockade or to cover an invasion of England, concentrated his efforts against the fighters and their airfields. Heavy attacks destroyed many fighters and rendered many fields in south and east England temporarily inoperative. But strenuous efforts by ground crews assisted by civilian volunteers reconditioned the fields, while industry replaced the planes in time to meet the Luftwaffe in the autumn and early winter. Foiled in efforts either to cut off British shipping or to soften up England for an invasion, Hitler made a final attempt to destroy cities and industry and thus break the British will to fight. Although many Nazi bombers got through and destruction was heavy, the Royal Air Force stayed aloft, perfected its techniques of defense, and staved off devastation. Losses in British planes, aviation supplies, and spare parts, necessary for the continuous operation of the Royal Air Force, were heavy; but the British Navy and merchant marine, in spite of attacks by German planes, submarines, and surface raiders, brought in the supplies that kept the fighting planes in the air.

Toward the end of 1940 the American aircraft industry was producing planes for Britain in quantity, especially the Lockheed-Hudson scout bomber, a twin-engined plane for the Coastal Command. Before the year ended these Lockheeds were being delivered across the Atlantic in 12-hour flights. Factories in the United Kingdom, Canada, and the United States could now replace British aircraft faster than they were being destroyed. The air force began to grow. A large proportion of British pilots whose planes were shot down would parachute to safety in their own territory; accordingly, although its personnel suffered severely, its losses were less than the German. Meanwhile, replacements were being trained in Canada as well as in England.

The Royal Air Force worked directly with the Navy and also regularly scouted and frequently bombed the so-called invasion ports, Hamburg, Antwerp, Flushing, Dunkirk, Calais, Boulogne, and Brest. During August and September information was obtained that German troops were embarking and disembarking from canal barges, apparently rehearsing for an invasion. In mid-September there were other indications, including the heavy attacks on English ports by the Luftwaffe, that an invasion was seriously contemplated. About this time British bombers sank a large number of barges and at least some of them were filled with troops equipped for landing on a hostile shore.

These indications of the planned invasion were confirmed after the war, by Grand Admiral Doenitz, who stated that tugs and landing barges had been assembled and army and navy detachments had practiced amphibious operations. The German Naval Command reported that the navy was too weak to protect a landing force against attacks by British men-of-war, and insisted that to invade England successfully it would be necessary for the Luftwaffe to annihilate the Royal Air Force, and then to attack all men-of-war in the English ports adjacent to the landing area so effectively that the British Navy would be forced to withdraw to distant bases. Doenitz claimed that by September the navy had completed preparations to transport the army of invasion across the Channel, but the Luftwaffe had not defeated the Royal Air Force. The autumn gales began in October, and Hitler countermanded the order to invade, but directed that the armed forces continue to simulate an invasion. But by mid-October the British authorities were convinced that if Hitler had ever intended to invade England he had abandoned the plan. Escort vessels that had been held in English waters returned to the convoys and merchant marine losses decreased. The battle of the Atlantic reverted to its former status of attack on and defense of sea-borne trade.

A regular feature of Hitler's technique was to divert attention from his failures by startling predictions of stupendous future successes. As the winter of 1940 drew to a close it was evident to him that the bombing attacks on cities of the United Kingdom would not alter the determination of the inhabitants to resist. Perhaps to distract the attention of the Germans from the failure of the Luftwaffe, perhaps in the hope of success, in February he proclaimed an ocean Blitzkrieg that was to win the battle of the Atlantic within 60 days. Grand Admiral Raeder had made unusually thorough preparations to coördinate U-boat wolf packs as attackers with Condor flying boats as scouts, for it had become evident that it was more difficult to locate than to attack convoys. The U-boats in groups of three, six, or nine, operating on the surface at high speeds, were directed to favorable attack positions by means of information supplied by the flying boats. The submarines usually attacked at night on the surface, submerging only to evade attack.

To assist the U-boats, Admiral Raeder first tried surface ships. In 1941 he unloosed the *Scharnhorst* and the *Gneisenau* on the shipping lanes. They inflicted severe losses on one convoy but were driven into Brest. Next Raeder despatched the *Bismarck* (May, 1941), which did not last as long, although it sank the *Hood* (see page 39). But wolf packs, led to the convoys by their flying boats, inflicted heavy damage in the spring of 1941. Allied, neutral, and

British losses rose from 300,000 tons in January to 600,000 in April, 1941, before countermeasures began to reduce sinkings.

The German war on all shipping supplying the British Isles was carefully planned, fiercely executed, and well sustained. At its height when a convoy was struck by a pack of submarines the losses were heavy, but they were never as large as the German radio claimed. On an average the Minister of Propaganda doubled the actual losses.

According to Admiral Doenitz, who directed U-boat operations until January, 1943, the year 1941 presented, on the whole, an almost insoluble problem to the U-boats. During the winter of 1940–41 the British concentrated more shipping in convoys, and increased the aircraft and patrol ships in the waters around the British Isles so that U-boats could no longer operate on the surface in the area where convoys converged. British long-range aircraft began to locate and attack wolf packs. These measures made it necessary for the submarines to operate at a greater distance from England, and for German planes to locate the convoys earlier. But Luftwaffe pilots had been primarily trained for flying over land and were not efficient in scouting over the ocean; and U-boats were still limited in number, for the building program begun in September, 1939, was not yet in production. There were not enough of the U-boats to scout the great ocean spaces.

Doenitz also complained that the United States had threatened to attack any German warship that entered the western Atlantic, and the political decision to forbid U-boats to operate west of Newfoundland was made in order to avoid any incident that might bring the United States into the war. In the four months ending September 30, 1941, the average British loss dropped to 180,000 tons. On the credit side was also another windfall of almost a million tons of Greek shipping that had joined the British pool after Mussolini's invasion of Greece the previous autumn.

The British added small planes that were catapulted from escort vessels to scout for or attack a submarine pack. When its air patrol was finished the plane would land on the water

SEA POWER SAVES GREAT BRITAIN 69

near a friendly ship and if weather conditions were favorable the pilot was picked up. Often the pilot went down with his plane. Soon, important convoys were all accompanied by a catapult ship; and planes searched well in advance of the convoy, driving off German air scouts and attacking U-boats. The radius of action of the flying boats of the Coastal Command operating from the British Isles continually increased; their searches were coördinated with those of the catapulted planes by the Operation Section of the Admiralty, which routed and often rerouted convoys to divert them from the paths of Doenitz' wolf packs.

Other measures were adopted that increased the shipping space available. The British combined the Ministries of Shipping and of Transport into the Ministry of War Transport, unifying the control of shipping, railway, and road traffic and reducing the turn around time in port. On March 11, 1941, the Lend-Lease Act became law; and to protect lend-lease cargoes going to Britain, American escort was extended further eastward. In April Marines were landed in Greenland with the consent of local officials and the Danish Minister in Washington. A month later a base was established in Iceland and American men-of-war escorted ships to that area, after which they passed to British escorts.

Under the terms of lend-lease a great many British ships, some of them capital vessels, were repaired in American shipyards. This timely assistance was badly needed, for the British combat ships of all types had suffered heavily in maintaining control of the Atlantic and the Mediterranean, and dockyards in the United Kingdom were overcrowded.

The result of British and American efforts to protect shipping in the north Atlantic became evident in the last half of 1941. In December, during his visit to the United States, Winston Churchill stated that the losses in the last five and a half months of 1941 were only one fifth those of the previous five months. As the year 1941 ended, Britain, assisted by the United States, had the battle of the Atlantic well in hand. It is obvious that the British Government was indebted to the United States not only for lend-lease material but for naval escort to protect it. It should also be remembered that no American shipments could have reached Britain if the Royal Navy had not controlled the Atlantic sea lanes.

Events in the Mediterranean, as the year 1941 opened, still favored the British and the Greeks. The latter drove the Italians back into Albania. On March 28 a British squadron under Admiral Cunningham, consisting of the battleships *Queen Elizabeth, Barham,* and *Malaya,* the aircraft carrier *Formidable,* four cruisers and accompanying destroyers, defeated two Italian squadrons with three battleships, several cruisers and destroyers. Among the Italian ships was the fast new battleship *Vittorio Veneto.* British planes sighted the enemy on March 27 and both squadrons were again located the following day. In spite of their higher speed, three Italian cruisers and as many destroyers were brought to action and sunk in the three-day battle.

In explaining Hitler's failure to invade England, Admiral Doenitz has asserted that the limited prospects of success could not justify the attempt because the Mediterranean offered another possibility of striking a decisive blow. Probably the reason for abandoning the attempt against England was Hitler's fundamental distrust of Stalin and his desire to obtain the Ukraine. He did not dare consume the bulk of his land and air forces against Great Britain with a possibly hostile Russia in his rear. But the immediate cause of Hitler's intervention in the Mediterranean was the success of the British and Greeks, compelling him to go to Mussolini's rescue. Although meanwhile preparing to invade Russia, in January, 1941, Hitler despatched a substantial force of the Luftwaffe to operate from the Sicilian airfields in an effort to gain control of the air in the central Mediterranean by destroying British airfields and planes in Malta. Simultaneously German ground troops were prepared for service in Africa and Greece.

Before the Germans reached Greece, revolt flared in Yugoslavia when the Cabinet signed a pact giving Hitler control of the country. The insurgent government was immediately recognized by Stalin. Beginning on April 6, the Wehrmacht

SEA POWER SAVES GREAT BRITAIN 71

overran Yugoslavia and Greece within three weeks; its mechanized and motorized infantry and armored divisions were still invincible. The painstaking Nazis had constructed tanks especially equipped for mountain warfare, and airfields in Bulgaria were used by squadrons of Stuka dive bombers until captured fields in the conquered countries were available. The British were compelled to evacuate Greece during the week of April 24–30, under cover of darkness. The campaign cost approximately 30,000 British troops; about 27,000 were evacuated to Crete but without their artillery, and 19,000 to Egypt at a cost of two destroyers and four transports.

The climax of the campaign in Greece was the capture of Crete by German air-borne troops transported across some 65 miles of water. This undertaking was a clear-cut victory for superior land and air forces operating against superior sea, inferior land, and no air forces. British land-based planes were first driven back to Africa, while the only British aircraft carrier available was unable to furnish air support because its squadrons had been depleted by steady operations. German air-borne troops in planes and gliders flew from Greece to occupy the airfields and form the spearhead of the invasion. They were followed by troops in small ships protected by dive bombers and fighter planes. First British destroyers and then cruisers attacked these small, troop-carrying *caïques,* sinking many, but the combat ships also suffered and eventually had to abandon the effort to intercept German reënforcements.

The British and Greek evacuation of Crete began on May 27, and during the next six days 17,000 men were taken off during darkness. This epochal campaign was hailed by air enthusiasts as the end of control of the sea by surface ships, but other observers noted that the loss of planes, air-borne troops, and specially trained units made it impossible for the Wehrmacht to exploit the victory by invading Cyprus 350 miles away. They noted further that with bearable losses the surface ships and transports were able to bring off 17,000 of a garrison of 27,000, although German aircraft were in undisputed control of the air and could follow the evacuating ships to the entrance of Alexandria before abandoning pursuit. One British division suffered more casualties from air attacks while embarked than it had sustained ashore during the fighting. The effort of surface ships unsupported by air to halt the air-borne invasion was so costly in ships it had to be abandoned; its unavailing effort to prevent the invasion and its relatively successful evacuation of the army cost the navy three cruisers and six destroyers.

To occupy Crete and assist the Greeks, it had been necessary to rob Wavell's army just after its triumphal advance to El Agheila early in February. In March Field Marshal Erwin Rommel, who had distinguished himself in command of an armored division in France, landed in Libya as Commander of the Afrika Korps which consisted of two highly trained armored divisions equipped for desert warfare. Late in the same month Rommel drove the British from Libya back into Egypt and laid siege to Tobruk, garrisoned by an Australian division. Before Rommel could organize an advance into Egypt the demand for German troops for the invasion of Russia deprived him of necessary reënforcements. In July the British took advantage of the German involvement in Russia to reënforce the Egyptian army. The British had fairly earned a breathing spell; their small and scattered armies in the Mediterranean had stood in the breach for over a year. General Sir Claude Auchinleck had succeeded Wavell in Egypt, the latter having taken command of all British forces in the Middle East. Nazi fifth columnists had provoked riots in Iraq; Arabs had seized the oil wells of Kirkuk and Mosul; and on June 1 Wavell drew upon the scanty stocks of troops in Egypt to retake those wells. The situation in the eastern Mediterranean was kaleidoscopic until the Germans invaded Russia and could no longer intervene effectively in North Africa.

Essential factors in British sea power were infantry divisions that were landed in strategic areas to assist in one forlorn hope after another. These soldiers knew they would fight without adequate air cover and probably be forced to evacuate. Defeat on land and evacuation by water became a regular British maneuver during World War II, as it had been during the Napoleonic Wars. But British soldiers were always ready for another landing after they had been evacuated and their ranks refilled.

The land campaigns in the Balkans cost the British two army divisions besides the loss of many ships and planes. The British estimated the German loss at 17,000 troops, mostly specially trained air-borne troops. On balance, the British gained. Hitler had hoped to be able to absorb the Balkans into the economic bloc of the Axis without resistance. The action of Mussolini made Greece an enemy; the intervention of Britain in Greece and the sympathy of Russia encouraged the revolt in Yugoslavia. Instead of obtaining economic coöperation Hitler had to occupy and garrison two countries that he had hoped to keep neutral.

In the autumn of 1940, immediately after abandoning the plan to invade England, Hitler had ordered the General Staff to prepare plans and provide the means to invade Russia in the following spring.[2] According to Admiral Doenitz the navy was not informed of the decision until January, 1941. Like all other military plans it was a close secret and Hitler did not inform Mussolini until a few hours before, and the Japanese Government after, the invasion occurred. Doenitz asserts that although in the beginning Russia "abided loyally by the terms of the Russo-German Treaty, she subsequently . . . exploited the position into which Germany had been forced [presumably by the campaign in western Europe and the inability to invade England] by withholding more and more of her supplies of wheat and oil to Germany and also by flagrantly violating various conditions laid down in the treaty relating to the Baltic States and Rumania."[3] There is no doubt that Russia took advantage of Germany's preoccupation in western Europe, but Doenitz need show no surprise at Stalin's failure to observe scrupulously all the provisions of a treaty obviously based on temporary expediency and without permanent basis.

2. See Colonel Truman Smith, U.S.A., "The German General Staff Abdicates," *Infantry Journal*, January, 1946.
3. Admiral Karl Doenitz, *The Conduct of the War at Sea*, p. 15.

Whatever Hitler's reasons for invading Russia, he underestimated Russian leadership, and the strength and equipment of Russian armies. He would not listen to the counsel of a few men of the General Staff who had the courage to advise him that Russia could not be defeated in three months.

The failure to conquer the British Isles left him with an open enemy in Great Britain, and a potential enemy in Russia who would certainly exploit the situation in eastern Europe and the Balkans if he exhausted his strength in the war with England. The British blockade, although very tamely applied, had reduced the supplies that formerly reached the Reich, particularly petroleum and its products. Oil from Rumania would sustain Germany in her war against Great Britain, but if operations were extended into North Africa, the Middle East, or Russia, more oil would be necessary.

In addition, according to Admiral Doenitz and Colonel Truman Smith, about this time Hitler succumbed to the military mirage that dazzled many others who overestimated the mobility of mechanized infantry and Panzer divisions, and described to his military cabinet how he would effect a junction of the Wehrmacht with the Japanese Army on the shores of the Indian Ocean. Undoubtedly Hitler had more than one motive when he launched the attack, but the military and economic factors predominated as he marched his armies into Russia the night of June 21–22.

Great Britain no longer faced Hitler's Europe alone. Churchill promptly pledged unlimited support to Stalin, and in a few days Roosevelt, in accordance with the declared American policy of furnishing economic assistance to all nations resisting an "aggressor," promised material aid from the arsenal of democracy.

Hitler's clash with his former so-called ally is reminiscent of Napoleon's break with Czar Alexander, and events leading up to the two famous ruptures are similar. The tempo of the later war was of course much faster, and the break between the quasi allies came much more rapidly. Very few observers seemed to note the historical parallel or recall the

SEA POWER SAVES GREAT BRITAIN 75

great difficulty of conquering Russia; the prestige of Hitler's armies was high, army officers all over the world predicted that the Soviet forces would be destroyed within six weeks to three months. In the autumn the Nazi armies stood in front of Leningrad, Moscow, and Rostov, but already they were almost exhausted by their efforts. The General Staff, convinced that a last push would win the war, ordered an advance on Moscow. But their armies were overwhelmed by a sudden change in the weather. Then they advised Hitler to go into winter quarters, for on the assumption that Russia would be defeated within three to four months, no plans had been made and no supplies provided for a winter campaign. Hitler would not listen. He committed the armies to a disastrous winter campaign.

It is true that Hitler invaded Russia without adequate preparations, but if he had waited to prepare his army, the defense of Russia would have been stronger. Time was no longer on his side. He had used as much of the Luftwaffe as he dared to expend in the vain effort to cut off the overseas supplies reaching England; even his willingness to gamble did not extend to risking the Wehrmacht in canal barges in the English Channel with the Royal Navy and Air Force in position to destroy it. Hitler could obtain more oil from either Russia or the fields of Iraq and Iran; to reach the latter he must invade Turkey, which would be helped by the British while Stalin's armies would be on his flank. And the further Hitler penetrated into the Balkans the more restive Stalin would become. Hitler had no choice except to attack Stalin; like Napoleon he had either to defeat Russia or admit his own defeat.

When Hitler invaded Russia the Royal Navy with its Fleet Air Arm had stood alone for a year between Hitler's triumphant armies and air forces. With sporadic but splendid assistance from the numerically inferior Royal Air Force, the Navy had evacuated British armies from Norway, France, Greece, and Crete. It had destroyed or demobilized practically all the French ships that refused to join General de Gaulle's Free French Navy. It had deployed all available British Army divisions and Royal Air Force squadrons to strategic areas in the Empire and thus made possible coordinated action of the three forces in the campaigns in North Africa, Syria, and the Balkans. And it had fought the battles at sea that secured British control of the Mediterranean.

While British control of the Mediterranean was one of the causes of the invasion of Russia, Britain's successful resistance to Hitler's attempts to starve or invade the home islands, or break the people's determination to resist, was a more fundamental reason. Officers and men of the Royal Navy assured immunity to invasion of the British Isles just as their predecessors in the wooden ships of the line had done in the days of Pitt and Nelson. They proved that the English Channel in the days of tanks and planes is a greater barrier to ground and air troops than a Maginot Line or the steppes of Russia, as long as Great Britain retains control of the sea.

Whatever the future holds for navies and sea power, it is clear that British sea power between June, 1940, and June, 1941, obtained and maintained by control of the sea and control of the air over certain strategic areas such as the Dover Straits, the English Channel, and the waters around Malta, was the decisive influence on the course of the war and the fate of the Empire. Further, the ability of Great Britain to save herself primarily by her own exertions and the intelligent use of sea power, which involved Germany in a war with Russia, forecast the downfall of Hitler's Europe, now enveloped by land as well as by sea.

VI

The Opposing High Commands

THE German victories in Europe encouraged the Japanese chauvinists to increase their demands on China and French Indo-China. Possession of Indo-China would threaten the Philippines and British Malaya. To meet a possible German-Japanese attack, President Roosevelt and Prime Minister Churchill, as heads of their governments, had in 1940 authorized their armed forces to prepare the Rainbow Plan for joint operation in case the United States and Japan became involved in the war. Under this plan the defeat of Germany was the first objective, of Japan the second. The Atlantic theater was given priority over the Pacific. Throughout the war the policy and grand strategy of Great Britain and the United States were controlled by this original concept.

Soon after Pearl Harbor, in December, 1941, Roosevelt and Churchill organized the Combined Chiefs of Staff, with headquarters in Washington, consisting of the United States Chiefs of Staff and representatives of the British Chiefs of Staff, with the necessary secretariat. It was the responsibility of the Combined Chiefs of Staff to consider the day-to-day problems of the war and determine a common course of action. The Combined Chiefs kept the President and the Prime Minister informed of the military and naval situation, and the two chiefs of state fixed Anglo-American policies and frequently suggested joint strategical operations. There was direct telephonic communication between the White House and 10 Downing Street, enabling Roosevelt and Churchill to confer at a moment's notice. Accompanied by civil and military advisers, they held several personal conferences on Anglo-American war problems, and on rarer occasions met with Stalin, and once with Chiang Kai-shek.

Frank Knox, publisher of the *Chicago Daily News*, became Secretary of the Navy just as plans for the two-ocean navy were formulated. The entrance of Knox and H. L. Stimson, both Republicans, into the Cabinet emphasized the unity of the country in the face of increasing foreign complications. Although convinced of the necessity of preparing the Navy for war and loyal to the President's foreign policies, Knox, as one of the leaders of the Republican party, could and on occasion did take issue with other members of the Cabinet. He knew that he needed strong and able assistants in the Navy Department and so delegated ample authority to Undersecretary Forrestal, his principal civilian assistant, and to Admiral King, his senior naval adviser.

James Forrestal had held a commission as lieutenant (junior grade) in the Navy in the first World War, and had subsequently been an investment banker in New York City. A friend and neighbor of Roosevelt, he was serving as one of the President's assistants when appointed Undersecretary. Forrestal's entire experience and personality enabled him to battle forcefully and successfully for the Navy's proper share of the national production during the difficult period of 1942–43 when the demand for war materials of all kinds far outran the supply. His success as Undersecretary led to his appointment as Secretary on the death of Knox. As Secretary, Forrestal's main responsibilities were to redeploy the Navy after the defeat of Germany, to help prevent any slump on the industrial front as the war drew to a close, and to prepare the Navy Department for demobilization and a return to peace.

Assistant Secretary of the Navy Ralph Bard supervised the activities of the shore establishments, and of naval personnel in civilian status. During the frequent absences of Knox and Forrestal on inspection trips, Bard acted as Secretary and he succeeded Forrestal as Undersecretary. Assistant Secretary of the Navy for Air Artemus Gates had served as a naval pilot in the first World War. His frequent visits to the fast carrier forces in the Pacific kept him vividly aware of the remarkable increase in the carrier forces of

THE OPPOSING HIGH COMMANDS 79

Admirals Mitscher and McCain. He quickly realized that American carrier planes could dominate Japan's Army and Navy land-based planes on Luzon and the Marianas, and that under the carrier planes' continuous air patrol Admirals Halsey and Spruance could bombard the coast and support a landing in Japan.

The American section of the Combined Chiefs of Staff in Washington, known as the United States Joint Chiefs of Staff, at first consisted of the Commander in Chief of the United States Fleet and Chief of Naval Operations, Admiral E. J. King; Chief of Staff of the United States Army, General G. C. Marshall; and Chief of the Army Air Corps, General H. H. Arnold. When Admiral W. D. Leahy returned from Vichy, the President appointed him Chief of Staff to the Commander in Chief of the Army and Navy, and throughout the remainder of the war these four officers constituted the United States Joint Chiefs of Staff. The British section of the Combined Chiefs of Staff were personal representatives of the staff in London. Its personnel, four in number like its United States counterpart, was changed from time to time. Radio, cable, telephone, and officer couriers facilitated communication between the Combined Chiefs in Washington and the British Joint Chiefs in London.

To coördinate the operations of the two navies at sea, the Atlantic Ocean was divided into two approximately equal zones. The British Navy assumed responsibility for the eastern Atlantic, the Mediterranean Sea, and the Indian Ocean, while the United States Navy took the responsibility for the western Atlantic and the entire Pacific. When ships of either navy entered the area of the other, they passed under the command of the controlling navy. This commonsense arrangement provided automatically for unity of naval command whenever Anglo-American ships met. When Anglo-American armies operated together ashore, special agreements were made and usually the nation providing the most troops selected the commander in chief, who was then provided with an Anglo-American staff.

Admiral Ernest J. King was serving as Commander in Chief of the Atlantic Fleet when, at one of the most critical periods in American history, he was appointed Commander in Chief of the United States Fleet and became "directly responsible, under the general direction of the Secretary, to the President of the United States" for the conduct of the naval war. Comparatively unknown to most of his countrymen, King was well known to his fellow officers who, almost without exception, approved the President's choice. Three months later, King was also made Chief of Naval Operations, and became responsible for the construction and maintenance of ships, and the procurement, training, and distribution of Navy personnel, as well as the strategic direction of the war at sea.

Decisions made by the Combined Chiefs of Staff that concerned American war operations were carried out by the American Joint Chiefs of Staff, operating through their Joint Deputy Chiefs of Staff. The Deputy Chief of Staff of the Army, acting for General Marshall, and the Vice-Chief of Naval Operations, Vice-Admiral Horne, acting for Admiral King, were authorized to interpret and implement the policies of the Joint Chiefs of Staff. As Commander in Chief, King depended upon his Chief of Staff to supervise the execution of his decisions and to coördinate his policies concerning the various fleets. Vice-Admiral Russell Wilson held this post until illness forced his retirement; he was succeeded by Vice-Admiral R. S. Edwards.

For the first time in American history, one admiral was simultaneously responsible "under the general direction of the Secretary" for expanding and maintaining the Navy and directing its fighting. King could meet this heavy responsibility because of his own professional capacity and also because he selected able assistants and delegated the necessary authority to them. Edwards assisted in the plans and operations of the various United States fleets; Horne, in the procurement of personnel and material. Edwards, familiar with the projected operations of the fleet, would anticipate the ships and personnel to be needed. Horne, working with Undersecretary Forrestal, would insure that ships, planes, and munitions were made ready and, working with Vice-Admiral Jacobs, Chief of the Bureau of Naval

THE OPPOSING HIGH COMMANDS

Personnel, that the required personnel were available. Horne synchronized the procurement of ships and crews, and despite many changes of program, when ships were completed crews were ready to man them.

In the struggle at sea Halsey, Spruance, Hewitt, Mitscher, McCain, Kinkaid, Fletcher, Turner, and a host of junior flag and commanding officers did the fighting. But it was Admiral King in Washington who made the over-all naval plans and distributed the ships between the Atlantic and the Pacific, while Admiral Nimitz was in operational command of the naval war in the Pacific and Admiral Ingersoll in the Atlantic. These three admirals controlled the general direction of the war at sea.

Although commonly regarded as supreme in military organization, the Axis Powers did not establish a combined staff to coördinate operations. There was some reciprocal activity; the Japanese sent Germany quinine and tin, and received optical instruments and plans for machine tools and airplanes. The Germans presented the Japanese with a D-9 submarine, but Admiral P. H. Weneker, the German naval attaché in Tokyo, reports that the Japanese would neither adopt the German design nor accept the suggestion to divert their submarines from attacking men-of-war to raiding merchantmen. At Germany's request Japan sent submarines into the Indian Ocean for a brief period in 1942, and for a time the two navies coöperated in unloosing surface raiders and running the Anglo-American blockade. Otherwise there was no coördinated action.

Under both the Kaiser and Hitler the German Navy had been subordinate to the Army General Staff. No admiral in the Reich was allowed a voice in the preparations for war. Only when the air marshals and field marshals were compelled to admit their inability either to blockade or to invade the British Isles did Hitler call in the navy. At that late date U-boat warfare was the only feasible resort. This German error in strategy reduced Admiral King's task in the Atlantic to a matter of overcoming the U-boat menace.[1]

1. See Chapter X.

The Japanese counterpart of the American Joint Chiefs of Staff was the Imperial General Staff, but it does not seem to have functioned as systematically as the American organization, although Admiral Nagano, who was Chief of the Naval General Staff and represented the navy on the Imperial Staff, stated: "The two staff headquarters were close together. Communication was easy and coöperation between the two went smoothly." And he is very positive that both the army and navy staffs agreed on the basic plan to secure the Philippines, Malaya, and the East Indies, generally called the "southern resources area." He also asserts that when the agreed-on perimeter of this area was secured by March 1, the army yielded to the navy's suggestion to extend it to include Midway, the Aleutians, and the Solomon Islands. Nagano states that the first suggestion of invading the Aleutians and Midway came from Admiral Yamamoto, Commander in Chief of the Combined Fleet, and that the Naval General Staff at first opposed and later accepted the plan.

Admiral Nagano's duties as Chief of the Naval General Staff corresponded with those of Admiral King as Chief of Naval Operations, and Admiral Yamamoto's as Commander in Chief of the Combined Fleet with those of Admiral Nimitz, the Commander in Chief of the Pacific Fleet. Vice-Admiral Fukudome, who served two tours as Chief of Staff of the Combined Fleet, reports that Yamamoto was the universal choice of the navy and Japanese people for Commander in Chief, saying, "There could be only one Yamamoto, and nobody could take his place." Fukudome also asserts that Admiral Nagano had full confidence in Yamamoto's judgment and if Yamamoto "said a certain plan promised success he [Nagano] was willing to let Admiral Yamamoto proceed with its execution." Nagano himself testified that he accepted Yamamoto's proposals for extending the territorial objectives.

The Imperial General Staff assigned two tasks to the navy, first to destroy the United States Fleet, and second to support the army in its occupation of the "southern resources area." Yamamoto was given a free hand to use the fleet as he saw fit to accomplish these tasks, and, beginning in January, 1941, he made the plan, obviously based on the strategic pattern set by Admiral Togo in the surprise attack on Port Arthur in the Russo-Japanese War, to prepare a similar surprise attack on the United States Pacific Fleet in Pearl Harbor and thus gain time for the Japanese Fleet to occupy the Philippines, Malaya, and the East Indies.

On his death Admiral Yamamoto was succeeded by Admiral Koga in April, 1943, and Koga by Admiral Toyoda a year later.[2] According to Admiral Fukudome, Koga was more "conservative and cool" than his predecessor, and Fukudome, who knew and admired all three, rated them professionally in this order: Yamamoto, Koga, Toyoda. In spite of Japan's overwhelming defeat, there has been no recrimination among the Naval High Command, no effort to lay the blame for failure on a particular admiral or naval group. It is fair to conclude that Japanese naval operations were planned and conducted by the ablest officers in the service, and that their Naval General Staff ashore and their admirals at sea retained the confidence of the officers and men until the end.

2. See Chapters XI and XII. Both Admirals Yamamoto and Koga were killed in airplane crashes.

VII

Procurement of Naval Material and Personnel

THE most efficient High Command would be useless without men and material. The War Production Board was established by the President to stimulate the maximum production from American farms, mines, and factories and then to divide the products between the operating agencies of the government, its Allies, and essential civilian consumption by controlling the distribution of American resources as they flowed into the industrial system. The responsibility of its chairman, Donald Marr Nelson, was to supervise the production of semifinished and finished materials and to maintain the nation's industrial plants in an efficient condition. The War, Navy, and Treasury Departments and the Maritime Commission acted as procurement agencies for the American Government, while the Foreign Economic Administration performed the same service for the Allies and for those agencies organized to wage economic war against the Axis. As the war progressed and labor and materials became scarcer, the President established the Office of War Mobilization and the Office of Economic Stabilization to settle conflicting claims of the military and home front.[1] These superagencies coördinated the activities and adjusted the problems that inevitably arose among the War Production Board, the War Manpower Commission, and the War Labor Board.

Duplication of effort and some conflict of authority was inevitable among the various departments and agencies. Unquestionably a more efficient organization could have been established if time had permitted. Nevertheless government, management, and labor—perhaps by "main strength and awkwardness"—did perform a miracle of production, and

---

1. These two offices were later consolidated under James F. Byrnes.

PROCUREMENT AND PERSONNEL 85

American farms, mines, factories, and shipyards did meet the almost insatiable demands of their own armed forces as well as those of their Allies, Great Britain and Russia. Production was slow in starting, but after the summer of 1943 American military leaders at the front—to a greater extent than any military leaders before in history—had but to ask to receive practically any quantity of ships, planes, munitions, and men. The best proof of the vastness of American production was the envy it excited among the Axis nations.

Undersecretary Forrestal was responsible for ascertaining the Navy's material needs and then for obtaining them from the War Production Board. This same problem had existed in the first World War and accordingly, as a part of their peacetime preparation for war, the War and Navy Departments had established the Army-Navy Munitions Board, headed by the Assistant Secretaries (afterward Undersecretaries) of War and Navy, to plan the industrial mobilization necessary to support a major war effort. In 1939 the board completed an Industrial Mobilization Plan. By then, it had outlined its organization and trained the necessary personnel to form the nucleus of a Joint Munitions Board that could define Army-Navy needs during a war and indicate what industrial plants could supply these needs.

The agency organized to coördinate the Navy's efforts in planning, procurement, and production in the second World War was the Office of Procurement and Material. Its head, Vice-Admiral S. M. Robinson, became the Undersecretary's "industrial Chief of Staff." The Navy members of the Joint Munitions Board were the nucleus of the new naval industrial staff; and to these Robinson added a group of civilians having business or professional experience, and naval officers with technical knowledge of the Navy's needs.

In war production, time is a most precious ingredient. To gear the Navy's procurement and production machinery to maximum speed and reduce the risk of fraud to a minimum, Forrestal established a general counsel's office. Struve Hensel, chief counsel, permitted Robinson's staff and all authorized bureaus to conduct direct negotiations with contractors. The Undersecretary simultaneously reënforced all technical bureaus with personnel qualified to solve the increasing problems of research, design, purchasing, production, and transportation which the war was imposing.

Since despite the prodigies of production there was a greater demand on the War Production Board than could be supplied, it became necessary for Forrestal and Patterson to support the Navy's and Army's claims. Before appearing as claimants, they always reconciled the demands of the two services and, fortified with the necessary data, were able to present irrefutable reasons for their requests. Other claimants could, however, frequently do the same thing and there were bitter engagements on this front, too.

The system of priority ratings, by which the board had allocated scarce materials, proved unworkable and was replaced in the second quarter of 1943 by the Controlled Materials Plan, which went into full effect July 1, 1943. The new arrangement fixed the distribution of all materials in short supply by controlling three strategic items—steel, copper, and aluminum. Availability of these three key materials determined production. The four major claimant agencies, War, Navy, and Treasury Departments and the Maritime Commission, were required to justify by January 1, 1943, their requirements of these three materials for a period of 18 months. By that time, the Navy's Office of Procurement and Material was prepared to predict its demands and justify them on the basis of directives it had received from the Combined Chiefs of Staff.

Once the Navy had been assigned its share of the nation's productive capacity, Forrestal assigned priorities to Navy bureaus and offices on the basis of strategic developments at sea. Thus these priorities reflected the strategic situation. For example, throughout the war—except in September, 1944, when attack transports and cargo ships were being constructed for the invasion of Iwo Jima and Okinawa and were given top priority—operational and battle damage made it necessary to give precedence over all new construction to repairs, alterations, and spare parts for ships al-

PROCUREMENT AND PERSONNEL 87

ready in commission. Until July, 1942, the four new battleships nearing completion were given Group One precedence; from July to September battleships gave way to landing craft for the North Africa and Pacific campaigns. In October the six aircraft carriers completing in 1942–43 took precedence (American carriers in the Pacific were dangerously low at that time), while late in November the carriers shared top place with destroyer escorts for Great Britain.

Forrestal and Robinson maintained close contact with Admiral Horne, Vice-Chief of Naval Operations, who was in turn kept informed by Admiral King and his Chief of Staff, Admiral Edwards, of the Navy's future strategic plans and the material needed to execute them. The Office of Procurement and Material enabled Forrestal to translate these requirements into the proper quantities of finished and semifinished materials, and to obtain these materials from the War Production Board. Within the Office of Production and Material Robinson organized committees which paralleled War Production Board committees and provided naval liaison officers for the board's committees. These officers presented the Navy's claims for its share of the nation's production.

Soon after coming into operation, the Office of Procurement and Material obtained at least six months in advance a schedule of the Navy's monthly requirements in ships, planes, guns, munitions, and principal components, such as batteries, boiler pumps, and armor plate. Officers then broke down these demands into facilities and materials, and arranged with the War Production Board for priorities and allocations. If the liaison officers could not obtain the Navy's share, it would be necessary for Forrestal or Robinson to take up the matter with Nelson. Forrestal's extensive knowledge of American industry made him an effective guardian of naval interests. He knew the capacity of American factories, mines, and farms, or knew the people who could tell him what they were.

To synchronize this procurement of ships, planes, ammunition, and other supplies with the procurement and training of officers and men required knowledge of future operational plans and close coördination of the two procurement programs. Admiral Horne, working with the Office of Procurement and Material and through the technical bureaus (Ordnance, Ships, Yards and Docks, Aeronautics, and Medicine), and maintaining constant touch with the Bureau of Naval Personnel, kept supplies in step with men and both in step with naval strategy. Occasionally the system failed, but by July, 1943, Admiral King could make strategic plans with the assurance that his logistic and personnel needs would be met. The Undersecretary and the Chief of the Bureau of Naval Personnel would procure the ships, the supplies, and the men; while Admiral Horne would keep the pipeline of supplies, which reached from the interior of the United States to the Pacific and finally to Tokyo, so filled that the needed supplies would be at hand, ready to land immediately after the first wave. A system of "functional components" was developed which, with the increase in national production, made the idea of the ever-filled pipeline—impossible of achievement early in 1942—a reality. Functional components were predesignated and standardized units of supplies for advance bases which enabled a prospective commanding officer to order delivery of an advance base, large or small, as needed.

The Bureau of Ships organized a similar standard personnel unit to man a repair base or a mother ship. These crews were pre-assembled and could be ordered as units, instead of having to be requested by each individual's rating, such as machinists mates, boilermakers, ship fitters, and so on. Only by these methods of standardization and synchronization could the enormous problems of providing material and personnel for Admiral Nimitz in the Pacific have been solved.

Statistics are usually dull, but the figures of combat ships provided by American industry are fascinating and approach the miraculous. Production in the United States reached its peak during the fiscal year that ended June 30, 1944. The Navy's share for this period included 24,000 new combat planes, 1 battleship, 6 27,000-ton carriers, 4 small carriers, 69 escort carriers, 115 destroyers, and 71 sub-

PROCUREMENT AND PERSONNEL 89

marines. Some of the records established in this period were unprecedented, as, for example, the 250 destroyer escorts, or 3 every 2 days, delivered during the first half of the period, or the 20,000 landing craft, 107 a day, launched during the second half.

Between December 7, 1941, and October 1, 1945, besides the 37 escort carriers and 86 destroyer escorts that were lend-leased to the Allies, there were added to the United States Fleet 8 battleships, 2 large cruisers, 13 heavy cruisers, 33 light cruisers, 1 large aircraft carrier, 17 aircraft carriers, 9 light aircraft carriers, 77 escort carriers, 349 destroyers, 412 destroyer escorts, 55 high-speed transports, and 203 submarines. This does not include the more than 100,000 small ships, such as mine craft, patrols, and large and small landing craft.

The demands of naval commanders are insatiable, for they can always use additional ships and men to increase the tempo and decrease the length of the war. On June 30, 1944, Secretary Forrestal reported to the President that, "having expedited one set of programs," the Navy faced another. Nimitz, Spruance, Halsey, Hewitt, Mitscher, and McCain were in continuous combat, and battle and operational losses were causing continuously rising logistical demands. They needed more assault ships, more rockets, and more high capacity ammunition, and the steadily increasing number of ships and planes operating under combat conditions required more spare parts.

The last bottleneck in logistics occurred in ports late in 1944. American industry could produce and railways could deliver to the docks more supplies than the port facilities and available stevedores could lift aboard the steamers. All available warehouses were soon overflowing. The congestion affected the Army, which was forwarding supplies to General MacArthur. Admiral Ingersoll was sent to the West Coast to take entire control of the Navy's deliveries, and the Army provided experts to control the routing of railway freight trains. The unhampered flow of supplies to Nimitz was soon resumed, but until the Japanese surrendered there was no end to the problems of production and distribution.

During June, 1944, while Hewitt and Kirk supported the landings in Normandy and southern France, King gave Nimitz, Spruance, and Mitscher the signal to take the Marianas in the western Pacific. No greater proof of the dependence of American sea power on production could be found than in this simultaneous climax in production and the initiation of the decisive overseas campaigns in the Atlantic and the Pacific.

The United States Navy began hostilities in 1941 with a serious reverse. Within a month it faced a U-boat offensive that threatened to cut communications with England; within three months the Japanese had established themselves in the western Pacific and were holding the approaches to the Indian Ocean. The American situation was critical; to some, the chances of victory appeared slim. However, a year and a half later the U-boats had been reduced to merely a nuisance, and two years after that Germany had been defeated, the Japanese Navy destroyed, and the Japanese Empire forced to surrender.

These naval successes in the Atlantic and the Pacific required a heavy expenditure of ships and men. There was no easy way to naval victory; the Navy learned to fight by fighting. It produced a brilliant galaxy of fighting admirals, and they would be the first to say that they could not have achieved victory had it not been for the continuous flow of ships, planes, and naval material. One example will suffice. Off Okinawa in the spring of 1945, approximately 250 ships were hit by Kamikaze. Many of the smaller ones sank; many of the larger were severely damaged. And except for the floating bases and the steady stream of replacements the war would have been prolonged indefinitely.

United States Marine Corps—Development of Amphibious Technique

For a century and a half the Marine Corps had specialized in making landings on hostile shores. The campaigns in Gallipoli, Mesopotamia, Salonika, and the Dardanelles had convinced many people that the new weapons and increased railway facilities had limited the possibilities of successful

PROCUREMENT AND PERSONNEL 91

overseas expeditions. The Marines had not, however, shared that point of view; they believed, rather, that these campaigns had demonstrated the need for adapting the new weapons to amphibious techniques and for peacetime training in amphibious warfare. In the period between the two World Wars the Marines in their Ship to Shore School at Quantico studied the amphibious operations of the first World War and began experimenting with the new weapons and using them in their practical exercises on the Potomac. Marine officers realized that the new weapons assisted the defenders, but they believed that these new weapons, particularly landing craft, tanks, and planes, could be even more effective on the offensive. They developed their own aviation arm, a field artillery especially designed for landing, smoke screens to cover their approach, landing craft for infantry, and amphibian tanks that could accompany the first assault wave and waddle ashore to give fire support to the leading elements.

Beginning about 1928, the Army and the fleet began to hold joint amphibious exercises, and some Army regiments participated in landing exercises on the West Coast and on Oahu. Between the two World Wars the Army was skeletonized; even the famous First and Second Divisions were not fully manned. Not until the spring of 1940, according to General Marshall, was it possible for the Army to assemble 70,000 regular troops for field maneuvers. Under these circumstances it is not surprising that the Army did not devote more time to amphibious operations. Later, when more troops were available, a number of divisions were trained for amphibious warfare. And as we shall see, Army divisions participated in practically every Pacific landing.

The Marines organized the East and West Coast Expeditionary Forces, the first at Quantico and the other at San Diego, which operated from 1920 to 1932. In Nicaragua, Haiti, Santo Domingo, Mexico, and China, Marines had landed and protected the lives and property not only of Americans but often of foreigners. Much of the technique of the Marine Corps was copied by the Japanese in their base forces and shore-based aviation, which were largely responsible for the early Japanese successes in the western Pacific.

During World War II the Marine Corps procured, supplied, trained, and distributed its own personnel under the direction of its Commandant, General Thomas J. Holcomb. When it appeared that the President might order the armed forces to anticipate the Germans at Dakar or land in Martinique, the Fleet Marine Force, although comparatively small, was in all respects ready. Later, the peacetime training of the corps was rewarded by an unbroken series of victories in the Pacific, to which should be added the repulse of the first Japanese assault on Wake Island. The Marines also had the honor of launching the first American land offensive of the war, at Guadalcanal.

The Marines demonstrated a stark courage by taking Tarawa—a small, heavily fortified atoll—by assault; they drove the enemy from Cape Gloucester on New Britain; and they then took the atolls of Roi, Namur, and Eniwetok in the Marshalls. Large-scale island fighting was resumed at Saipan, Tinian, and Guam, followed by the bitter assaults on Peleliu and Iwo Jima, and ending in the combined Army and Marine Corps victory at Okinawa. At the end of the war the Marines were organized in six divisions, with their own aviation in addition to their carrier-based squadrons, and every division had seen combat in the Pacific.

The United States Coast Guard

The United States Coast Guard was another autonomous component of the Navy, coming under naval control in November, 1941. Like the Marines, Coast Guard personnel made a major contribution to amphibious warfare. Some of them participated in every major landing operation. Personnel rose from 13,800 to 171,000, over 51 per cent of the larger figure being employed on sea duty.

The Coast Guard has always joined the Navy when the guns begin to shoot. Their men and officers are trained along Navy lines and have the same traditions of service. They had no difficulty in "shaking down" and beginning promptly to make one of their important contributions to the war:

teaching inexperienced naval crews to steer small boats through the surf.

The Bureau of Naval Personnel

Although the Navy Department was expanded and functions of certain of its bureaus and agencies were modified during the war, Secretary Knox did not scrap the bureau system, and Undersecretary Forrestal and Admiral King worked through the bureau chiefs, who in many instances are the legally constituted agents of the Secretary.

The Bureau of Naval Personnel was primarily responsible for the procurement, training, and distribution of naval personnel. Under its general direction all bureaus and naval districts had prepared plans, during the peace years, for procurement of personnel in time of war. Many of the bureaus and districts had been authorized to procure qualified reserves to fill war billets and relieve regular officers for sea duty. When the President declared a limited emergency in September, 1939, the expansion of personnel began, and it was accelerated in July, 1940, to meet the needs of the two-ocean navy. In the summer of 1941 the bureau instituted an intensive advertising campaign for more recruits.

After Pearl Harbor the rate of expansion was again increased and commandants of naval districts and chiefs of the bureaus enrolled additional personnel. By January 1, 1942, the enlisted force had reached 332,000 men. Until February 1, 1943, the Navy recruited volunteers, accepting about 900,000. After that date, under an agreement with the Army, the Navy ceased recruiting men between the ages of 18 and 37. During the next six months the Navy received roughly 780,000 men from Selective Service and accepted 206,000 volunteers outside the draft-age limit. In the summer of 1943 the Navy had difficulty in obtaining the necessary men from Selective Service, and in February, 1944, a call for 100,000 produced only 37,000. Still, the bureau managed to man the ships. By April, 1945, it was able to reduce its calls on the draft board. On June 30, 1945, the Navy numbered about 3,000,000 personnel, including nurses and

Waves, but excluding the Marine Corps and Coast Guard.

To train these recruits the Bureau of Naval Personnel expanded the four training stations already in existence at Newport, Norfolk, Great Lakes, and San Diego, and established three new ones at Bainbridge, Md., Sampson, N. Y., and Farragut, Idaho. After recruit training, enlisted men were sent, depending upon their aptitudes, to special schools, to be trained for example as electricians, machinists, or radio operators. Radio schools were among the largest and most important, because of the extensive use of radar and other electronic instruments. Other bureaus, notably Ordnance, Ships, Yards and Docks, and Aeronautics, ran their own technical schools, based on policies established by the Bureau of Naval Personnel.

In peacetime the Naval Academy had supplied practically all the regular line officers. During the last war, commissioned officers were obtained from four additional sources: civilians qualified by business or professional experience for a particular shore billet or duty aboard ship, ex-enlisted men who had reached Petty Officer First Class rating, graduates of various officers' schools (usually men immediately or recently out of college), and officers from the merchant marine.

Beginning in 1924 the Navy had established Reserve Officers' Training Units in various colleges and universities where reserve midshipmen were trained to meet wartime needs. As early as 1940 it became evident that many more officers would be needed than the Navy had previously anticipated. In 1940 and 1941 intensive courses were given to young collegians at Annapolis, Northwestern University, and aboard the U.S.S. *Prairie State*. By the summer of 1941 these three sources had provided over 5,000 reserve junior officers. Approximately the same number was graduated by the summer of 1942. After Pearl Harbor it became necessary to establish offices in various cities to procure civilians whose experience or professional training qualified them for receiving direct commissions and filling certain billets, some of which were aboard ship, but most of which were ashore.

PROCUREMENT AND PERSONNEL 95

On December 31, 1941, there were some 38,600 commissioned officers; on June 30, 1945, there were 317,000. The number procured in each of the years 1942, 1943, and 1944 was approximately the same, 95,000. The number of officers required for the wartime Navy explains why two thirds of those obtained in 1942 were commissioned directly from civilian life. As late as 1944 one third of the officers procured came directly from civilian life, and for the war period as a whole over half came directly from that source. The regular Navy provided 17 per cent of the officers in 1942, by training and promoting petty officers, and in 1944 this proportion was increased to 25 per cent.

Newly commissioned reserve officers destined for sea duty were given an indoctrinational course of instruction, followed wherever possible by a period of operational duty on the type of ship on which they were to serve. Destroyer officers, for example, before going to their own ships, would be ordered to Norfolk to take short training cruises on destroyers operating from that base. Whether they came through a reserve training unit or were commissioned directly, most sea-going reserve officers "learned by doing," and qualified themselves for a particular duty aboard ship, such as battery officers, communications, destroyer duty, watch and division duty, or as commanding or executive officers of small ships such as submarine chasers, PT boats, and later, landing craft.

Officers destined for the submarine service were given the most exacting examinations. Perfect physical condition and a high mechanical aptitude were demanded. It is an interesting fact that throughout the war the number of applicants for this most important but also extremely hazardous and arduous duty continued to be so numerous that it was never necessary for the Navy to lower its standards. The prewar requirements of two years previous sea duty were, however, first reduced and then abandoned. The Training School at New London provided the necessary training. Its instructors were drawn from officers and crews of submarines operating in the Pacific, and its training program was based on experience gained under war conditions.

Only in the most exceptional circumstances was an officer ever assigned to submarine duty without special training. Combat service on any type of ship or plane is exacting—sweating out a battle in the turret or engine room, flying a plane or fighting gasoline fires on a carrier, escorting convoys, or night fighting in a destroyer or PT boat—there are no easy billets. Destroyers, incidentally, saw the most action and sustained the heaviest losses of the war. Wherever there was a battle, there was a screen of destroyers. They were the first in and the last out of all engagements, particularly the night battles. Service on a submarine, however, probably exacts a shade more than does service in air or on surface craft. Just as it became necessary to limit the tours of duty in planes, it became the policy to encourage submarine officers, after five to ten patrol cruises in the Pacific, to ask for quieter service in the Atlantic.

The Bureau of Aeronautics

In 1935 the Bureau of Aeronautics had been authorized to train naval aviation cadets. Selection boards chose the candidates, who were given 12 to 15 months' training, the first six months in preliminary and ground-school subjects. The cadets were then advanced successively to primary, intermediate, and advanced flying training. In 1940 and 1941 neither planes nor pilots were available to equip existing units fully, due partly to the number of experienced flyers required as instructors in the continuously expanding training program. Just before Pearl Harbor, however, the number of pilots being graduated from the training schools exceeded the demands of the fleet, and new pilots were formed into squadrons or groups ready to relieve those serving afloat.

Before the war the Bureau of Aeronautics had made an arbitrary estimate of the number of pilot replacements required because of combat losses, battle fatigue, and other forms of attrition. This allowance proved adequate as to individual pilots, but since individual replacement pilots were not qualified to take their places in operating units without further training with a specific unit, it became neces-

PROCUREMENT AND PERSONNEL

sary to organize special training squadrons to train pilots and air crews assigned to replacement pools and to maintain them in a state of combat readiness. Even with this careful planning it became difficult to maintain a flow of squadrons and groups toward the combat area, because the demand for replacements varied with the intensity of flight operations in the combat zone. However, the organization was flexible and close coördination was established between planning and procurement divisions of the bureau and the carrier task forces in the Pacific. When the period of intense and prolonged carrier operations began in June and July, 1944, the bureau's training program had reached its peak and not only furnished replacements for carriers already in commission but provided squadrons and groups for the carriers going into commission. During 1944 six large 27,000-ton carriers and 38 escort carriers were completed, which gives an idea of requirements in personnel and planes.

Until the Marianas campaign, attrition due to combat losses, fatigue, and other causes was less than estimated. In the spring of 1944 the number of personnel in training was accordingly reduced. The Philippines campaign and the cumulative effect of combat fatigue proved, however, that four instead of six months was the desirable limit on tours of duty in the combat area, and that pilots should be required to make only two tours, with a third tour in exceptional cases for men who volunteered. On account of these new provisions, the bureau was compelled to increase the quota for its training program from 6,000 to 9,000 pilots.

The ability of the Bureau of Aeronautics to provide pilots to meet the stupendous increase in the number of carriers is in striking contrast to the failure of the Japanese Navy to meet a much smaller demand. As will be seen, Admiral Nagano bewailed Japan's inability to replace pilots and carriers.

The Seabees

Beginning in January, 1942, the Bureau of Personnel and the Bureau of Yards and Docks recruited the construction battalions, soon nicknamed the Seabees, to construct port facilities, airfields, and other service establishments in combat zones. These men were largely civilian artisans, i.e., carpenters, mechanics, metal workers, divers, etc. They were trained and commanded by officers of the Navy's civil engineers. In amphibious operations Seabees landed soon after the first wave. Their first task was to get equipment ashore, clearing underwater obstacles as necessary and setting up pontoon assemblies. At Saipan, Tinian, and Guam, they landed with the assault troops, brought equipment and supplies ashore over pontoon causeways they had constructed, and then built the airfields. They had been sufficiently drilled to protect themselves and their equipment, and on at least one occasion a Seabee bulldozer fought it out successfully with a Japanese tank. Before the war was over the Seabees consisted of 250,000 men and 8,000 officers, most of whom were serving overseas.

The Bureau of Yards and Docks was also responsible for much of the construction of advance bases, from Quonset huts to advanced base docks (a type of floating drydock), of which 150 were completed, with a lifting capacity of over one million tons. Operating closely with Mobile Squadrons Four and Ten, organized by Admiral Nimitz in 1943 to provide logistical support for the advance of the combat ships from the Solomons to Okinawa,[2] the Seabee battalions supplemented the squadrons' work of furnishing advance base facilities for the Third and Fifth Fleets.

The Bureau of Medicine and Surgery

The Bureau of Medicine and Surgery, under the general policy of the Bureau of Naval Personnel, has always supervised the procurement and training of its officers and of its nurses and hospital corpsmen. During the second World War, which was largely amphibious, the bureau organized a chain of medical facilities which reached from hospital corpsmen advancing with the assault waves, to the field hospitals, then to various types of hospital ships, to the fleet, and to advance base hospitals. The Personnel Bureau's stand-

2. See Chapter XII.

PROCUREMENT AND PERSONNEL

ard unit for operation nearest the scene of combat was a mobile hospital, staffed with officers of the Medical, Dental, Supply, Civil Engineer, Chaplain, and Nurse Corps, with essential enlisted men such as hospital corpsmen, electricians, cooks, and bakers. These mobile hospitals were despatched to the combat areas as needed.

A mobile hospital provided 8 hospital corpsmen per infantry company (1 corpsman to 25 privates) to land with the assault troops. These corpsmen were the first to care for the wounded. By using blood plasma, controlling hemorrhages, giving other first aid, and evacuating the wounded promptly, they saved hundreds of lives.

These medical shock troops advanced inland with the first wave, and were quickly followed ashore by the battalion aid station with two medical officers, eight hospital corpsmen, stretcher bearers, and jeep ambulances. The battalion aid station was reënforced by the regimental and finally the field hospital. Jeep ambulances proved their value on Guadalcanal and thereafter were standard equipment for evacuating casualties from the front lines. Evacuation seaward would begin as soon as casualties arrived at the beach. A medical platoon attached to the shore party commander would prepare the wounded for evacuation to ships which had been designated and equipped, and their crews trained before the invasion. These craft included assault transports, hospital carriers, and finally hospital ships, which took the most seriously wounded.

In the bloody assaults on the Pacific islands, the Marines knew they had a water-borne hospital service directly behind them and that the wounded would receive efficient and almost immediate assistance.

The Bureau of Ordnance

The Bureau of Ordnance provided the guns, ammunition, and other offensive and defensive ordnance for the ships and planes of the Navy. The task was fourfold: it involved research and design, manufacture, procurement, and maintenance. The bureau had representatives with the fleet and was so organized that the constantly changing character of naval warfare could be immediately reflected in changes in design and procurement. For example, the Navy's destruction of large enemy naval vessels lessened the need for armor-piercing ammunition, while amphibious operations increased the need for large quantities of underwater demolition equipment for use on enemy inshore defenses, and bombardment ammunition and barrage rockets for reducing shore installations. Again, as the fleet approached closer to the islands of Japan, the bureau had to meet new demands for both offensive and defensive weapons: the latest type of mine to block enemy harbors and shipping lanes, additional 40 mm. guns, new radar-controlled, blind-firing directors, and improved fuses to meet the threat of enemy air attack and Kamikaze suicide planes. The enormous fire support given by surface ships to landing parties is sharply revealed by the fact that it required 109,000 tons of bombardment ammunition to take Guam, Saipan, Tinian, Peleliu, Iwo Jima, and Okinawa, besides that expended in the final bombardment of the home islands.

Navy research helped to develop and worked out new uses for radar, rockets and rocket launchers, torpedoes, mines, fuses, and intricate fire-control and gun-director systems, to mention only the most important, and placed new fighting weapons and more deadly power in the hands of the fighting men. Ordnance centralized its research, design, and development activities in a new research division early in 1941, and maintained liaison with the Office of Scientific Research and Development, the National Defense Research Council, and Army Ordnance, as well as with many private and commercial research institutions and laboratories, thus greatly extending the scope of its endeavors.

The magnitude of the work done by the Bureau of Ordnance can be measured by the fire power of all guns of the Navy, which in mid-1940 approximated 411 tons of projectiles in 15 seconds, and five years later aggregated 4,500 tons for the same period.

Unquestionably the new weapons which contributed most to victory in World War II were radar and other equipment based on electronics. The Bureau of Ordnance and also the

PROCUREMENT AND PERSONNEL 101

Bureau of Ships and other divisions of the Navy had pioneered in research in new types of vacuum tubes, on which electronic instruments are based. Thus the United States Navy was the first to install radar in submarines and, at the outset of the war, American ships were the only naval vessels having a search radar specifically designed for shipboard use.

The Rapid Expansion of United States Naval Reserve Officer Personnel

The most modern ships and equipment would be useless without competent officers and men. The demands of the latest war on the abilities of commissioned officers were tremendous, yet former enlisted men from the fleet and young Americans from civil life were quickly trained to perform their particular naval duties extremely well.

During the critical period of the submarine war in 1942, priority was given to reserve officers for the armed guard and submarine chasers. Reserve officers trained for destroyer escorts were in greatest demand and their number almost tripled in 1943; calls for reserve officers for carriers doubled in the first half of 1943 and *tripled* again in the second half; those for officers for amphibious craft were increased tenfold in 1943, and *fourfold again* in 1944. The Bureau of Naval Personnel modified its training program to meet changing strategic situations.

By 1945 the proportions of reserves among the officer complements of the various types of ships were as follows: battleships and cruisers, 2/3; carriers, 3/4; submarines, 3/5; destroyers, 5/7; auxiliaries, 7/8; landing craft, 19/20; and escort and patrol vessels, 24/25. Probably only the United States could have provided a sufficient number of men with the native capacity to qualify for such heavy responsibilities in such a short time.

No one realized, even in June, 1942, what the needs of the Navy would be for commissioned officers; but provision had been made to expand and the Navy knew where to obtain and how to train its officers, and 85 to 90 per cent of its commissioned ranks in wartime were new men. Graduates

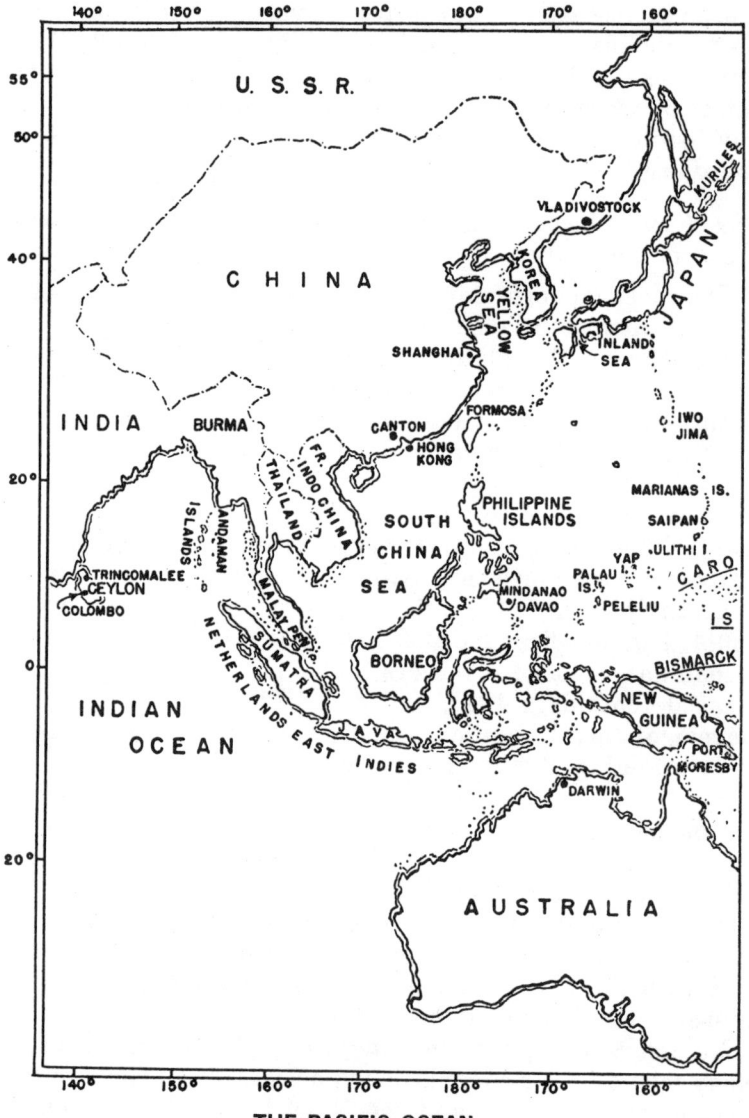

THE PACIFIC OCEAN

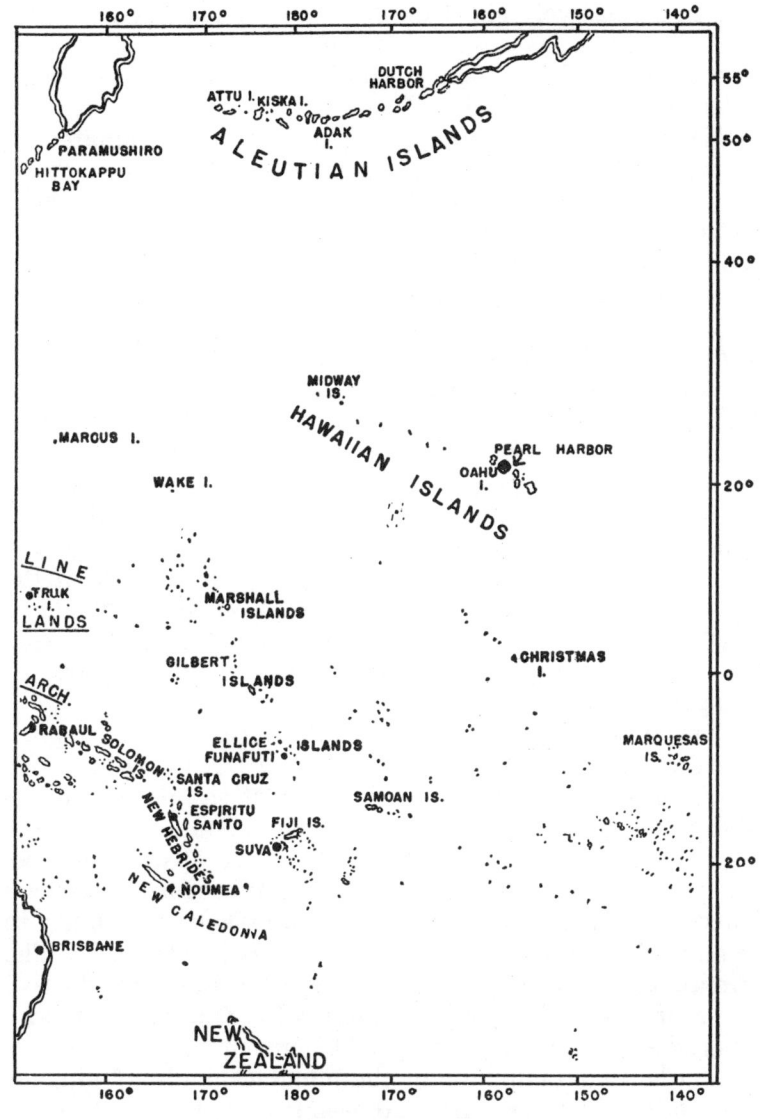

THE PACIFIC OCEAN

of Reserve Officers' Training Units and specialty schools were in a relatively short time given command of PT boats and submarine chasers, and if the war had lasted another year many of these officers would have qualified for command of destroyer escorts.

Officers of the regular Navy naturally predominated in command of larger ships and in positions of high authority, for these were the senior officers who had devoted their entire lives to the theory and practice of naval warfare, and who quite understandably possessed the over-all knowledge and experience that qualified them for these duties.

However, these regular Navy officers, practically all graduates of the Naval Academy, constituted approximately only one in twenty officers in the naval service during the war. They were the "leaven which seasoned the loaf." But after full credit is given to the "regulars" who in the piping days of peace prepared the Navy for war, it was the civilians who, responding promptly and patriotically, absorbed specialized training quickly or turned their previous experience to the Navy's use, and furnished the bulk of the Navy's officers. Neither regulars nor reserves could have won the war alone; the rapid growth of American sea power, and final victory, required the concerted efforts of both groups.

The United Kingdom needed roughly a century and a quarter, from 1660 to 1783, including nine wars, three of which were global, to become the preponderant sea power and to establish the British Empire. The United States became the preponderant sea power between 1941 and 1945. This phenomenal achievement was possible only because American industry and the Navy revealed an unprecedented ability to expand without losing their characteristic efficiency. The ultimate source of American sea power lies in the productive power of the nation and the high caliber of the men who officered and manned the ships. The output of farms, mines, shipyards, and factories, in the capable hands of citizens whose latent fighting spirit had been grossly underestimated by the Axis nations, endowed the United States with one of her most priceless possessions, sea power.

VIII

Japanese Sea Power in the Western Pacific

State of United States Armed Strength in the Pacific

WHILE the British Navy, with the help of the United States Navy in the Atlantic, was still engaged in a desperate struggle to maintain control of that ocean and the Mediterranean, the Japanese began a campaign that demonstrated the decisive influence of sea power in the western Pacific. Political, military, and naval factors conspired to dramatize the demonstration. Officials in Japan's Foreign Office and War and Navy Departments all believed that a nation whose foreign policy was thwarted by another power should make every imaginable preparation for war and then seize the most favorable opportunity to attack. The constitution of the Imperial Government facilitated positive decisions in foreign affairs and methodical preparations by the army and navy to support them. This advantage in going to war was enhanced in 1941 by the determination of the American administration to have the enemy strike the first blow. The result was a Japanese sea, land, and air blitz that dwarfed Germany's campaigns in Europe.

The Rainbow Plan of the Allies, formulated in the spring of 1941, provided that in the event of war the United States Pacific Fleet based on Pearl Harbor would conduct a limited offensive in the central Pacific in an effort to divert Japanese forces from their anticipated invasion of the Philippines, British Malaya, and the East Indies. American forces in the Far East would join the British and the Dutch in the defense of their territories. It was assumed that American reënforcements in the Atlantic would permit the British to strengthen their forces in the Far East.

Throughout the remainder of 1941 the American armed

forces were raised, equipped, trained, and deployed in accordance with this concept of an Anglo-American war against the Axis. The British forces already in combat were given priority in supplies and equipment. The Atlantic Fleet was utilized to escort supplies in the western Atlantic and to maintain American bases in Iceland and other Atlantic islands. By autumn the United States Navy was almost equally divided between the Atlantic and the Pacific. The Pacific Fleet was directed to hold itself in readiness to reenforce the Atlantic Fleet still further and was relieved of all responsibility for the Far East.

In the Philippines Admiral Thomas C. Hart's combat force was disposed as follows: 2 destroyers, 29 submarines, 6 motor torpedo boats and tenders in Manila Bay; and Patrol Wing Ten distributed between Manila, Subic Bay, and Laguna de Bay, with a small detachment operating an air patrol from Davao. The heavy cruiser *Houston,* the light cruisers *Boise* and *Marblehead,* and 11 destroyers were in the southern Philippines and at Balikpapan. The Japanese did not conceal the movements of their forces through the South China Sea into Indo-China; they wished to draw American attention to operations in the western Pacific in order to conceal their thrust at Pearl Harbor. The flying boats (PBY's) had been observing the Japanese in the South China Sea, and Admiral Hart was aware of the increase of their forces in Indo-China. His men were alerted, and he anticipated that with air protection from the Army he could operate his submarines from Manila. He organized the destroyers and cruisers into Task Force Five, commanded by Rear Admiral W. A. Glassford. The 16th Naval District (Philippine Islands), with headquarters at Cavite, was assigned to Rear Admiral F. W. Rockwell. Rear Admiral W. R. Purnell became his Chief of Staff, and he retained personal command of the submarines, Patrol Wing Ten, and the PT boats. It was Hart's intention to remain in Manila as long as the submarines could base there.

General MacArthur commanded American and Filipino land forces in the Philippines. His ground troops included 19,000 American regular and national guard troops, 14,000

Philippine scouts trained and officered by American regulars, and about 100,000 Filipinos who had been recruited by the government to protect the islands after they became independent. In addition, MacArthur had 8,000 air troops with 250 combat planes, including 35 Flying Fortresses and about 100 P-40 pursuit planes.

On November 5, in a joint estimate of the situation in the western Pacific submitted to the President, General Marshall and Admiral Stark reaffirmed their conviction that the Anglo-American plan adopted in March was still "sound." They reported: "The Philippines are now being reenforced. The present combined naval, air, and ground troops will make attack on the islands a hazardous undertaking. By about the middle of December, 1941, United States air and submarine strength in the Philippines will have become a positive threat to any Japanese operations south of Formosa. The U. S. Army Air Force in the Philippines will have reached its projected strength by February or March 1942, . . . it might well be a deciding factor in deterring Japan in operations in the areas south and west of the Philippines. By this time [March, 1942] British Naval and air reenforcements to Singapore will have arrived. The general defensive strength of the entire southern area . . . will then have reached impressive proportions." This official estimate of the ability of air forces and submarines to make the Japanese attack on the Philippines hazardous was submitted to the President the same day that Admiral Yamamoto issued detailed orders to his fleet and task force commanders for the surprise attacks on Pearl Harbor, Guam, Wake, the Philippines, and Malaya, and 32 days before the Japanese avalanche started rolling in the western Pacific. When General Marshall and Admiral Stark, on November 26, requested the President to prolong Japanese negotiations, arrangements had been completed for 21,000 troops to sail for the Philippines by December 8. When Pearl Harbor was attacked, six troop transports and nine supply ships were at sea en route to the Philippines. All but one supply ship reached a friendly harbor.

The Imperial General Staff had ordered the Japanese

108   SEA POWER IN WORLD WAR II

Navy to be ready in the event of war with the United States to destroy the enemy fleet and in coöperation with the army to occupy the "southern resources area" (see page 112). In January, 1941, two months before the Anglo-American Rainbow Plan was completed, Admiral Yamamoto, Commander in Chief of the Combined Fleet, began to make preliminary plans to attack the United States Pacific Fleet, to attack simultaneously the British, Dutch, and American forces in the western Pacific, and to invade Wake, Midway, Guam, the Philippines, British Malaya, and the Dutch East Indies, in case pending negotiations with the United States failed.

Pearl Harbor

The Japanese Foreign Office had not abandoned hope of reaching an understanding, but the navy and army, in accordance with custom, were preparing to attack in the event that their diplomats failed to gain their objective. When Secretary Hull's note of November 26 was received, the Tokyo Cabinet decided that further negotiations were useless; the Naval General Staff upon being informed requested that the parleys be continued until the fleet had completed its arrangements to attack. Accordingly the Foreign Office instructed its envoys in Washington to prolong the negotiations, prepared a note rejecting Hull's proposals, and planned to have the answer delivered to the State Department immediately before the attack on Pearl Harbor. The Embassy staff were slow in decoding this very long message, and its delivery was delayed until after the bombs had fallen, but the Japanese planes were launched on time and struck on schedule.

Yamamoto's plan was simple but comprehensive. A Pearl Harbor attack force was especially trained to disable the Pacific Fleet at anchor with aerial torpedoes. Obviously modeled after the British torpedo plane attack on Italian ships in Taranto, it was a more concentrated attack. Simultaneously, on the assumption that the Pearl Harbor attack would succeed, a South Sea attack group was to invade the Philippines and British Malaya. A northern defensive group

JAPAN IN THE WESTERN PACIFIC 109

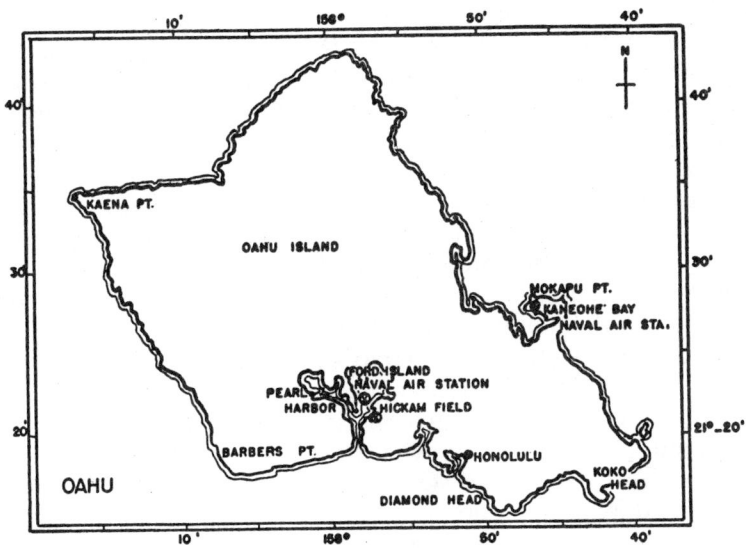

was stationed to guard against a Russian attack from Vladivostok. And a southeastern group was set up to capture Guam and Wake.

Admiral Yamamoto retained under his personal direction in the Inland Sea the main body of the Combined Fleet, and undertook to maintain the coherence and security of his widely deployed forces. As events developed this main body was not needed, but to appreciate the Japanese plan and the ensuing naval panorama it is essential to remember that the Pacific campaign was planned by Yamamoto and his staff, and its execution controlled from his flagship, the newly commissioned battleship *Yamato*.

The Pearl Harbor attack will be described first, for upon its success depended the rapidity and extent of the Japanese penetration in the western Pacific. While it was under consideration, a proposal to land an expeditionary force on

Oahu was rejected on account of the delay and the increased risk of detection involved. Hitokappu Bay, a remote harbor in the Kuriles, was chosen for the base of operations, and the northern route to Pearl Harbor between Midway and the Aleutians was selected to reduce the chances of detection while preparing and executing the surprise attack. Training the pilots of the torpedo planes from six carriers had begun in August. To provide against the contingency that the ships in Pearl Harbor might be protected from aerial torpedoes by steel nets, dive-bombing squadrons accompanied the torpedo planes. There were no nets in Pearl Harbor, and both torpedo and bombing attacks were effective.

The capital ships participating in the attack had to be rapidly redeployed to take part in the operations in the southwestern Pacific; this required them to fuel at sea. In the actual attack fueling was facilitated by the smooth seas, but the ships had been repeatedly exercised until they were proficient even in heavy weather. The willingness and capacity of the Japanese Navy to take almost infinite pains were largely responsible for their successful assault on Pearl Harbor.

Surprise was the essence of the plan. It was agreed that if the striking force were discovered at least two days' steaming from the take-off point, the attack would be abandoned; if discovered only one day's steaming distance, the commander would decide whether or not to continue the operation. This was the only important decision permitted Vice-Admiral Nagumo, commanding the Pearl Harbor attack force.

The striking force consisted of 2 fast battleships, the *Hiyei* and the *Kirishima*, 6 carriers, the *Kaga*, the *Akagi*, the *Hiryu*, the *Soryu*, the *Shokaku*, and the *Zuikaku*, 1 heavy cruiser, 2 light cruisers, and 16 destroyers; it was accompanied by 3 fast fleet tankers and 1 supply ship. The force left Hitokappu Bay on November 23, Japanese time, reached the stand-by position in latitude 42° North and longitude 170° East on December 4, and refueled. By December 6 the pilots were informed that 8 battleships and 15 cruisers were in the harbor but no aircraft carriers, and they were fur-

JAPAN IN THE WESTERN PACIFIC 111

nished with charts of Pearl Harbor showing the berths of the various ships. Each pilot was assigned his target.

All the members of the Cabinet, particularly Prime Minister Tojo, favored hostilities against the United States and the Cabinet Council formally approved this course on December 1. The Imperial Headquarters on December 2 directed that "The hostile action against the United States of America shall be commenced on December 8 [Japan time]." But not until December 6, Japan time, did the Navy Department in Tokyo issue the final order to attack.

Japanese pilots began taking off the six carriers for Pearl Harbor at 6 A.M. on December 7, Honolulu time. By 7.15 two waves aggregating about 400 planes were air borne and proceeding toward their objective, 200 miles due south. The first wave consisted of 50 fighters, 50 high-level bombers, 50 dive bombers, and 40 torpedo bombers. The second wave included 40 fighters, 50 high-level bombers, 80 dive bombers. At 7.55 the first wave struck the Naval Air Station on Ford Island, Kaneohe Bay Naval Air Station, and Hickam Airfield; dive bombers and torpedo planes next fell upon major units of the American Fleet. At about 8.15 there was a high-altitude bombing attack. Finally there was a dive-bombing and strafing attack about 9.10. Training planes were then sent to photograph the damage done.

In the absence of aircraft carriers, the enemy's objective was battleships, eight of which were berthed in Pearl Harbor. Between 7.55 and 8.15 A.M. the Japanese sank four, badly damaged one, and let none of the rest escape injury. Before the attack, the United States Navy had 301 planes; afterward only 52 were fit for service.

President Roosevelt, Congress, the War and the Navy Departments have each conducted an investigation of the Pearl Harbor disaster. The Navy Department has officially censured the admirals most directly responsible. Most of the official testimony taken at the investigations has been released to the public, and anyone wishing further information on the causes of the débacle has easy access to official accounts based upon sworn testimony.

The consequences of the attack on Pearl Harbor are more

essential to a study of sea power than its causes, and succeeding pages will tell the disastrous effects the attack had on the Pacific Fleet during the first months of the war. At this point it is necessary only to emphasize that in war on the sea strategic or tactical surprise is almost a guarantee of tactical victory. Therefore an aphorism attributed to Frederick the Great can be applied with greater force to admirals: "A great general may sometimes be defeated but never surprised." If the Navy Department had in any way condoned the conduct of the officials it considered responsible for Pearl Harbor it would have fatally lowered the standard of conduct expected of its high commanders.

After launching the planes the Japanese striking force steamed northwest at over 25 knots. Thirty planes were lost in the attack; the rest were recovered between 10.30 A.M. and 1.30 P.M. Returning to Kure by a circuitous northerly route, the task force escaped detection by American planes that scouted to the southwest of Oahu. En route two carriers, the *Hiryu* and the *Soryu*, two cruisers, and two destroyers were sent to the assistance of the task force whose attack on Wake Island had been beaten off. The Marines on Wake resisted until December 23, but Guam fell within two days. Nagumo abandoned the plan to attack Midway, possibly because of the presence of an American task force south of that island. Otherwise the project was executed as planned.

Kondo's Offensive in the Western Pacific

The spectacular success of Nagumo's attack on the American Air Force and Fleet in Oahu has obscured the achievements of the forces which, commanded by Vice-Admiral Kondo, spearheaded the invasions of Malaya, the Philippines, and the Netherlands East Indies, overran British New Guinea, New Ireland, and New Britain, and climaxed their campaign by a raid in the Indian Ocean that destroyed all British combat and merchant ships in the Bay of Bengal. Kondo garnered the fruits of Nagumo's attack on Oahu.

Yamamoto had assigned Kondo two battleships, two aircraft carriers, two heavy cruisers, and a division of de-

JAPAN IN THE WESTERN PACIFIC 113

stroyers to observe and, if necessary, to attack the *Prince of Wales* and the *Repulse,* known to be at Singapore. Kondo was also given Carrier Division 12, which maintained and operated a force of seaplanes similar to American flying boats. These accompanied the base forces and gave local air reconnaissance and observation until land-based planes could be established ashore.

Japanese base forces had been developed and standardized during the ten-year war with China. Fleet Base Force One and Two were prepared for the invasion of Luzon. A special base force included two groups of paratroopers. In these forces were troop transports, ordnance ships carrying shore guns and ammunition, supply ships, mine sweepers, and a variety of landing craft which enabled their sea infantry (sailors trained to fight ashore like American Marines) to land through the surf and along open roadsteads. Usually these sea infantry were the first wave of a landing force to secure a bridgehead. Army troops would then land to complete the operation.

The Japanese Army and Navy had evolved a sound system of command of joint expeditions. The admiral commanded en route to and during the landing of the sea infantry. As soon as conditions ashore permitted, the sea infantry were relieved by regular army units, and when the general reported that he could maintain his position or advance, the command of the landing force passed to him. Thereafter the navy was responsible only for maintaining the line of communications in order to provide reënforcement and supplies. If the landing was repulsed, as at Wake Island, the admiral retained command and was responsible for the evacuation. After a successful landing the infantry was reëmbarked, reënforced, and refitted if necessary, and despatched to the next landing place. Artillery support was given by light cruisers and destroyers, for the Japanese could not afford to risk their heavy cruisers and battleships against shore batteries or land-based planes.

Admiral Kondo had also been given the 11th Air Fleet, Vice-Admiral Tsukahara commanding. Headquarters of the 11th were in Formosa; the 21st and 23d Flotillas were sta-

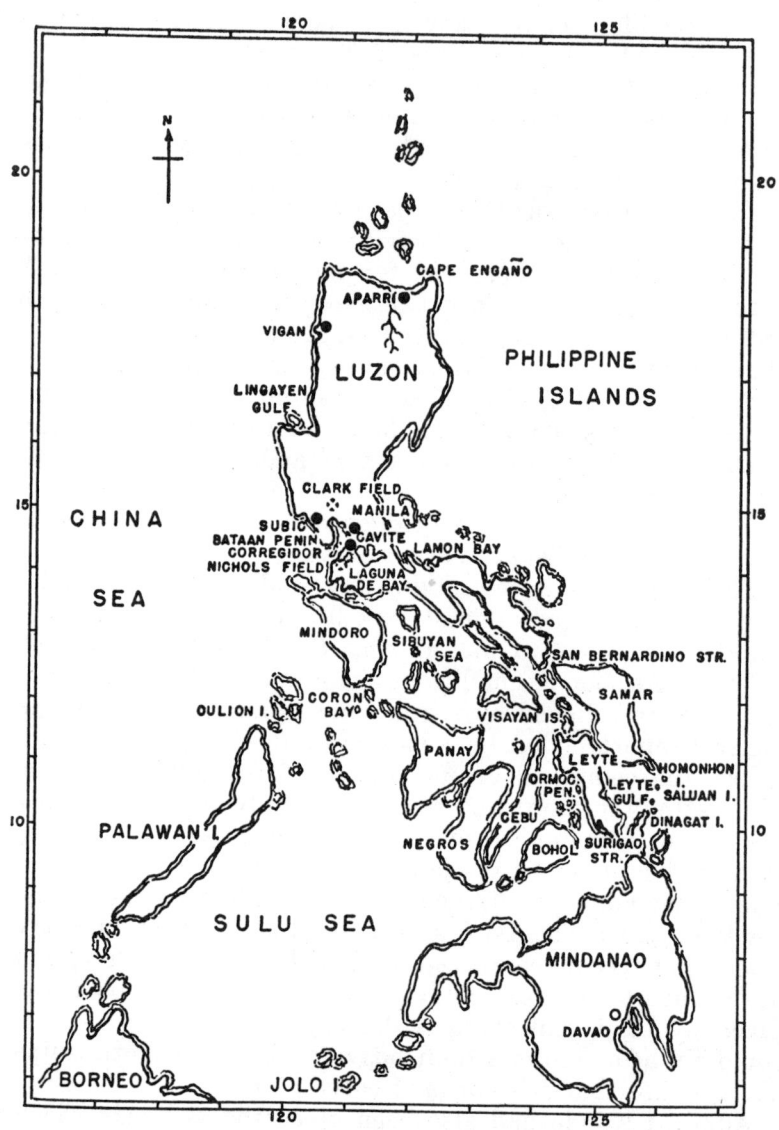

THE PHILIPPINE ISLANDS

JAPAN IN THE WESTERN PACIFIC 115

tioned there with some 300 land-based naval planes ready to attack the United States air forces in Luzon and support the invasion of the Philippines. Tsukahara's 22d Flotilla was stationed on Saïgon with orders to attack naval forces in Singapore and support the invasion of Malaya. This air fleet was manned by naval personnel, and was trained in high-level and dive bombing, and in torpedo attacks on ships. According to Captain Sonokawa, commanding officer of the air group covering Saïgon and Korea, the standard procedure of the 22d Flotilla required pilots to drop torpedoes at an altitude of 20 to 50 meters, a range of 400 to 600 meters, and a speed between 160 and 170 knots. Under these circumstances, if properly aimed, a torpedo would hit the target immediately after it leveled off at the proper depth. The Japanese Ordnance Department had believed that the torpedoes could be successfully dropped from a much higher altitude—200 to 500 meters—but in actual operations Japanese pilots proved that only 10 per cent exploded when dropped from these heights.

The Japanese Army had its own integrated aviation to provide air support for the ground troops, so the navy was only required to furnish air support during landings. Then the air fleets were transported by the navy to the next theater of operations. Japanese air fleets combined the advantages of land planes flown by naval personnel qualified to navigate over water areas and to locate, identify, bomb, and torpedo enemy ships. The Japanese had other air fleets but the 11th was a crack organization and the 22d Flotilla was one of the best trained in Japan. Captain Shibata, at that time senior staff officer of the 21st Flotilla, testifies, and their successes in Luzon prove, that the 21st and the 23d Flotillas were proficient in day and night bombing attacks.

A number of submarine squadrons were allotted to Admiral Kondo. He stationed a few in the South China Sea to strike British merchant ships, an exception to the general practice of employing them against enemy combat ships. The remainder he employed to scout for air and surface forces and to attack enemy combat ships under favorable conditions. On several occasions when overcast or rainy weather made Japanese air scouts ineffective their submarines found hostile ships.

While Admiral Kondo was stationing his forces to overrun Malaya and the Philippines, Admiral Hart was planning to use his "S" boats in direct defense of Luzon, his larger submarines against enemy lines of communications, and his flying boats against enemy ships and as scouts for his submarines.

About 3 A.M. (Manila time) on December 8 Admiral Hart learned of the attack at Pearl Harbor. He informed General MacArthur and his fleet units, and directed his officers and men to operate according to plan. Soon after daylight Admiral Hart was advised that Japanese aircraft had attacked Davao and destroyed two of his PBY's, and that the destroyer *W. B. Preston,* acting as seaplane tender, had narrowly escaped being overwhelmed by four Japanese destroyers. Other PBY's continued their patrols. The submarines, except two under repair at Cavite, quickly took station, and Glassford's Task Force Five departed for Soerabaja, Java, where he established his operational headquarters and cooperated with Dutch and British forces in escorting convoys and opposing Japanese invading forces.

American submarines were also ordered to attack Japanese merchantmen that carried strategic materials, such as oil, rubber, tin, and edible fats, from the East Indies. These undersea boats began the first offensive by American ships against Japan. As the war progressed American submarines steadily reduced the tonnage the Japanese could ship into the home islands for civilian and industrial use.

In contrast, throughout the war the Japanese used their submarines against American combat ships, although they were advised by the German Ministry of Marine to employ them against merchant ships in the convoys between the West Coast and the Hawaiian Islands. The strategy of the Japanese, who possessed a powerful surface fleet with at least seven aircraft carriers, was correct. They hoped to reduce the United States Pacific Fleet by submarine and air attack until they could attack with the surface fleet and thus

JAPAN IN THE WESTERN PACIFIC   117

gain control of the Pacific. On the other hand, the Germans had no aircraft carriers and only enough surface ships to attack merchant shipping. Fleet Admiral Raeder could never have hoped to attack the British Fleet successfully. During the first week of the war Admiral Yamamoto was almost overwhelmed with good news. The Russians remained quiet at Vladivostok. He had damaged the United States Pacific Fleet more than he dared hope, while his attack group had escaped with negligible casualties. He had gained a free hand for Admiral Kondo in the western Pacific.

Kondo's forces also made excellent progress. The 21st and 23d Flotillas of the 11th Air Fleet, based on Formosa, after being delayed several hours by bad weather, took off and caught the American planes at Clark and Nichols Fields on the ground about 12.30 P.M., December 8. Seventy-two fighters and 100 bombers took part in these attacks; their losses were small and they reported that they had destroyed 45 bombers and 5 fighters.

The afternoon of the 10th the 22d Flotilla, based on Saïgon, reported to Admiral Yamamoto that they had sunk the *Prince of Wales* and the *Repulse*. This disaster requires some explanation. The tentative Anglo-American Rainbow Plan had contemplated that a substantial British naval force would reach Singapore in time to participate in the defense of the western Pacific. British naval losses and the situation in the Mediterranean in 1941 reduced this force to two capital ships, the *Prince of Wales* and the *Repulse,* with no aircraft carriers or antisubmarine screen. The force was commanded by Admiral Sir Thomas Phillips. On December 5 Admiral Phillips was in Manila conferring with Admiral Hart, when word came that a large Japanese Expeditionary Force was steaming toward the Kra Peninsula. Phillips departed by plane for Singapore immediately. If the landing was not prevented the Malay Peninsula would soon be overrun and Singapore doomed. On the 9th the admiral sailed without air cover but with a British destroyer screen in what was to be a futile attempt to intercept and destroy the Expeditionary Force. He knew that Japanese air forces were strongly established in Indo-China. But the weather was overcast; during maneuvers off Singapore tropical rain squalls and low ceilings had frequently grounded Royal Air Force planes. Phillips had reason to hope that his ships might escape detection long enough to break up the projected landing on Malaya.

Phillips also knew that Admiral Kondo's force included at least one *Kongo* class battleship. He was ready to shoot his way through the Japanese escort. He did not know that his vessels had been photographed in Singapore by a Japanese plane on the 8th and that, as he sailed, the 22d Air Flotilla was loading bombs to attack his ships in harbor.

In the afternoon of the 9th Phillips became convinced that the Japanese knew his position and strength, and therefore could easily divert their transports beyond striking distance, whereas, since the weather was clearing, his surface ships would be exposed to air attack. Deciding to abandon the attempt, he headed for Singapore after dark. The position of his force was reported to Captain Sonokawa, and about noon on the 10th the British ships were found and sunk by bombs and torpedoes.

Phillips has been generally criticized for his attempt to attack the Expeditionary Force. However, if he had remained in harbor his ships would almost certainly have been attacked at anchor on the 9th. And since the antiaircraft batteries at Singapore were as inadequate as the fighting squadrons, under the circumstances it was not a foolish decision to attempt to break up a landing of vital importance instead of waiting to be bombed in a vulnerable harbor or trying to escape. Phillips could not have based surface ships on Singapore any longer than Hart could on Manila, both ports being within easy bombing range of the 11th Air Fleet.

The Expeditionary Force that Admiral Phillips failed to intercept landed without naval opposition at Kota Bahru on the northeast side of Malaya on the 9th. Within ten days they had occupied Peñang Island and were astride the peninsula in force, while their planes, using airfields on

JAPAN IN THE WESTERN PACIFIC 119

Peñang and in the Kota Bahru area, guarded both flanks of the ground troops as they advanced toward Singapore.

Army forces from Canton attacked Hong Kong with dive bombers on December 8, and within 48 hours ground troops had driven the British garrison onto Hong Kong Island. Japanese infantry landed on the island on the 18th, and the artillery and air force of the Japanese Army methodically cut to pieces both defenses and defenders, although two destroyers and four motor torpedo boats managed to escape before Hong Kong was invested by sea. On Christmas day the city surrendered unconditionally.

In the early afternoon of the day the 22d Air Flotilla had sunk Phillips' force off Singapore, the 21st and 23d Flotillas circled over Cavite beyond the range of the 3-inch antiaircraft batteries. They had no fighter opposition; in leisurely and accurate fashion they bombed the naval shore establishment. The large submarine *Sealion* was destroyed in dock, while the *Seadragon* was towed to safety and by a miracle the destroyer *Peary* suffered only minor injuries. The Cavite Navy Yard was demolished. Admiral Hart realized of course that Manila Bay was no longer safe for surface ships. After dark he despatched all surface ships except the submarine tender *Canopus* south; the next day merchantmen aggregating 200,000 tons escaped in the wake of Glassford's Task Force Five that had preceded them and cleared a path. On the 12th Hart's PBY's were followed in from sea by Japanese fighters and seven were sunk on the water; Japanese fighters raided Manila and Subic Bay the day after and sank more PBY's. Hart reluctantly ordered the remainder to Soerabaja; only the submarines and PT boats were now operating from the Manila area. A few PBY's were under repair. The absence of the flying boats further handicapped the submarines by depriving them of their scouting force. Admiral Tsukahara was fully aware of the damage his planes had inflicted; he considered American air resistance ineffective on the 11th and negligible on the 18th, just ten days after hostilities began. By the middle of December Admiral Kondo's air and naval forces had completely invested

Luzon, and his submarines were surrounding the southern islands while base forces and army troops from the Palau Islands strengthened their hold on Mindanao and landed in Jolo.

On December 22 the Japanese made their first landings in force on Luzon at Lingayen Gulf in the northwest and Lamon Bay in the southeast. Landings had been anticipated in both places; 20 submarines were deployed, some in the direct route of the Japanese convoys. These underseas craft made determined attempts to get to the enemy transports. The Japanese had foreseen these attacks and had provided heavy escorts for the transports, with ample air cover from planes operating from Formosa, Vigan, and Aparri in the north and from Palau and Davao in the south. The distance to be traversed by the convoys was short, air scouts had small opportunity to obtain information in time to be useful, and the ability of the Japanese to land on open beaches enabled them to avoid some of the landing places where they were expected. These factors hampered Hart's submarines and they succeeded in sinking only one transport of the many that entered Lingayen Gulf.

The High Command had also expected much from the Army air force on Luzon, but the Japanese planes on Formosa alone exceeded them in strength and had been rehearsed for the invasion and, by bombing MacArthur's planes on the ground in the initial attacks, this superiority was greatly increased. During the landing at Lingayen Japanese planes operating from the near-by fields easily provided air cover. Even so the Japanese heavy cruiser *Ashigara* while en route from Formosa was attacked by five or six American bombers; and throughout the first day of landing in force Japanese ships were repeatedly bombed, but the Japanese claim they landed on schedule and that only smaller ships including one light cruiser were damaged.

General Jonathan Wainwright, commanding the field army in the north, fought a series of delaying actions, retiring upon Manila, while simultaneously the armies resisting the Japanese forces in south and east Luzon also fell back toward the city. The capital was the rail and road cen-

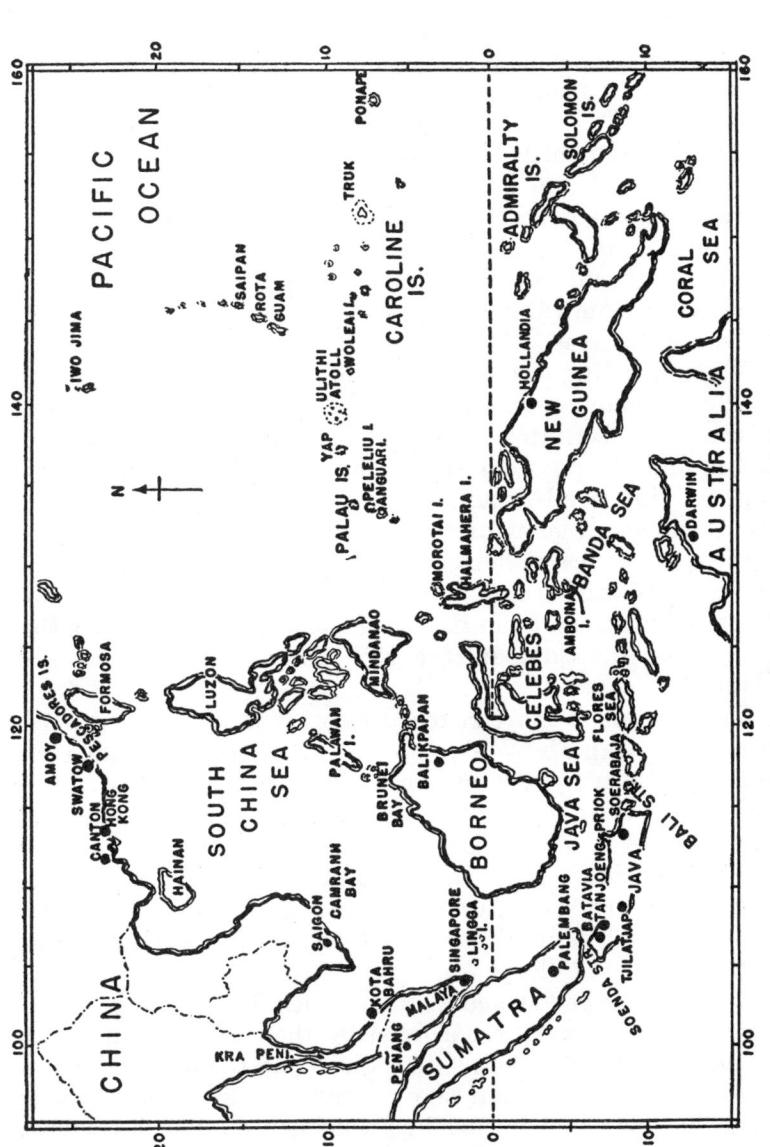

AREA OF JAPANESE CONQUEST IN THE WESTERN PACIFIC

ter of Luzon, and the transportation system was a primary military objective. The attacks by Japanese planes were justified but caused many casualties among civilians in Manila. On December 24 General MacArthur decided to withdraw the armies to Bataan Peninsula and to take the Government of the Philippines with him to Corregidor; subsequently he declared Manila an open city. At an Army-Navy conference on the same day it was decided that Admiral Hart would move his headquarters to Soerabaja and leave Rear Admiral Rockwell in command of naval forces in the Manila area.

While directing the movements of his ships in the western Pacific, Yamamoto, who fully realized the potential strength of the United States, was watching for the reaction of Nimitz and the possible approach of naval reënforcements. Neither King nor Nimitz could be lured into false moves by any of his stratagems or taunted into premature action by newspaper critics at home. King directed Nimitz to secure first the Hawaiian and Midway Islands and then the line of communications from the West Coast to Australia via the Marquesas, the Samoan, the Fiji, and the New Caledonia Islands.

When Admiral Hart reached Soerabaja on December 31 he ordered Captain Wilkes to transfer the American submarines to Java, thus concentrating practically his entire force there, with a temporary repair base at Port Darwin, Australia. Again he confronted superior forces, for the leading elements of the Japanese Second and Third Fleets, commanded by Vice-Admiral Kondo, had already established themselves in Mindanao, Jolo, and Borneo, and were threatening the Celebes.

Kondo's forces arrived in the Palau Islands late in January where they were reënforced by the *Kirishima* and the *Hiyei*, two fast battleships, the *Akagi* and the *Kaga*, the two largest carriers, and four heavy cruisers. The crews of these ships had all participated in the attack on Pearl Harbor. Kondo still had, in the Second Fleet, the 11th Air Fleet and Carrier Division 12 of seaplanes. He was ordered to destroy the Allied air forces and surface ships, and then to give nec-

JAPAN IN THE WESTERN PACIFIC 123

essary assistance to Vice-Admiral Takahashi, whose Third Fleet of cruisers and destroyers was to furnish the escort for the enemy transports carrying the landing forces destined for the Netherlands East Indies.

In addition to supporting the invading troops, Kondo was specifically ordered to prevent the escape of Allied ships operating in the Java Sea, and then to hold his force in readiness to raid British ships and bases in the Indian Ocean. Kondo was given ample strength to carry out his orders, and the naval campaign for the Dutch East Indies followed the identical pattern of the one for the Philippines.

In spite of enemy superiority, Hart planned, Glassford commanded, and Commander P. H. Talbot executed a successful destroyer attack on Japanese transports off Balikpapan on the night of January 23-24. Without damage to any of his four destroyers, Talbot led his force between the Japanese destroyers and transports. By Japanese admission he sank four transports and one escort vessel. The Japanese claimed that the transports were empty.

When Prime Minister Churchill visited President Roosevelt in December they organized the Combined Chiefs of Staff of the United States and Great Britain (see Chapter VI). Other members of the Allied nations, notably Holland, participated in plans and operations when their armed forces or national interests were involved. Russia, at peace with Japan, could not become a full-fledged member, and China took part only in consultations involving the Far East.

A subsidiary of the Combined Chiefs of Staff, known as the ABDA Command, was set up in Java early in January to coördinate the efforts of the Australian, British, Dutch, and American forces opposing Japan in the western Pacific. General Wavell of the British Army was made Supreme Commander; Lieutenant General Brett, U.S.A., Deputy Commander; Admiral Hart exercised operational control of the naval forces; Lieutenant General Heinter Pooten, of the land forces; and Air Chief Marshal Sir Richard Pierse, of the air forces. The ABDACOM had limited strength but unlimited responsibilities. When Hart arrived at Soerabaja the British, Dutch, and American ships were busily engaged in escorting troops and supplies to Singapore, although it was being bombed daily and obviously could not be used for a naval base even if the British Admiralty had been able to spare enough ships from the Mediterranean to contest Japanese control of the western Pacific. Despite desperate efforts to relieve Singapore, 70,000 British land, sea, and air forces on the Malay Peninsula were compelled to surrender on February 15. Under the existing circumstances, Singapore was doomed no matter who was commander in chief, but it is hard to understand why in a theater of operations where control of the sea and of the air over stratègic sea areas was the decisive factor, a general was given supreme command.

The British cup of defeat was running over. A few days before the Union Jack came down in Singapore, the *Scharnhorst,* the *Gneisenau,* and the *Prinz Eugen,* which had been bottled up in Brest for almost a year, sortied from the French port, ran through the English Channel and Dover Straits under the protection of the Luftwaffe, destroyers, and motor torpedo boats, and successfully reached German ports. Squadrons of Nazi fighting planes, rising in succession from one after another of the airfields that dotted the European side of the Channel, drove off bombers of the Coastal Command, torpedo planes of the fleet air arm, and the British destroyers and PT boats. With the numbers of airfields and planes they had available, it was easy for the German naval and air staffs to synchronize the movements of their ships and planes. The result was an air fight between the Royal Air Force and the Luftwaffe; the German ships served as bait to lure a gallant squadron of unescorted naval torpedo planes to destruction. A British official report made after the war reveals that the Royal Air Force had agreed to furnish a certain number of planes for joint action with naval aircraft and surface ships, and then ordered three quarters of their quota of planes to other duty without informing the Admiralty. The Luftwaffe was as independent as the Royal Air Force but it operated under the German High Command and coördinated its operations with the land and sea forces. Some injury was suffered by the

German ships, but their successful passage through the English Channel under the guns of the Royal Navy, and the bombs of the Air Force was resented all over Britain.

Some time later Churchill defended the government's conduct of the war in the House of Commons. He told the members how he had planned to get the United States into the war and how he had succeeded; he confessed that his efforts to keep Japan out of the war had failed. He emphasized the catastrophes that had befallen British arms, but claimed that the entry of the United States into the war, with its vast industry, finance, and man power, more than compensated for the immediate defeats and the addition of Japan to the Axis. Churchill obtained a vote of confidence, not on his conduct of the war, but on his success in getting the United States into it.[1]

Amid the news of continuous victories in the Far East, Yamamoto heard the sound of American guns and bombs. When Nimitz took command late in December, his entire fleet was required for escort duty to reënforce the line of communications. Nevertheless he determined to take the tactical offensive at the first opportunity. Two task forces returning from escort duty were despatched to strike the Marshall and the Gilbert Islands on February 1. Japanese ships, planes, and naval bases were successfully bombarded, American losses were small, and the effect on the officers and men was exhilarating. For the first time, Admiral Halsey and Admiral Spruance had carried the fight to the enemy.

On February 24 and March 4 Halsey extended the raids to Wake and then to Marcus Island. Yamamoto did not alter his plans; he had anticipated an American reaction and probably hoped that public opinion might influence Admiral King to order a further advance before proper preparations had been made.

The surrender of Singapore released a number of Japanese ships, planes, and divisions for service elsewhere. The pressure on Java was increased, but not that on Bataan, for the Imperial General Staff and Yamamoto knew that Luzon

1. See Churchill's article, ''Secret War Speech,'' in *Life*, January 28, 1946.

was isolated. They could safely by-pass the ground forces on Bataan, already bereft of sea and air support. The fall of Singapore also convinced the British that Java could not be held, and both the British and American naval commanders were authorized by their governments to evacuate their forces when it became necessary.

Admiral Hart made another attempt to delay the Japanese, using the *Houston,* the *Marblehead,* the *De Ruyter,* and the *Tromp,* and an American destroyer division, plus three Dutch destroyers. Rear Admiral Doorman of the Royal Netherlands Navy commanded the force. On February 4, the 21st Air Flotilla bombed Doorman's force for about two hours, striking both the *Houston* and the *Marblehead.* It was necessary to abandon the attack. The Dutch cruisers and American destroyers escorted the American cruisers to Tjilatjap on the south coast of Java, where a naval base had been established. The cruisers docked, still within easy bombing distance of Japanese air bases. The *Marblehead* had been seriously damaged; Captain Arthur G. Robinson hastened temporary repairs and on February 13, with a disabled rudder that necessitated her being steered by her engines during half the trip, and with leaks the pumps could barely control, the *Marblehead* limped off on her epic 9,000-mile cruise home.

On February 4 Admiral Hart was ordered to Washington and Admiral C. E. L. Helfrich of the Royal Netherlands Navy succeeded as Commander of the Allied Naval Forces. Ten days later Governor General Van Mook succeeded General Wavell as Allied Supreme Commander. Helfrich, convinced that Java could be held, ordered the *Langley* and the *Seawitch,* together carrying 59 planes, diverted from Colombo to Tjilatjap. He stationed Allied submarines in defensive positions off the Java coast, planted the last remaining mines in a field off Soerabaja, and distributed between Tandjoeng Priok, and Soerabaja the additional British cruisers and destroyers that had become available after the fall of Singapore. He concentrated every ship and plane for the defense of Java; he was fully supported by his British and American colleagues, but the Japanese were greatly

JAPAN IN THE WESTERN PACIFIC 127

superior in land, sea, and air forces, and operated them skillfully.

Allied submarines operating along the Japanese lines of invasion delayed the enemy's schedule about a week, but by February 5 Amboina, the Dutch stronghold guarding the eastern approach to Java, was taken with its garrison of Dutch and Australian toops, and a few days later Palembang in Sumatra was captured. Java was in the Japanese pincers, and their land and sea planes bombed the Allied surface ships and bases there at will. The remainder of the Java Sea campaign was a series of determined but vain efforts of smaller naval and air forces to break through superior naval and air forces to attack enemy transports and prevent the invasion of the island.

Admiral Kondo extended his assault to Australia. On the 19th 290 planes from the carriers *Akagi, Kaga, Junyo,* and *Ryujo* attacked the ships and port facilities at Port Darwin. Two waves of high-level bombers circled deliberately over their targets and dropped bombs with deadly accuracy. Dive bombers followed and ended their runs by machine-gunning survivors trying to reach shore in small boats. The destroyer *Peary* was sunk, while the *W. B. Preston* escaped to Broome after being hit. The Japanese sunk or beached every merchantman in the harbor, wrecked port facilities, heavily damaged the airport and hospital, and set the city afire.

Just before noon on the 26th, as the *Langley* and the *Seawitch* approached Tjilatjap, Japanese planes attacked and the *Langley*, America's first aircraft carrier, on which pioneer carrier pilots had been trained, was hopelessly disabled and had to be sunk by the destroyer *Whipple*.

As Helfrich took command the situation was critical, and it grew steadily worse. On February 26 he had available two heavy cruisers, three light cruisers, ten destroyers, a few American and Dutch Catalina seaplanes, several army bombers, and about a dozen fighting planes. Nevertheless he ordered Rear Admiral Doorman, who commanded the Allied Fleet at Soerabaja, to make a night attack on an enemy convoy of 30 transports escorted by cruisers and destroyers, reported north of the port.

On February 26 and 27 Doorman made a determined effort to carry out his orders, but Admiral Takahashi, with complete control of the air, continually interposed his cruisers and destroyers between the Allied ships and the Japanese convoy. On the afternoon of the 27th Doorman became involved in a day engagement in which the *Exeter* was disabled, two destroyers sunk, and all but two of the remaining destroyers expended their fuel and torpedoes in fruitless attacks on enemy combat ships. Nevertheless about 9 P.M., with two destroyers and four cruisers, Doorman again attempted to evade the Japanese cruisers and destroyers and to deliver a night attack on the transports. The Japanese cruisers and destroyers, aided by parachute flares from their planes that almost continuously illuminated Doorman's force, torpedoed and sank one destroyer and both Dutch cruisers before midnight. Only the *Houston* and the Australian cruiser *Perth* remained. They made a final futile attempt to evade or break through the Japanese cruisers and destroyers. About 1 A.M. on February 28 their commanders informed Admiral Helfrich of the loss of the Dutch cruisers and that they themselves were proceeding to Tandjoeng Priok.

Still undaunted, Helfrich ordered the remaining ships to assemble in Tjilatjap. The immediate problem was to get these vessels out of the Java Sea; Japanese surface and air forces controlled both exits, Bali and Soenda Straits. The *Exeter* at Soerabaja was routed north of Bawean Island and given the *Encounter* and the *Pope* as escorts. All three were intercepted north of Bawean Island about noon on March 1 and quickly sunk.

The *Houston* and the *Perth* left Tandjoeng Priok at 9 P.M., February 28, followed two hours later by the Dutch destroyer *Evertsen*. En route, they surprised and attacked a long line of enemy transports. Unfortunately they had been sighted and followed by the destroyer *Fubuki*, which torpedoed the *Houston*, reducing her speed to 10 knots.

The *Perth* slowed to keep company, and both were engaged at close range by the heavy cruisers *Mogami* and *Mikuma*. The *Perth*, hit by several torpedoes, went down first. The

JAPAN IN THE WESTERN PACIFIC 129

Houston split her battery between the two enemy cruisers and went down firing 15 minutes later, about 2 A.M., on March 1. Almost simultaneously, Japanese cruisers ran the *Evertsen* ashore. Of about 50 Japanese transports, two certainly, perhaps three, were sunk, all loaded with the Mikado's soldiers. Captain Rooks of the *Houston* and his gallant colleague, the captain of the *Perth,* went down with their ships but had the satisfaction of knowing they had finally achieved their objective: they had evaded the combat ships long enough to attack enemy transports.

Of the ten ships that tried to escape from the Java Sea, only Binford's four American destroyers succeeded in fighting their way out. The destroyer *Ford* was first sent to the westward as if the force would proceed to Batavia, then, turning about, rejoined the others. Led by the *Edwards,* the four destroyers hugged the coast of Java until, emerging from Bali Strait, they dashed full speed for the open sea. Sighted by three enemy destroyers, they engaged in a running gun duel and simulated firing torpedoes from their empty tubes. According to Admiral Helfrich's directive, the four destroyers then proceeded to Australia for torpedoes.

Governor General van Mook and Admiral Helfrich were finally convinced that Java could not be saved. The admiral dissolved the Allied Naval Command. Rear Admiral Glassford and Rear Admiral Pallisier, R.N., ordered their respective forces in and en route to Java to go to Australia, where Allied naval forces were gathering. But Admiral Kondo's Second Fleet, operating south of the barrier, cut off and sank the American destroyers, the *Edsall* and the *Pillsbury,* the gunboat *Asheville,* several British corvettes, and numerous auxiliary ships and merchantmen. On March 9 Java surrendered.

A month later, soon after a force of British battleships, one carrier, and some heavy cruisers had arrived in the Indian Ocean, Admiral Kondo made his long-planned raid into that area. Planes from his four carriers attacked Colombo on April 9. Royal Air Force fighters and antiaircraft batteries shot down 37 planes. The surface ships had left Colombo to escape air attack but in the afternoon Japanese scouting planes found the heavy cruisers *Cornwall* and *Dorsetshire* at sea and dive bombers sank them. An attempted counterattack on the carriers by Royal Air Force bombers failed when the British scouting planes could not find the enemy. For three days Kondo's planes operated without resistance in the Bay of Bengal, sinking all shipping and bombarding two coastal cities in Madras. On April 9 the naval base and airfield at Trincomalee were bombed; Royal Air Force bombers attacked the carriers but were driven off by Japanese fighters that shot down most of the bombers. On the same day Japanese scouting planes located the *Hermes,* a veteran British carrier; 70 Japanese bombers soon sank her and her destroyer escort, the *Vampire*. This triumphant raid was the high-water mark of the westward advance of Japan.

Rangoon had fallen the same day Java surrendered. A Chinese army under General Stilwell that went to the assistance of the British in Burma became involved in a hasty evacuation. By April 26 Lashio on the road to Chungking was taken, and Chungking and Free China had been cut off from the western Allies, except for a precarious route over the Himalaya hump in army bombers. The Andaman Islands, Peñang, and Singapore, with Christmas Island and the East Indies, seemed to give the Japanese complete control of the western Pacific.

Yamamoto had made good use of the first three months of hostilities. By March his air and sea forces had enabled the Japanese Army to consolidate its positions in Malaya, Burma, and the East Indies and to tighten its grip on the Bataan-Corregidor section, while his own base forces advanced into the Lae-Salamaua area and Rabaul and threatened the Solomons.

Yamamoto's vision of 1941 had, in the spring of 1942, become reality: he had struck the United States Pacific Fleet a heavy blow, and Japanese amphibious forces had exploited this success to the utmost. They had secured Japan's original territorial objectives, and the Empire extended from the home islands to Sumatra.

The Japanese Second Fleet left for the Inland Sea in mid-April to prepare to capture Midway. In view of previous Japanese achievements, the seizure of this island did not seem a difficult undertaking.

IX

The Struggle for the Central Pacific

EVEN before Kondo's Second Fleet raided the Indian Ocean the Japanese appeared to some American pessimists to be irresistible. Radio commentators were predicting a junction of the German and Japanese Armies in India. But even then many Japanese Army and some Navy officers doubted the wisdom of extending their conquests. Actually the Japanese High Command faced a very difficult decision. If the advance were halted, Allied forces would remain in shorter striking distance of the heart of the Empire. If the offensive continued, combat ships would be stretched dangerously thin, and the merchant marine, already overburdened, would be further strained. As has been stated, probably Admiral Yamamoto, his task force commanders, and the staff officers of the Combined Fleet, flushed with their remarkable series of victories, supplied the impetus for enlarging the territorial objectives of the Empire.

While Japanese forces were sweeping over the southwest Pacific, King and Nimitz had strengthened the line of communications from the West Coast of the United States to Australia by establishing bases in the Fiji, Samoan, Ellice, New Hebrides, and New Caledonia Islands. Since further Japanese advance east or south obviously would threaten that line of communications, Vice-Admiral Wilson Brown was ordered to halt any attempted progress of the enemy forces gathering in Rabaul and New Guinea. This would automatically protect the passage of American troops en route from Australia to Nouméa, New Caledonia. Brown's force, which included the carriers *Lexington* and *Yorktown*, hit the enemy on March 10. The *Lexington's* planes struck first, bombing enemy transports and escort cruisers in Nassau Bay, in the Lae-Salamaua area of New Guinea, where the Japanese, under air cover, had landed troops a few days earlier. The *Yorktown's* planes followed shortly afterward, inflicting further damage on transports, cruisers, and destroyers as these vessels milled around Lae Harbor trying to evade attack.

This raid had been planned and supervised by Commander W. B. Ault, who commanded the *Lexington's* planes. While the carriers remained in the Coral Sea, their planes had reached the Lae-Salamaua area by direct route over the difficult Owen Stanley Range. Ault's preliminary reconnaissance and skillful conduct of the strike reduced American risks and increased the damage inflicted upon the enemy. The score was 1 light cruiser, 1 destroyer, and 5 transports or supply ships sunk; 1 mine layer probably sunk; 2 heavy cruisers, 2 destroyers, 2 gunboats, and 1 seaplane tender damaged. Brown's task force lost 1 scout bomber, and 11 other planes were damaged.

Brown's successful raid delayed the progress of the Japanese in their sweep toward Australia; nevertheless while General Homma overran Bataan, the Japanese Army had sufficient ground troops to strengthen their position in the Lae-Salamaua area and the northern Solomons, and to provide another invasion force for Port Moresby, all of which brought on the Coral Sea action. Meanwhile, on April 2, Vice-Admiral Brown turned over command of Task Force "B" to Rear Admiral Fitch, who reported to Rear Admiral Fletcher, the senior American Commander in the Coral Sea.

The Battle of the Coral Sea

Vice-Admiral Inoue, who was Commander in Chief of the Southeastern Fleet, commanded the Japanese force, including the *Shokaku* and the *Zuikaku*, the most modern carriers with 80 planes each, three heavy cruisers, and ten destroyers. He was ordered "to defend the Port Moresby Invasion Force and to attack any American Force that interposed." When the Coral Sea campaign opened, the large carriers lay north of Tulagi in the Solomons while the invasion fleet of five transports, the small carrier *Shoho*, four heavy cruisers, two light cruisers, and a seaplane tender was over 400 miles to the westward, just north of the Louisiade Islands off the

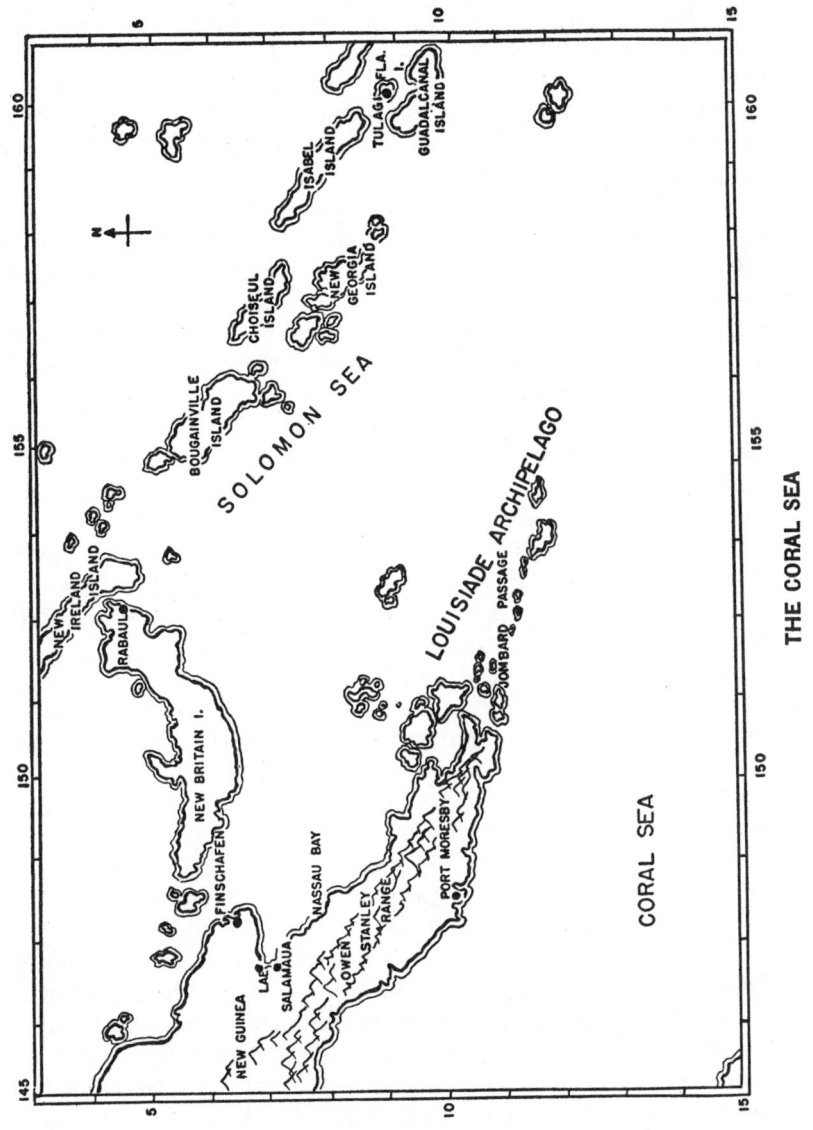

southeastern tip of New Guinea. Other troop transports were landing soldiers at Tulagi. When information of this landing reached Admiral Fletcher on May 3, he took a small task force, with only one carrier, the *Yorktown,* and steamed north at full speed. The next day the *Yorktown's* planes damaged and sank a number of ships in Tulagi Harbor, with very light American losses.

Admiral Fletcher then proceeded southeast to join Australian and American forces under Admiral Fitch. One or the other of the Allied groups was spotted and the rendezvous was reported by a Japanese "snooper" plane, probably from Admiral Inoue's carriers which still lay north of Tulagi. Meanwhile Fletcher fueled his ships,[1] despatched the tanker *Neosho* and the destroyer *Sims* southward in accordance with fueling rendezvous provisions, and informed his forces he would "attack enemy ships, shipping, and aircraft in order to check the Japanese advance in the New Guinea-Solomons area."

The Allied forces, designated as Task Force "F," were organized into three groups, the air group, around the carriers *Lexington* and *Yorktown,* under Fletcher's command, and two groups of cruisers and destroyers, one under Rear Admiral Kinkaid, U.S.N., and the other under Rear Admiral Crace, R.N. Kinkaid's and Crace's groups were similar in composition and interchangeable. Learning of the presence of the invasion force off the tip of New Guinea, Admiral Fletcher steamed toward the point during the night and early on the 7th detached Crace's group to operate south of Jombard Passage which led into the Coral Sea south of the Louisiade Islands, where any enemy surface ships would have to pass to reach Moresby.

The small carrier *Shoho* of the invasion force, assisted by the 25th Air Flotilla based on Rabaul, furnished planes to scout for American submarines and to provide air cover for the transports. Inoue's carriers, also proceeding toward the Louisiades to join the invasion group, launched search planes from the *Zuikaku* and the *Shokaku;* at almost

1. Fueling was a continuous operation in Pacific campaigns. Destroyers had to be refueled almost every 48 hours; cruisers and carriers had greater radius but required replenishments almost as often.

STRUGGLE FOR THE CENTRAL PACIFIC 135

the same time Fletcher sent his scouts aloft. The American scouts found the *Shoho* group about 9 A.M. and erroneously reported two carriers present. Fletcher knew he had three to deal with, so immediately launched bombing and torpedo planes from both carriers. Admiral Fitch on the *Lexington* was given tactical command, and between 11.30 A.M. and noon a coördinated bomber and torpedo attack sank the *Shoho*.

Meanwhile, Japanese scouting planes had found the *Neosho* and the *Sims* and reported them as a carrier force; they were attacked, and the *Sims* was sunk and the *Neosho* disabled at about the same time that the *Shoho* went to the bottom.

The Japanese heavy carriers were situated to the eastward in an area of low visibility. The American carriers were also in an area of low visibility, but it was clearing. Both sides launched scouting and fighting planes. About 4 P.M. the Japanese launched an attack group of bombers and torpedo planes, but they did not find the American carriers until they had jettisoned their bombs and were returning to their own carriers after dark. During the night the opposing admirals knew that enemy carriers were in easy striking distance. Their two forces were evenly matched, but the Japanese had a small advantage in their land-based planes and seaplanes from Rabaul, and a distinct advantage in the weather. Their carriers were operating in an area of overcast and rain, while the *Yorktown* and the *Lexington* were now in the clear.

An around-the-clock search was launched by the Americans and probably by the Japanese at daylight on the 8th. Shortly after 8 o'clock an American scout reported the position of the two enemy carriers; almost simultaneously an enemy message was intercepted indicating that one of their scouts had found Fletcher's carriers. Admiral Fitch on the *Lexington* was again given tactical command and planes were launched at once. While fighters took station to break up the expected attacks, a coördinated bomb and torpedo assault was launched against the *Shokaku* at 11 o'clock. She took six sure hits by bombs and, according to Japanese accounts, almost capsized. The *Zuikaku* took refuge in a rain squall. The *Lexington* attack group had not been furnished with accurate position reports and the bombers did not find the target; Commander Ault, who, as in the March 10 attack, commanded the *Lexington's* planes, finally found the *Zuikaku* through a break in the clouds and tried to coach the bombers to the target by voice radio. He failed, but did concentrate a small group of torpedo planes that attacked the *Zuikaku*. Having exhausted his gas supply in the effort, Ault went down radioing this farewell message: "Remember —we got a thousand-pound hit on a flat top."

Meanwhile the *Yorktown* and the *Lexington* had been attacked by enemy planes almost simultaneously, about 11.15 A.M. The *Yorktown* received one direct bomb hit and several near misses. Her speed was reduced to 30 knots, but her damage control party extinguished fires and made emergency repairs. The *Lexington* was hit first by two torpedoes, then by several bombs. Fires were started in various parts of the ship; by 12.40 P.M. the damage control had all fires out but one. A list of 6 degrees was rectified, and she made 25 knots under good control. However, about 1 P.M. a terrific explosion occurred between decks on the *Lexington,* probably from gasoline leaks. Many fires were started and before they could be controlled there were other minor explosions. Shortly after 5 P.M. Admiral Fitch ordered Captain Sherman to abandon ship. While destroyers went alongside in succession, taking off members of the crew and picking up others from the water, another enormous explosion rocked the sinking ship, tossing the remaining planes high in the air for their last flight. Pulling boats then circled the ship to pick up the rest of the crew. It required four torpedoes from the *Phelps* to send the *Lexington* to the bottom. Over 92 per cent of the crew of approximately 3,000 men were saved. The score of the four days' actions was enemy ships sunk: 1 small carrier, 1 light cruiser, 2 destroyers, a cargo ship, and 4 gunboats; ships damaged, *Shokaku* severely, *Zuikaku* slightly; aircraft destroyed, 104. American losses were: sunk, 1 carrier, 1 destroyer, and 1 tanker;

STRUGGLE FOR THE CENTRAL PACIFIC

damaged slightly, 1 carrier; planes lost, 66. Enemy personnel lost were estimated between 2,000 and 5,000; American, 545.

Of the battle of the Coral Sea Admiral Nimitz reported that "Admiral Fletcher between May 4th and 8th won a victory with decisive and far-reaching consequences for the Allied cause." The immediate effect was to stop all further attempts of the Japanese to reach Port Moresby by sea. Commander Sekino, staff officer of the cruiser squadron which had escorted the carrier *Shoho,* testifies that they gave up the attempt to reach Moresby because they could not destroy Crace's surface force, and their carrier-based planes were of little use because they were running out of fuel. The Coral Sea action is significant as the first major naval battle in which surface ships did not exchange a single shot. But Crace's ships did bar the advance on Moresby.

The failure to reach Port Moresby by sea compelled the Japanese to undertake to cross from Lae over the Owen Stanley Mountains. Meanwhile, however, Allied naval victories had been giving MacArthur time to build up his land forces. Accordingly, before the Japanese could assemble strength for their undertaking, a combined American-Australian force under MacArthur, operating from Moresby, turned them back by land.

Of even greater consequence was the damage to the two carriers *Shokaku* and *Zuikaku* which were expected to take part in the Midway invasion. The *Shokaku* required three months for repairs and missed the entire campaign; the *Zuikaku,* superficially damaged, did not reach the Aleutians until late in June. The *Yorktown,* thanks to the efforts of her officers and men and Rear Admiral W. R. Furlong's navy yard at Pearl Harbor, was able to get into the thick of the fighting at Midway. Thus Fletcher and Fitch, during the week that Corregidor surrendered, sank the first enemy carrier, stopped the Japanese advance toward Australia, denied them the Coral Sea and deprived Yamamoto of two, perhaps three, of his carriers that could otherwise have fought in the decisive battle of Midway Island.

The Battle of Midway*

Meanwhile, about the middle of April, Vice-Admiral Kondo and Rear Admiral Takahashi returned to Japan with the Second and Third Fleets after accomplishing all the tasks which had been given them by their Commander in Chief. While the two fleets were refitting, Doolittle's medium bombers took off from the carrier *Hornet,* and, escorted part way by fighters from the *Enterprise,* bombed Tokyo. According to Captain Watanabe, gunnery officer of the Combined Fleet, Admiral Yamamoto thought these planes had flown from Midway Island, and his resolve to invade that island hardened.

Yamamoto's plan included the capture and occupation of Kure, Sand, and Eastern Islands in the Midways, and attacks and if possible landings on Attu, Kiska, and Adak in the Aleutians. Air forces and submarines would then be based on the Aleutians to protect Japan from American planes or invasion forces, while Japanese planes operating from Midway would attempt first to neutralize Oahu and perhaps make its eventual capture possible.

Yamamoto realized the importance of the operations. He took personal command, gathered his war-tested flag officers and concentrated most of the navy for the great attempt. While plans were being completed news of the battle of the Coral Sea arrived. Yamamoto despatched Watanabe to inspect the damaged carriers *Shokaku* and *Zuikaku.* Although he learned that the *Shokaku* definitely could not and the *Zuikaku* probably would not be ready on the date of sailing from Japan to Midway, Yamamoto adhered to the tentative schedule. He had some reason for haste; time was definitely on the side of Nimitz, yet the absence of these two ships deprived the Japanese commander of 160 planes and two of his best carriers.

Admiral Yamamoto commanded the Expeditionary Force and also the main body, Battleship Divisions One and Two, consisting of seven battleships, two heavy cruisers, a destroyer squadron, and the small carrier *Zuiho,* which was to provide antisubmarine reconnaissance and air cover for the main body and its supply ships. Vice-Admiral Nagumo,

* For map, see p. 158.

STRUGGLE FOR THE CENTRAL PACIFIC 139

commander of the air fleet at the Pearl Harbor attack, again commanded the same force, less the *Shokaku* and the *Zuikaku*. As direct escort, he was given two fast battleships, two heavy cruisers, and a destroyer squadron, and was assigned his own supply ships. Yamamoto undertook to give Nagumo additional security by having the main body steam on parallel courses between him and the estimated positions of the American forces.

Kondo and Takahashi, who had respectively given direct and indirect support to the forces that had invaded the Philippines, Malaya, and the East Indies, had the same tasks and practically the same strength for the Midway operation, except that they had no carriers. However, the 11th Air Flotilla of seaplanes with three tenders (not to be confused with the 11th Air Fleet of shore-based planes), the 24th Air Flotilla from the Marshalls, and the 26th from Marcus Island operated with Kondo's force en route. Possibly some of these flying boats accompanied Kondo to Midway. Seaplanes were used for distant scouting to relieve carrier planes of the task; according to Rear Admiral Nomura (not the Ambassador), the seaplanes failed to find the American ships on account of poor visibility.

The landing force, carried in 16 transports and supply ships, consisted of 1,000 marines (sea infantry) ordered to capture Sand Island and 50 to take Kure Island, while 1,000 army troops were considered enough to seize Eastern Island. In all, the Japanese provided only 2,050 troops to take three islands. These were accompanied by a meteorological group, surveyors, and laborers. Equipment and stores for three months were provided. Destroyer Squadron Four furnished direct protection en route and was prepared to lend artillery support for the landing. Cruiser Division Seven, Rear Admiral Kurita commanding, with four heavy cruisers, including the *Mogami* and the *Mikuma,* was prepared to clear the advance and if necessary bombard the objectives. In advance of his surface ships Yamamoto sent ten of his largest submarines to patrol northwest of Midway, and a single undersea boat to serve as an aid to navigation west of the islands.

Admiral Hosogaya, Commander of the Vladivostok Observation Force during the Pearl Harbor attack, commanded the Aleutian Diversionary and Landing Group. According to Captain Watanabe, Yamamoto intended first to make diversionary air attacks on Dutch Harbor in the hope of luring American ships into that area so they could be attacked; later, if events favored, landings would be made at Attu, Kiska, and Adak. Hosogaya was given initially 5 heavy cruisers, 2 carriers, the *Ryujo* and the *Junyo,* with a total of 30 fighters and 36 bombers, and each of the cruisers had 2 observation planes, while several of the 20-odd submarines carried small planes. En route Hosogaya was reënforced by Battleship Division Two, Destroyer Squadron Three, and the small carrier *Zuiho* from Yamamoto's main body.

The Aleutian force set out from Hokkaido, the main body and the air force from the Inland Sea, the carriers from Hiroshima, and the landing forces and escort from Saipan. En route the task forces were widely separated but within supporting distance of one another. Yamamoto knew that no American battleships were west of Honolulu, and he was prepared to interpose fast battleships and heavy cruisers between any of his task forces and hostile cruisers. He had deployed the carriers to provide air cover for ships on the northern routes; seaplanes from shore bases and tenders provided air scouts and cover for the southern routes.

As Yamamoto approached Midway his dispositions invited some criticism. In the hope of enticing Nimitz into dividing the American carriers, he detached the *Zuiho* to join Hosogaya's two carriers in the diversionary force, as has been said. In the raid on Pearl Harbor he had assigned Nagumo six carriers; for the more difficult seizure of Midway he gave him only four. Nagumo had to destroy the defenses of Midway, and, if American carriers appeared, destroy them or at least neutralize their planes.

While the Japanese High Command were preparing and launching their invasion force, Admirals King and Nimitz had not been idle. Both noticed the absence of Japanese strength in the southwest Pacific after the battle of the Coral Sea; they felt sure the enemy was regrouping his

STRUGGLE FOR THE CENTRAL PACIFIC 141

ships for another advance. The question was, in what direction? Early intelligence reports indicated an attack in the central Pacific, and when later information confirmed this, Nimitz recalled Fletcher's task force to Honolulu. Repairs on the *Yorktown* were rushed, and a squadron of torpedo planes from the carrier *Lexington* filled some of the *Yorktown's* vacancies caused by the battle of the Coral Sea.

Within a short space of time Nimitz concentrated his air, surface, and undersea craft in the vicinity of Midway. Even then the American forces were outnumbered by the enemy, and King was constrained to limit Nimitz "to strict attrition tactics." With his responsibilities in the Atlantic and the Pacific, King could not afford to risk carriers and cruisers unduly. He suspected that Yamamoto might attempt to cut off part of the Pacific Fleet. As is now known, this is precisely what Yamamoto hoped and planned to do by using his Aleutian Diversionary Force to lure part of the American Fleet to Dutch Harbor.

In addition to the forces and planes ashore, Admiral Nimitz had 25 of the latest submarines commanded by Rear Admiral English. These were stationed on the anticipated line of approach of the enemy forces. The surface fleet was divided into Task Force "F" under Rear Admiral Fletcher with the *Yorktown* as flagship and a mixed force of cruisers and destroyers under Rear Admiral W. W. Smith; and Task Force "S" under Rear Admiral Spruance with two carriers, the *Enterprise,* flagship commanded by Captain G. D. Murray, and the *Hornet* under Captain Marc A. Mitscher. Each carrier had 35 dive bombers, 14 torpedo planes, and 27 fighters. Rear Admiral Kinkaid commanded the escort of Task Force "S," consisting of six cruisers and nine destroyers.

Many of these officers and ships had served in the Coral Sea with Fletcher. Rear Admiral Spruance had commanded the escort force that had bombarded the Marshall Islands in January. Practically every officer present at Midway subsequently rendered distinguished service, and probably each recalls with peculiar pride being present at the most critical and decisive naval engagement in the Pacific. In no subsequent action, not even in the hotly contested Guadalcanal campaign, was the margin of victory so close or the results more far reaching. Fletcher, senior to Spruance, took command when the two task forces joined on the afternoon of June 2, some 350 miles northeast of Midway.

As evidence of an attack on Midway accumulated, Nimitz reënforced the island's Marine battalion, and Coast Artillery personnel fortified their positions and placed underwater obstructions. Information of the enemy's approach was essential. To obtain it, Admiral Nimitz strengthened the air forces on Midway by bringing the Marine air group to full strength and adding four Army B-29's under Colonel Sweeney and six improved Navy torpedo bombers, the new "Avengers." Later, during the battle, additional planes flew in from Oahu.

On June 3, Honolulu time, the Aleutian force bombed Dutch Harbor. Fog hampered the operation and the attack was repeated the following morning. No American ships were lured into the trap, but the enemy was operating on schedule and according to plan. Meanwhile Admiral Nagumo, taking full advantage of the weather, was approaching Midway behind an area of low visibility.

American PBY's, scouting northwest of Midway on May 31 and June 1, were thwarted by the same weather front that Admiral Nagumo was utilizing. Army B-17's scouted on the same days; they also had negative results. On the morning of the 3d, however, American scouting planes sighted two enemy cargo vessels 470 miles west of the islands and shortly afterward the main body[2] of Kondo's force was discovered 700 miles due west of Midway. Colonel Sweeney led the first group of B-17's to attack it; three groups bombed the enemy force late in the afternoon, reporting hits on a heavy cruiser and a transport. After midnight two Navy pilots made torpedo attacks against the same formation. These were the first night torpedo attacks ever delivered by flying boats. Captain Toyama testified that the

---

2. The Japanese overwork the term "main body"; nearly every formation has a main body. Yamamoto and Kondo each had a main body. We are using the Japanese terminology here.

STRUGGLE FOR THE CENTRAL PACIFIC 143

high-level bombers (B-17's) made three near misses that did no damage, that the PBY's made one torpedo hit in the bow of a tanker that reduced its speed, and that one of them turned its machine guns on a transport.

June 4 was the day of decision. A résumé of the fierce air fights of that date will assist an understanding of the four-day battle for the central Pacific. Before daylight on the 4th long-range aircraft taking off from Midway located the hostile air fleet at 5.45, just as it emerged from the mists, with its fighting patrol aloft and its bombers ready to launch. These bombers, protected by fighting squadrons, broke through the American fighters defending Midway and delivered a devastating attack on the island. By 7 A.M. torpedo and bombing planes from the American carriers were launched to attack the enemy carriers, which were already being attacked by bombers from Midway. Japanese fighters not only beat off the attacks of the Midway planes but practically annihilated torpedo squadrons from the *Hornet,* the *Enterprise,* and the *Yorktown.* At 10.20 the Japanese had every reason to be pleased; their attacks on Midway had devastated the island and they had repulsed American attacks and inflicted heavy loss. But within the next 20 minutes dive bombers from the *Enterprise* and the *Yorktown* completely disabled three out of four enemy carriers. All three were subsequently sunk. Never in naval history had such decisive results been obtained in such a short time. The fourth carrier was disabled in the afternoon and scuttled on the 5th.

The details of the June 4 action will now be related. That morning, even before the American scouting planes had returned to the island, Midway was under heavy attack by planes from the Japanese carriers that, as has been related, had approached under cover of the fog. But the Japanese were expected; the Midway fighters were in the air and took toll of the enemy bombers. And it was long-range planes from Midway that had discovered the enemy carriers and enabled the American carrier planes to make their successful attacks. Furthermore, by absorbing the first blow from the Japanese carriers, Midway Island probably saved the *Hor-*

net, the *Enterprise,* and the *Yorktown* from a heavy enemy carrier strike. Midway and its planes made a substantial contribution to the victory.

Of the 290 planes the Japanese had brought in their force, about 140 attacked Midway at this time. The enemy fighters and bombers were accustomed to working together; when an American fighter attacked an enemy bomber, Zero fighters immediately counterattacked. Although numerical odds were against the American fighters, they inflicted heavy losses on the enemy fighters and broke up the bomber formations. Japanese bombers could not circle leisurely over Midway as they had done over Cavite and Port Darwin. Nevertheless Midway took a terrific pounding, almost every structure being destroyed or badly damaged. Apparently expecting that the island would be captured, the bombers did not attack the airfields.

By 7.15 A.M. the last enemy plane had departed; shortly thereafter Yamamoto's carriers began to receive return visits from American planes. Between 7 and 8.15, Army, Navy, and Marine Corps planes from Midway attacked the enemy carriers. Visibility was excellent. Four Army B-26's and six Navy TBF's attacked simultaneously at 7 o'clock; only one of the Navy planes survived and the pilot had been unable to observe the results of the attack on account of enemy fighter interference; two B-26's were lost diving to avoid the fighter screen, the other two reported they were pursued by 50 fighters. The first Marine wave attacked about 8 o'clock in a gliding dive; their pilots were not sufficiently trained to dive bomb; only 8 of 16 planes returned and only 2 were operable. Shortly afterward Colonel Sweeney with 15 B-17's struck; the B-17's approached in two groups of six and one of three; Japanese fighters did not press home their attacks on the B-17's, probably on account of the altitude involved. The second wave of Marine dive bombers appeared just as the B-17's departed. Driven off by enemy fighters from the carriers, they made a low-level attack on a battleship. There had been no report from the Navy torpedo bombers; the four B-26's could not ob-

STRUGGLE FOR THE CENTRAL PACIFIC 145

serve the results of their torpedoes; the first wave of Marines reported three direct hits and several near misses. Colonel Sweeney's squadron reported three hits on two carriers; and the third Marine force reported two hits on a battleship that began to smoke.

These reports led Admiral Nimitz to estimate that one or two transports or cargo ships had been sunk and about eight other combat and cargo ships damaged, but according to subsequent information from Japanese officers only one enemy tanker had been hit and it was only reduced in speed. Every Japanese officer interviewed, except one, testified that none of the carriers, battleships, or cruisers had been hit by high-level bombers.

The land-based planes supplied essential information; they located the enemy transports and main body 700 miles at sea, and confirmed the earlier intelligence of the enemy's approach. This was their main contribution, although they were also used to attack enemy ships and aircraft.

Meanwhile the American carriers were coming into the action. While operating to the northward of Midway on the 3d, the two task forces under Admiral Fletcher and Admiral Spruance learned that the enemy transports and the main body, but not the carriers, had been sighted. At 4.30 A.M. on the 4th, about 200 miles north of Midway, the *Yorktown* launched a search to the northwest as well as a fighter patrol to protect the three carriers. Planes of the *Hornet* and the *Enterprise* were in readiness to take off. At 5.25 A.M. the position of two enemy carriers was received. Spruance, directed to attack, proceeded westward at 25 knots until within 150 miles of the enemy. About 7 o'clock the *Hornet* launched 35 dive bombers carrying 500-pound bombs, 15 torpedo planes, and 10 fighters; simultaneously the *Enterprise* launched 33 dive bombers, 15 carrying 1,000-pound bombs, 12 with one 500-pound and two 100-pound bombs, and six with 500-pound bombs, 14 torpedo planes, and 10 fighters. As 9 o'clock approached, the captain, fearing the *Yorktown's* planes might be bombed aboard, launched 12 torpedo planes, 17 dive bombers, and 6 fighters, retaining a reserve of 17 bombers to attack the other two carriers when discovered. Thus shortly after 9 o'clock all American carrier planes except the *Yorktown's* reserve were in the air.

Enemy carriers, assuming that American carriers had been diverted to the Aleutians by the attack on Dutch Harbor, did not anticipate their presence at Midway, and apparently learned of their proximity only from the Japanese planes that attacked the island, or from one of the Japanese seaplane scouts. While Spruance was steaming westward, the Japanese steamed north. Unfortunately the *Hornet's* group commander, with the entire group of 35 dive bombers and 10 fighters that had been launched, did not find the enemy at the reported position; he turned south and never sighted the carriers. His fighting planes ran out of gasoline, although eight of the ten pilots were rescued after landing in the sea; all but two of the bombers reached Midway, refueled, and returned to the *Hornet*. Torpedo Squadron Eight from the *Hornet* turned north instead of south, and found the carriers, now a group of four. Despite the fact that the squadron had no fighters to protect them, they attacked. Captain Ohara of the *Soryu* reports that they flew low and straight for the carriers and were shot down one after another by the Japanese fighter patrols. Only a few were able to launch their torpedoes. The sole survivor of Torpedo Squadron Eight, a young ensign, crashed near the *Akagi* and from his rubber life raft witnessed the subsequent attacks of American planes.

The torpedo squadron of the *Enterprise* lost its fighters but attacked. The Japanese carriers turned away and, according to their officers, evaded the torpedoes. Only four of the squadron's 14 planes survived. About this time the *Yorktown's* torpedo squadron approached. It had some fighter protection but suffered heavily. First the squadron commander leading the formation was shot down; then almost in a row six more planes went down. Of the five that remained to pursue the attack, three were shot down and two survived. A fighter pilot thought he saw two carriers hit. But Captain Aoki of the *Kaga* and Captain Yamaguichi of the *Hiryu* testified that the torpedo planes made no hits on

STRUGGLE FOR THE CENTRAL PACIFIC

the carriers. Three torpedo squadrons had been practically annihilated. One pilot and no planes of the *Hornet* survived; only two planes of the squadron that flew from the *Yorktown* returned, only four of the 14 from the *Enterprise*.

In this kaleidoscopic battle between enemy carriers and American carrier planes, the Japanese had to that moment been winning. But Lieutenant Commander C. W. McClusky, Jr., group commander of the *Enterprise,* and his pilots, flying the 33 dive bombers from the *Enterprise,* changed the situation almost in the twinkling of an eye. Failing to find the carriers at the reported position, McClusky had steered north, making "the most important decision of the action." About 10 A.M., immediately after the few surviving American torpedo planes had left the scene, McClusky's group sighted the four enemy carriers. Two sections of the dive bombers struck the *Kaga* and the *Soryu* almost at the same time. Pilots reported they made eight hits on the *Kaga,* whose Captain Amagai admitted that four direct hits were made while practically all his planes were aboard being serviced for an attack on the American carriers. Many of his planes caught fire, and the *Kaga* sank in the afternoon taking most of them with her. Sixty pilots and 700 of the crew were saved. Not a plane from this ship had been used on the offensive.

Some of the *Enterprise* pilots who attacked the *Soryu* thought they were attacking the *Akagi* and reported three hits. The *Akagi* was in the vicinity, and the pilots may have been right, but the captain of the *Soryu* reports that his ship received three hits at that time. The planes and fuel tanks of the *Soryu* were ignited; when the fires had been extinguished the *Soryu* crept away from the scene of carnage, only to be sunk that afternoon by three torpedoes from the submarine *Nautilus.*

The captain and the crew of the *Nautilus* had earned their triumph; they had made a determined effort to reach a carrier in the forenoon only to be forced by destroyers to submerge. After being heavily depth charged, the *Nautilus* emerged and returned to get her carrier. The *Soryu's* planes had already struck Midway in the attack described earlier in this chapter. They had returned and were being fueled and armed to attack American carriers when the *Soryu* was struck. Her planes went down with her, but 30 pilots and 700 of the crew were saved. Captain Ohara attributes the loss of his ship to the delay in servicing the planes.

At about 10.30 the *Yorktown's* 17 bombers, 15 carrying 1,000-pound bombs, descended upon the *Akagi* as she launched the first planes of her second flight. The first bomb from the *Yorktown's* planes converted the flying deck into a mass of flames and four other hits made it an inferno. Captain Aobi of the *Akagi* states that 40 planes were being serviced when she was hit by two bombs; fires were started and planes exploded. The engines went out of commission and many engineers were killed. She floated during the night but had to be sunk by Japanese torpedoes the next morning.

It was the dive bombers that decided the battle of Midway. The same Japanese officers whose testimony, already given in this chapter, emphasized that the high-level bombers operating from Midway earlier in the day had not hit the Japanese carriers, battleships, or cruisers, also state that the torpedo planes did no damage to these ships.

This evidence from Japanese sources was confirmed by the dive-bombing pilots of the *Enterprise* and the *Yorktown,* who reported that the enemy carriers showed no visible sign of damage before the dive-bombing attacks. The sweeping success of the dive bombers was undoubtedly partly due to the fact that from about 7 to 10.30 that morning the four Japanese carriers had been under intermittent attack that had kept them maneuvering, disarranged their fighter patrols, and facilitated the attacks of the dive bombers. It should be recalled that when bombers of the Royal Air Force had attacked a similar carrier group in the Indian Ocean in April, with its fighter patrols on station to repel the assault, practically every British bomber had been shot down before it could reach the carriers. Japanese fighter squadrons were a formidable force at that time.

While her three sisters were being struck, the *Hiryu* steamed northwest and escaped into the area of low visibility. Soon after, she learned from her scouts of the posi-

STRUGGLE FOR THE CENTRAL PACIFIC 149

tion of the *Yorktown* and shortly after noon her dive bombers struck. Her pilots thought they were attacking the *Enterprise*. In spite of fighter protection and antiaircraft batteries, the ship that had survived the Japanese attack in the Coral Sea took three direct hits and several near misses. The damage from Japanese bombs was not great. By 1.30 P.M. the engines were making 20 knots and the fires were sufficiently under control to begin refueling fighters on deck. Again enemy planes were reported and despite stubborn resistance a few torpedo planes got through. About 2.45 two torpedoes hit the *Yorktown* amidships on the port side. She developed a list and it increased until it appeared that she would capsize; her engines were dead, and the ship stopped. The order to abandon ship was given and executed about 3 P.M., with destroyers coming alongside to pick up survivors.

The *Hiryu's* successful attack was her last. Just as her torpedo planes hit the *Yorktown* the Japanese carrier's position was reported, probably by scouting aircraft from the *Enterprise* that were searching for her; an hour later 24 bombers took off from the *Enterprise*. They struck the *Hiryu* at about 5 o'clock. Two were shot down by enemy fighters; the remainder made six direct hits. Half an hour later the *Hornet's* squadron arrived, but the *Hiryu* was burning so fiercely she was not considered a useful target. The *Hornet* planes attacked a battleship and a cruiser, estimating that they made two hits on each. According to the captain of the *Hiryu* only the battleship was hit; she received a glancing blow on the stern that did no material damage. Despite six hits the *Hiryu* remained afloat, but during the night fires reached her engine room, and she was sunk by a Japanese torpedo the next morning.

Meanwhile, on Midway Island, working parties had begun restoring facilities as soon as the Japanese planes had departed. In the afternoon six Army B-17's took off to attack the three enemy carriers, the *Kaga*, the *Soryu*, and the *Akagi*, that were still burning. Their pilots reported at least one hit. At almost the same time Major G. A. Blakey, bringing a reënforcement of six B-17's from Oahu, struck at the same targets; after shooting down four enemy fighters the pilots estimated that their bombs hit a damaged carrier and a destroyer. Japanese officers are positive, however, that in neither of these attacks were their ships hit. Soon after dark the Marine Bomber Squadron and 11 PT boats left Midway to strike the enemy who was now retreating. But apparently Yamamoto's battleships found cover in the same area of low visibility that had concealed the approach of his carriers; neither the Marine flyers nor the captains of the PT's found them.

After the *Yorktown* was abandoned, Admiral Fletcher shifted to the *Astoria*. At nightfall on the 4th American admirals knew their planes had disposed of four enemy carriers, but they had indications that another carrier was in the vicinity. Yamamoto could have had three more carriers, the *Ryujo,* the *Junyo,* and the *Zuiho,* off Midway; actually there was no enemy carrier in operable condition nearer than Dutch Harbor.

Admiral Spruance with the *Hornet* and the *Enterprise,* six cruisers, and seven destroyers had to consider the possibility that another carrier was present and that Yamamoto would still attempt to seize Midway. Spruance wished to avoid a night engagement with enemy battleships, cruisers, and destroyers, and be in easy supporting distance of the island at daylight, so he set his courses for the night accordingly. During the night Spruance received contradictory messages, the first in a series of baffling intelligence reports about the enemy, that, as events developed, caused him to waste the 5th and the early hours of the 6th making sure that no enemy carrier was in the vicinity.

According to Captain Watanabe, who was staff gunnery officer of the Combined Fleet, 1940-43, and aboard the flagship with Yamamoto at Midway, Yamamoto held a two-hour conference with his staff late on June 4, and accepted the recommendation of his Chief of Staff, Rear Admiral Ugaki, to retreat. At the same time Admiral Kurita, commanding the Seventh Cruiser Division, was ordered to bombard Midway, probably to cover the withdrawal of the others. Kurita proceeded at high speed toward Midway but the

STRUGGLE FOR THE CENTRAL PACIFIC

heavy cruisers *Mogami* and *Mikuma* collided during an emergency turn away from an American submarine. The *Mogami* was badly damaged and her speed reduced; the *Mikuma* was only slightly hurt. On his own initiative Kurita turned about and steamed west at about 15 knots during the night with four cruisers and destroyer screen. Yamamoto ordered the submarines to retire at the same time; during the retreat at about 1 A.M. on the 5th, a submarine bombarded Midway. This piece of bravado ended the Japanese effort to capture that island.

On the 5th, while Spruance searched for the main body of Yamamoto's force in the area of low visibility to the northwest, Midway planes found and attacked Kurita's damaged cruisers. Army B-17's made two attacks, Navy PBY's one. According to American pilots, two hits were made on one cruiser, or one hit on each of two cruisers: the *Mogami* and the *Mikuma* were sister ships, alike as two peas, and the difficulty in identification is understandable. Admiral Soji confirms some of the details of the attack, namely, that the dive bombers dove out of the sun, but that only near hits were made except in the case of one plane which dove into the after turret of the *Mikuma*. Captain Fleming, U.S.M.C., was the pilot of this plane, and was awarded the Congressional Medal of Honor posthumously. The *Mikuma* was slightly damaged. This attack caused the two uninjured cruisers to increase speed to join Yamamoto's main body, leaving the *Mikuma* and the *Mogami* with two destroyers.

Early on the 6th Spruance decided to abandon the search to the northwest, where he was still hampered by the weather, and despatch his scouting planes to search westward where the atmosphere was clear. The damaged cruisers were promptly found. The *Hornet* delivered two attacks; the *Enterprise* one, and then photographed the enemy ships. The last flight of planes barely got back to the carriers; many of the pilots made their first after-dark landing. Some American planes had trouble finding their own carriers and landed on whatever ship could be found in the darkness, or on Midway.

The testimony of Admiral Soji provides details of the

three attacks delivered by the *Hornet* and the *Enterprise* dive bombers against the crippled ships on the 6th. On the first attack, at 7 A.M., the *Mogami* was hit twice, one turret was disabled, and fires were started but soon extinguished; the *Mikuma* was struck two or three times, and a destroyer was hit once but was able to keep up with the cruisers. On the second attack, between 9 and 10 A.M., the *Mogami* was again hit twice and fires were restarted. The *Mikuma* fared worse, being hit several times. She burned so fiercely that destroyers could not go alongside to rescue the crew, who jumped overboard and were picked up by small boats. During the third attack the *Mogami* was hit only once, the *Mikuma* several times, and the destroyer *Arashio*, whose deck was crowded with survivors of the *Mikuma*, was hit, with heavy casualties. The *Mikuma* sank in the late afternoon or night. The *Mogami* and the two destroyers were joined by a detachment from the main body some time afterward and were escorted to port.

Spruance now turned his force around and headed east. He had already been forced to send some of his destroyers to fuel, and his carriers and cruisers had consumed much of their oil. Since submarines were in the vicinity, it was not prudent for the carriers to proceed without a full antisubmarine screen of destroyers, and if the pursuit had continued much farther west American carriers would have come within range of Japanese planes based on Wake Island.

When the *Yorktown* had been abandoned on the evening of the 4th, three destroyers had set up a patrol around her to prevent capture or destruction by the enemy. On the 5th she had been taken in tow by the mine sweeper *Vireo*. At daylight on the 6th Captain Buckmaster returned with a picked salvage crew of 180 men; the destroyer *Hammann* came alongside to furnish power and fight the flames. By early afternoon considerable progress had been made, the list had been reduced, and some of the fires extinguished; but shortly before 2 P.M. a submarine hit the *Yorktown* with three torpedoes and the *Hammann* with one. The destroyer broke into two parts and sank immediately. Buckmaster and

STRUGGLE FOR THE CENTRAL PACIFIC   153

his salvage crew continued to work desperately to save the thrice stricken *Yorktown*. For a while it seemed they would succeed; but at 3 A.M. on the 7th the list began to increase, and two hours later she rolled over on her port side and quietly sank. It was heartbreaking to lose the *Yorktown* after the herculean efforts to save her. However, the experience gained in such early and unsuccessful attempts to save American carriers was to make possible the almost miraculous salvaging of combat ships later, in battles with Kamikaze planes off Okinawa.

After their second attack on Dutch Harbor, Hosogaya's forces cruised between Midway and the Aleutians for ten days in the vain hope of luring some American ships to their destruction, but as a diversionary attempt the entire action failed.

After Yamamoto lost his carriers off Midway he ordered the landing in the Aleutians canceled, but was later persuaded by Hosogaya to permit the occupation of Kiska and Attu on June 7. A few Americans operating a weather station were captured. Tokyo propagandists emphasized these landings to conceal their Midway defeat from the Japanese public. The navy went even further; according to some ranking army officers, even the army was not informed of the full extent of the naval losses.

It was galling to American pride to have a foot of territory in enemy possession, but possession of those unimproved Aleutian ports had no effect on the strategical situation and compelled the Japanese to expend ships, planes, and troops to maintain them. The Aleutians have long been likened to an arrow pointing at the heart of either Japan or the United States. They are on the shortest route between the two nations, but the climate hampers all operations, and the total lack of natural facilities makes this route practically worthless compared with the longer but more convenient passage via the middle Pacific.

According to Captain Watanabe, some of Yamamoto's staff wished to land on Midway without the carrier support. However, as has been pointed out, Yamamoto apparently was influenced by his Chief of Staff to retire and he was certainly persuaded by Hosogaya to land in the Aleutians. Whether or not these decisions were wise, they indicate that Yamamoto was swayed in his most important decisions by his task force commanders and staff. This was not true of Admiral Togo, who, in one afternoon in the Russo-Japanese War, lost two battleships in a Russian mine field off Port Arthur, which left his fleet inferior in battleships to the fleet he was blockading. Without asking his staff's opinion Togo decided to maintain the blockade and then impressed his views upon them.

Although gratified with the result of the battle of Midway, American naval commanders were not at all satisfied with the performance of certain material and personnel. After the action, records of both material and operation were subjected to rigorous analyses, so successfully that battle clinics became a regular feature of the Nimitz program. King and his staff would weigh the recommendations of the clinic carefully, after which the Deputy Chief of Naval Operations would initiate improvements in materials, and Nimitz would effect the necessary changes in methods of operations. More than any one factor, these analyses contributed to the steady increase in the ruggedness of the material and the operating efficiency of the personnel.

In the battle of Midway, as in that of the Coral Sea, planes from carriers decided the outcome; surface ships did not exchange a single shot. After these engagements Admiral King had every reason to believe that the naval aviation of the Pacific Fleet was more effective than that of the enemy. The Japanese Navy had combined air, surface, and undersea craft into an instrument of war which, until it encountered a fleet equally air minded, was irresistible. It is true that the Japanese had imitated many American methods but certain of their arms—shore-based naval aviation, for example— had been equal, and perhaps superior, to the American when the war started. In this connection it may be pointed out that the Japanese Navy had met no opposition from the Army or budget director in developing its shore-based air fleets. Unfortunately the feud between the American Army Air Corps

STRUGGLE FOR THE CENTRAL PACIFIC 155

and the Navy, and the insistence of the Director of the Budget that there be no duplication of effort, had curtailed the development of naval shore-based planes as an integral part of the United States fleets.

In a larger sense the battle of Midway opened a struggle between the smaller Japanese Navy, which had shown consummate ability in extracting the utmost from its temporary control of the sea, and the larger United States Navy which for a time had had to abandon the western Pacific. In spite of aviation, steam, oil, and modern weapons, the Japanese confronted the same insoluble problem that the French had encountered much earlier on various occasions in the West Indies when, having temporary control of the Caribbean, they occupied British islands only to lose them again when the British Navy returned in greater and permanent strength. The only hope of ultimate Japanese victory lay in greater tactical skill of the Japanese, basic strategic errors by the American High Command, or the unwillingness of the American people to continue the war. Nimitz, Fletcher, and Spruance, their officers and men, were as courageous as the Japanese and more skillful. The United States Navy had many temporary reverses ahead, but after Midway there could be no doubt of the final outcome.

Rear Admiral Takata, who served successively on the staff of the Air Fleet, the Combined Fleet, and as a member of the Navy General Staff, attributes the Japanese defeat at Midway to strategical inefficiency and careless handling of the navy. He places the blame squarely upon Yamamoto. Captain Aobi of the *Akagi* thinks overconfidence caused the defeat, saying, "Because we had suffered so little at Pearl Harbor we thought we could get away with the same thing at Midway." It would have been natural for Yamamoto, Nagumo, and the Japanese pilots to be overconfident. Yamamoto had planned and supervised, and Nagumo and his pilots had taken the decisive part in an unprecedented series of naval triumphs. Except for their reverse in the Coral Sea, their navy had executed practically on schedule a program of conquest from Burma to the Solomons, and was threatening Australia. Japanese carrier planes were a deadly combination; the fighters protected their own floating homes as well as guarded the bombers on their missions of destruction. Along with Japan's shore-based naval planes, which were equally proficient, the carrier planes had with ease destroyed British, Dutch, and American air opposition in the western Pacific and the Bay of Bengal, enabling her surface ships to demolish or drive from the Far East all Allied surface craft. Only Spartan self-restraint would have saved Yamamoto, Nagumo, and their pilots from overconfidence, and this they lacked.

Yamamoto must also bear the blame for not making a greater effort to repair the *Zuikaku* in time to participate in the campaign. Nagumo's tactical handling of his carriers is also difficult to justify. In spite of the fact that the diversionary attack on Dutch Harbor had been launched in the express hope of luring carriers away from Midway, the bulk of Nagumo's planes attacked without ascertaining whether American carriers were in the vicinity. Half of the planes on the *Akagi* and the *Soryu* made attacks on Midway; only the *Hiryu* attacked both Midway and the *Yorktown;* the *Kaga* made no attacks.

Even if Yamamoto had taken Midway there was not enough space on its islets to maintain an air force large enough to neutralize the Hawaiian Islands. Only as a preliminary outpost for an immediate follow-up attack on Oahu would Midway have been valuable. If he had attempted to maintain an air force at Midway, he would have brought on a series of sea and air actions in an area where American forces were stronger. Attrition suffered by the Japanese in the Solomons campaign was heavy, but it would have been greater in a campaign to hold Midway.

Rear Admiral Takata testifies that the pilots were overtrained for attack and not proficient in scouting. Japanese scouting planes did mistake the tanker *Neosho* for a carrier, but they had no difficulty in finding British ships in the Indian Ocean. Most pilots prefer fighting and bombing to the equally essential but more prosaic work of scouting and directing batteries. Both Yamamoto and Nagumo had had ample authority to prescribe the scope and quantity of training. These same officers had prescribed the training pro-

STRUGGLE FOR THE CENTRAL PACIFIC 157

gram for carrier and shore-based naval planes in the spring and summer of 1941 preparatory to the successful attack on Pearl Harbor, the Philippines, Malaya, and the East Indies.

Admiral Nimitz reported with customary modesty that the decisive battle of Midway "was essentially a victory of intelligence." Information of enemy intentions in that campaign was very accurate and for that the intelligence officers earned his generous praise. But intelligence is only the servant of a commander in chief. If Nimitz had hesitated to act promptly or had lacked the courage to uncover both the north and the south Pacific in order to be able to repel a probable attack in the center, the best intelligence officers in the world would have been useless. Yamamoto attempted surprise; Nimitz achieved it.

When his force was concentrated Nimitz could oppose only three American to the four Japanese carriers; and Yamamoto could have had seven, possibly eight, carriers present. The basic reason for the defeat of Yamamoto was the reasoned decision of Nimitz and his willingness to accept a calculated risk, plus the loyal and efficient execution of his plan by Admirals Fletcher and Spruance at sea, and by the Army, Navy, and Marine commanders ashore, who took full advantage of enemy overconfidence and mistakes. But Americans should always remember the dive bombers who turned an apparent defeat into decisive victory, the torpedo squadrons who without fighter cover flew straight and low at the enemy, the Marine flyers led by Fleming, and those Army airmen symbolized by General C. L. Tinker, who relentlessly pursued the fleeing enemy. For they were all necessary to defeat the Japanese at Midway.

Admiral King and Admiral Nagano both agreed that this American victory removed the Japanese threat to the Hawaiian Islands, gave the United States Navy control of the central Pacific, and placed the Japanese on the defensive. Also, by depriving Japan of carriers and restricting her freedom for aggressive action, it relieved the British from further raids in the Bay of Bengal. Midway was fought the first week in June; by opening the campaign for the Solomons in the first week of August King retained the initiative. The loss of four carriers compelled Nagano to take drastic measures to replace them; two battleships, the *Ise* and the *Hyuga,* were converted into "hermaphrodites," half battleship and half carrier. During the year required for conversion they were of no use, and when completed they were not successful. Also it was necessary to convert seaplane tenders like the *Chitose,* into carriers, permanently depriving the very useful seaplanes of their tenders and reducing their efficiency on the eve of a campaign in the Solomons.

Approximately 30 per cent of Japan's carrier pilots were killed at Midway, and another 30 to 40 per cent were sent to Japan on sick leave. The remainder were returned to Kyushu for additional training in a refresher course beginning July 15. Two months were allotted for the course, but these pilots were sucked into the Solomons campaign, which began August 7, and were killed either at Rabaul or Port Moresby, or in the Solomons.

King's move into the Solomons immediately after the battle of Midway placed a tremendous strain on the resources available to Nimitz and Halsey in the Pacific; but it forced Nagano and Yamamoto to dance to the American tune. The Japanese Navy was never allowed to recover from the consequences of its defeat at Midway.

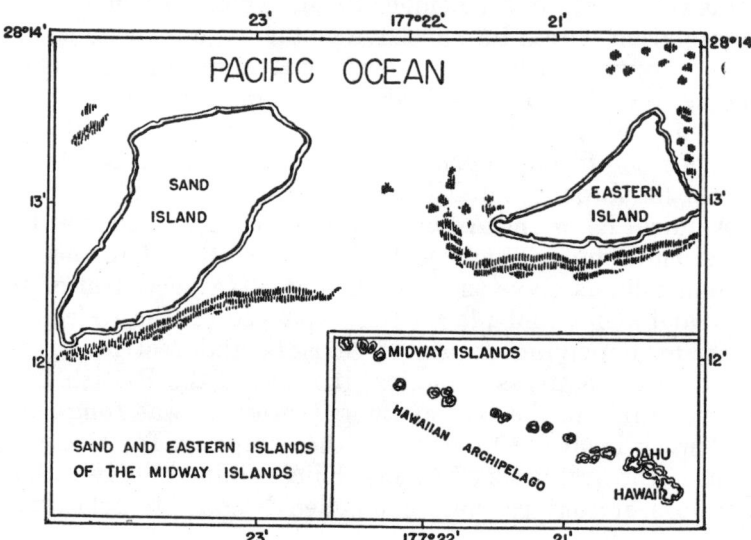

SAND AND EASTERN ISLANDS OF THE MIDWAY ISLANDS

X
The Battle of the Atlantic

U-Boat Warfare in the Atlantic

WHEN Admiral King ordered plans made for the invasion of Guadalcanal he was in the midst of a desperate struggle to rid the Atlantic Coast and—in coöperation with Britain—the Atlantic Ocean of U-boats. This part of the battle of the Atlantic was first and last a contest between Anglo-American surface ships and aircraft and German U-boats supported by the Luftwaffe operating from air bases along the coasts of France and Norway.

The Nazis had tried other means. Occasionally an armed German merchantman would evade the cordon of British warships that barred its way to the ocean, but if it operated along the regular sea lanes it was soon discovered and run down, and if it avoided these routes it found few victims. After the conquest of Norway, German battleships and cruisers attempted to operate against merchant ships. But by March the *Bismarck* had been sunk and the *Scharnhorst,* the *Gneisenau,* and the *Prinz Eugen* driven from Brest to Germany and Norway. Systematic and repeated attacks by the Royal Air Force and the fleet air arm prevented these combat ships from getting to sea. Thus they also proved ineffective. After the Japanese occupied Malaya, the Philippines, and the East Indies, German and Japanese blockade runners provided a useful exchange of strategic materials; but by the spring of 1943 Japanese and German raiders, supply ships, and merchantmen had been sunk in such numbers that they ceased to operate. Only the U-boats, protected by their concrete pens from air attacks in harbor and escorted through the Bay of Biscay by PT boats, continued the battle.

According to Admiral Doenitz, the Japanese did not give the Germans advance information of their intention to attack the American armed forces in the Pacific. But the record shows that, a few days before Pearl Harbor, the Japanese Ambassador to Berlin reported to Ribbentrop that Japanese-American negotiations were deadlocked and asked what action Germany would take in the event of a war. It is scarcely possible that officials of the German Foreign Office did not anticipate hostilities in the Pacific.

When Germany declared war on the United States, shipping in the Atlantic coastal waters became a valuable and vulnerable target for U-boats just at the time when countermeasures had made it very dangerous for them to operate in the waters surrounding the British Isles. In September, 1941, well before the first ship was sunk off the American coast (January, 1942), Admiral King had established the convoy system between the East Coast and Iceland. When Germany declared war he had anticipated the U-boat invasion of American coastal waters and had collected the scanty supply of antisubmarine vessels and aircraft available to protect American coastal shipping. Most of the effective escort vessels were already assigned to the ocean convoys. Submarine chasers, PT boats, and escort vessels were on order and building, but not enough were available. As quickly as possible King armed fishing boats and pleasure craft, borrowed planes from the Civil Air Patrol and escort ships from England and Canada, and obtained from the Army the First Bomber Command especially trained to operate against U-boats. With these he organized the antisubmarine defenses.

In January Admiral Doenitz despatched six U-boats, commanded by some of his most experienced captains, to attack shipping along the eastern Atlantic seaboard. The U-boats cruised on the surface, boldly approaching close to shore where traffic was most dense. Their phenomenal success inspired Doenitz to order every available U-boat to these lucrative waters. British coastal areas and approaches to the Channel were thus temporarily relieved of U-boats. Immediately the Admiralty and Air Coastal Command reduced

THE BATTLE OF THE ATLANTIC 161

some of the pressure on American shipping by sending ships and aircraft to attack the submarines as they crossed the Bay of Biscay—en route to American coastal lanes.

Shortage of escort vessels at first prevented the establishment of coastal convoys. The Navy could patrol only a few of the most dangerous stretches of coast. After assembling every small craft that would float and carry a gun, King was compelled to rob the ocean convoys to protect coastal waters. By the middle of May he had enough escort vessels to establish convoys between Norfolk and Key West, and between Boston and Halifax. The relief along these routes was immediate: sinkings in May along the Atlantic Coast were only one quarter the previous monthly average, partly because of the disinclination of U-boats to attack vessels under escort and partly because, in accordance with the German plan, the submarines were moving toward the Gulf of Mexico and the Caribbean Sea where the Germans had discovered that American defenses were even weaker than they had been along the north Atlantic Coast. Sinkings in the Gulf and Caribbean areas caused the total loss of tonnage to be greater in May than in April, but the convoy system was obviously the solution to the U-boats' coastal campaign.

Tankers were always preferred targets of the U-boats, and the major oil-loading ports were in the Gulf and Caribbean Sea. King immediately reënforced the Gulf, but losses reached a peak in June. In July convoys were established between Key West and Trinidad, the Canal Zone and Guantánamo, and between certain ports in the Gulf of Mexico. Later, they were established between the Caribbean oil ports and Halifax, and from the Caribbean to Recife, Brazil, where the Brazilian Navy took charge. As an ever greater number of escort vessels became available, first the Atlantic coastal routes, then the Gulf, and finally the Caribbean were made comparatively safe from U-boats. They made their last major offensive stand in the Western Hemisphere in the Trinidad area.

By the end of October King considered the U-boats under sufficient control to enable America to launch, in coöperation with Great Britain, the amphibious expedition that captured

North and West Africa.[1] However, the U-boat menace continued, and while providing support for General Eisenhower's campaigns in Africa, Sicily, and Italy, Admiral King was obliged to continue his relentless war against it and to provide escorts for coastal and ocean convoys.

By the end of 1942 all the well-traveled coastal routes in the Western Hemispere were provided with frequent sailings of well-protected convoys. Thereafter, American coastal waters were relatively safe. Admiral Doenitz, the most vigorous advocate in Germany of U-boat warfare as the only means of defeating Britain, had seen his submarines driven from the western approaches to the English Channel and the coastal waters of the British Isles in 1941 (see Chapter V) and from the seaboards of the Americas in 1942. He attributed the defeat in coastal waters to the Allies' combination of aircraft scouting with surface craft equipped with submarine-location equipment. Undiscouraged, he then calculated that if he despatched his U-boats in combat groups, called wolf packs, to the mid-Atlantic, they would be free from the deadly combined air and surface attacks. This shift would compel the U-boats to do their own scouting, for the Luftwaffe could not cover the mid-Atlantic.

Doenitz convinced Hitler that his new plan would succeed, and was given supreme command of the navy, superseding Grand Admiral Raeder in January, 1943. Hitler also directed Armament Minister Speer to give priority to U-boat production. Designs of the new types XXI and XXIII were rapidly completed and brought into production. In 1917 the Kaiser, after failing to win with a superior army, had turned to the submarines; in 1943 Hitler, having failed to gain the decision with a superior army and air force, had recourse, equally futile, to the same weapon.

The time Doenitz chose to launch the grand attack was a very favorable one. The number of Nazi U-boats had increased; German losses in 1942 had been comparatively slight, and the construction program was providing ample replacements. Crews had gained experience in maintaining their boats and operating under war conditions. A technique

1. See pages 168–178.

THE BATTLE OF THE ATLANTIC 163

of controlling the submarines from shore had been perfected by the Nazis. Wolf packs were directed from Lorient by the commander of U-boats, who could use his shore-based radio without divulging the presence or location of the submarines. Admiral Doenitz reported that the commander of U-boats ashore was always able to obtain tactical coördination of the veteran U-boat commanders at sea.

At the very time, however, that Admiral Doenitz calculated his U-boats were ready to strike a deadly blow in the mid-Atlantic and cut the vital line of communications between the United States and the United Kingdom, Admiral King completed preparations with the British Admiralty to provide continuous air patrol over the convoys throughout the entire Atlantic crossing. Allied production had increased the number of escort ships available, including the first contingent of escort carriers, which soon came to be known as "baby flat-tops." Planes from these escort carriers could locate the U-boats well away from the convoys, make the first attack, and summon escort destroyers equipped with radar and depth charges.

Thus the U-boat campaign reached its peak in the spring of 1943. The Nazis struck at the Allied convoys with all their force, skill, and cunning. But the U-boats, from which so much had been expected, failed again. They were beaten by a combination of measures: by an increased surface escort, land-based air coverage at the convoy terminals, and new carrier-based air coverage in mid-voyage; by an increased employment of radar and other warning devices; and, perhaps chiefly by the increased efficiency of Allied personnel. The U-boat changed from pursuer to pursued. German losses rose from 13 per cent of those available in 1942 to 30 to 40 per cent in 1943. Admiral King, confident of the coming victory, told Undersecretary Forrestal in April that the U-boat "was being dealt with" and would be "in hand" within four to six months. Admiral Doenitz admits the loss of 43 U-boats in 1943; actually over five times that number were sunk. The toll of German submarines taken by the Allies was increasing, and this trend was to continue. Only 85 U-boats had been sunk in 1942; but in 1943 the number was 237, and in 1944, 241. In the first four months of 1945 a total of 153 were sunk, or 1.25 submarines per day.

By May, 1943, Doenitz was forced to recognize that his plan of changing the area of attack to the mid-Atlantic had failed. However, he did not give up easily. He increased the antiaircraft batteries on the U-boats and developed a new form of attack to be tried against the escort ships and planes of the north Atlantic convoys. Captains of U-boats were ordered to remain on the surface and to use their additional antiaircraft guns to fight enemy aircraft. They were directed to drive off planes, then to concentrate their attacks against the surface escort ships, using acoustic torpedoes. This done, the U-boats were to strike their ultimate objective, the transports carrying troops or the cargo vessels loaded with foodstuffs, raw materials, or munitions. According to Doenitz, the first attack using the new tactics was a partial success; the U-boats fought the aircraft and successfully attacked the escort ships, but did not break through and reach the convoy. The American record of a trans-Atlantic convoy attacked at that time partly confirms the German account. The U-boats attempted to fight off the aircraft and to torpedo their way through the surface escort. They did torpedo several of the escorts, but only three U-boats of this particular pack of 25 succeeded in launching torpedoes at merchant ships.

The American defense against this new form of attack was to provide more planes, with heavier bombs. When a second attack was tried in September, the "air force," Doenitz admits, "was so powerful that had the U-boats remained on the surface they would in all probability have been completely destroyed." King's prediction made in April, that within four to six months the U-boat situation would be "in hand," was confirmed. By early winter over 150 U-boats had been sunk, carrying to the bottom some of the most experienced German crews.

Within ten months of having been given supreme command of the German Navy by Hitler, on the basis of his argument that, properly employed, the U-boats could win

THE BATTLE OF THE ATLANTIC 165

the battle of the Atlantic, Doenitz admitted that "Surface warfare for U-boats had come to an end."

Still Doenitz did not abandon hope. German scientists developed and Speer began construction of a new type of U-boat which could recharge its batteries under water. This improved model could operate close inshore where the sea lanes to the Irish Sea and the English Channel converged, without having to rise to the surface when batteries were exhausted. But this craft, known as the Schnorckel class, was not ready for service in 1943. Doenitz resigned himself to a waiting period, during which he kept just enough U-boats operating to compel the Allies to maintain their convoys and other antisubmarine measures.

British and American naval leaders knew they had beaten the particular type of U-boat then in service. They also knew that German scientists were seeking to improve both the U-boat and its weapons. Accordingly Allied scientists and naval leaders increased their efforts to improve the weapons and methods of attack against the submarine.

In May, 1944, American escort commanders protecting the Atlantic convoys knew they had routed the U-boats. The commander of the U.S.S. *Guadalcanal* (an escort carrier) Task Group, not content with sinking, determined to capture a U-boat and bring it into port. Before leaving the East Coast he explained his ideas to his commanding officers. The skippers, enthusiastic over the prospect, arranged to board a U-boat after it had been disabled and before its crew could scuttle it. However, for over a week their search for a victim was unproductive. Fuel ran low. Then, on June 4, their patience was rewarded. At 10 A.M. a possible contact was reported; the escort carrier immediately despatched a bomber and a fighter (in Navy vernacular, a killer group) and directed other fighter planes, already in the air, to assist. Six minutes later depth charges were fired at the estimated position of the U-boat. The location was accurate, the aim was good. The fighter plane sighted the submerged submarine and indicated its position to the destroyer *Chate-*

laine, which dropped a full pattern of depth charges, forcing the submarine to surface. She proved to be the *U-505*. Over the radio the task group commander again told the skippers and pilots, "I want to capture this buzzard!"

The U-boat captain put up a good fight, firing an acoustic torpedo at the *Guadalcanal,* but he was surrounded by three destroyers, and two fighter planes were circling overhead. Destroyers and planes, ordered not to use any weapons that would sink the submarine unless she started to submerge, fired only machine guns. They poured bullets toward the German sailors as they scrambled on deck until the "cease fire" order was given. This was the signal for the armed boat crews to board the *U-505*.

The U-boat was turning in small circles, and most of its crew had dived overboard. After sending his boatload of boarders, the captain of the *Pillsbury* (second destroyer of the name) followed and, like a good ranch hand, roped the U-boat, to the great glee of the escort commander, who broadcast, "Ride 'em, cowboy!" Meanwhile the *Pillsbury's* boat was alongside and the boarding party dived down the hatches, closed the valves, and replaced the cover on a bilge strainer, shutting out a six-inch stream of water that would soon have sunk the ship. Boarding parties from the *Guadalcanal* and other ships promptly followed and all hands quickly disconnected the demolition charges, closed valves and watertight doors, rigged hand pumps, and started some of the gasoline pumps.

It was necessary to take the prize in tow to keep her afloat, and this required skillful seamanship. The captain of the *Guadalcanal* made fast a heavy wire towline to the submarine, maneuvered the carrier to recover its planes, and then proceeded with the captive U-boat trailing astern, the Stars and Stripes flying where the Swastika had flown.

This achievement of the *Guadalcanal* Task Group definitely proved that the U-boats were no longer a menace, and that the spirit of John Paul Jones, Stephen Decatur, John Trippe, and others like them still persists. They and most of their contemporaries were skilled in a yardarm to yardarm fight, but their victory was sealed by boarding the enemy

THE BATTLE OF THE ATLANTIC 167

and towing him into port. In addition, the capture of the *U-505* provided valuable technical information.

Part of the story of victory in the battle of the Atlantic is a narrative of production. The years 1943 and 1944 saw a reduction in sinkings by U-boats, and they were also marked by an increase in shipyard construction. The Maritime Commission and American management and labor contributed greatly to the ultimate victory. After January 1, 1943, American shipyards produced a monthly average of a million tons of new merchant ships. The table below illustrates how both British and American production increased during the 1942–45 period, while conversely the number of U-boats killed off by the Allies constantly grew and Allied tonnage sunk showed a steady decline:

Year	German Submarines Sunk	Allied Shipping Sunk	New Construction			Net Gains or Losses
			United States	British	Total	
	(Number)		(In thousands of tons)			
1942	85	8,245	5,339	1,843	7,182	−1,063
1943	237	3,611	12,384	2,201	14,585	+10,974
1944	241	1,422	11,639	1,710	13,349	+11,927
1945 (4 mos.)	153	458	3,551	283	3,834	+3,376
Totals	716	13,736	32,913	6,037	38,950	+25,214

In June, 1944, the U-boats made a desperate effort to intervene during the landing in Normandy, but a combined Anglo-American air and sea offensive against them in the approaches to the Channel effectively kept them down. The landing in France compelled the U-boats to retire to Norway. The recently perfected Schnorckels could operate with immunity close inshore, but experience was showing that the strain of continued submergence on the personnel did not permit of extended operations. In the spring of 1945

Doenitz was still urging German scientists and industrialists to perfect and construct a new type of submarine with a high submerged speed, but the Reich collapsed before it could become a menace.

In both the first and second World Wars the U-boats were defeated but fought to the end. In the forenoon of November 11, 1918, just before the signing of the Armistice, a German U-boat sank a British battleship in the Strait of Gibraltar. On May 6, 1945, the day after Admiral Doenitz, successor to Hitler as Chief of State, had signed the unconditional surrender of the Reich, the *U-853* sank a merchant ship near Point Judith, Rhode Island, and was itself sunk a few hours later by an American destroyer, thus ringing down the curtain on the battle of the Atlantic.

The Anglo-American Landings in North Africa

In December, 1941, Churchill and Roosevelt had agreed that within a year an Anglo-American force would land in either Europe or Africa. In June, 1942, the Combined Chiefs of Staff decided upon the landings in North and West Africa during the following November. It was time to end the fluctuating warfare in North Africa and secure control of the Mediterranean. From June, 1940, to June, 1942, the war in the Balkans and the Middle East, like a running sore, had drained the Allies of about 1,000,000 men (British and American), 6,000 planes, 5,000 guns, 50,000 machine guns, 4,500 tanks, and more than 100,000 army vehicles, with heavy operational and combat losses.[2] In addition, the Royal Navy had suffered severely. The great bulk of these troops and munitions had not gone through the Mediterranean but had traveled the long distance around the Cape of Good Hope, for Axis planes and submarines in the central Mediterranean had inflicted almost unbearable losses on British convoys using that sea. British submarines and aircraft also inflicted heavy losses on Axis convoys proceeding from Italy and Sicily to Tripoli and sometimes, with the connivance of Vichy France, to Tunisia. Control of the oceanic routes had enabled Great Britain, with the aid of the United States, to

2. See Roger W. Shugg and H. A. DeWeerd, *World War II*, pp. 155–156.

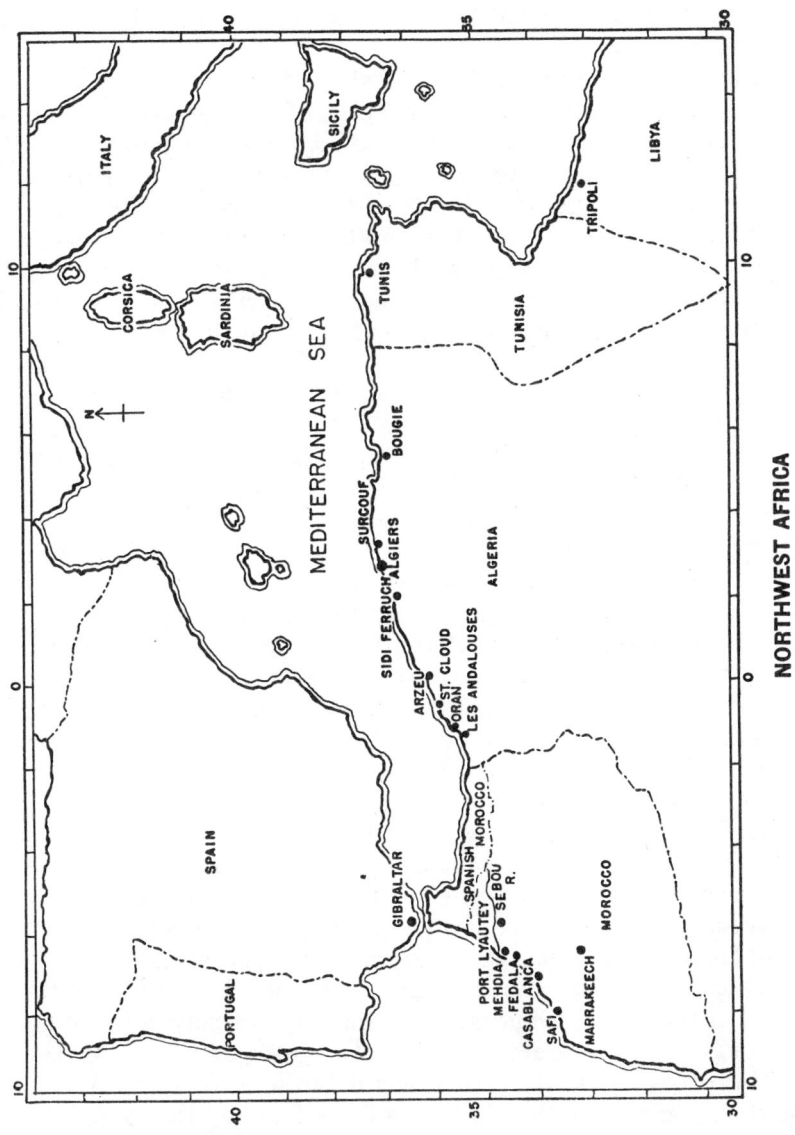

send halfway around the world more tanks and planes than the Axis Powers could send across the central Mediterranean.

The tide of battle in Tripoli shifted monotonously until the autumn of 1942, when in spite of the severity of the U-boat offensive in American coastal waters, Admiral King completed the plans and provided the ships and escorts for the greatest trans-Atlantic armada ever seen to that time.

From their inception the landings in Africa were enmeshed in diplomacy. French colonies loyal to the captive Government of Vichy constituted the territorial objectives. It was extremely desirable to keep the French armed forces in the African colonies from opposing the invaders, whose eventual object was the overthrow of Hitler and consequently the restoration of France. In Vichy Admiral Leahy was striving to keep Marshal Pétain from yielding to Hitler; and General Eisenhower, describing the delicate situation, has told how he, accompanied by his political adviser, Robert Murphy, advanced upon North Africa with a rose in one hand and a rifle in the other.

The immediate objectives of the Allied Expeditionary Force were the capture of the Oran-Algiers-Tunis area in Algeria and the Casablanca area in Morocco. No one could predict the result of the negotiations under way with the French colonials; reports that they would resist were followed the next day by information that they would yield. Plans were made on the assumption that the objectives would have to be taken by assault.

After securing the initial beachheads in Algeria and Morocco, the two forces were to form a junction in Algeria, leave a force to observe Franco's army in Spanish Morocco, and then proceed eastward as rapidly as possible.

It was hoped that the Anglo-American forces in Northwest Africa and General Montgomery's army advancing through Tripoli could close like the jaws of a vice on the Axis forces in North Africa. If the landing in North Africa had been made farther to the east, in Tunisia, this objective might have been attained. But since this would have exposed the transports to Axis land-based planes operating from

THE BATTLE OF THE ATLANTIC 171

Sicily and Italy, it was decided to land at Algiers instead, and advance overland through Tunisia.

General Eisenhower, with an Anglo-American staff, became Commander in Chief of the Allied Armies after they were landed. En route the Anglo-American Army coming from England was escorted by a British task force commanded by Admiral Sir Andrew Cunningham, while the amphibious force coming from the United States was commanded by Rear Admiral H. K. Hewitt, U.S.N., who subsequently commanded the American amphibious forces during their landing operations in Italy and Sicily. Lieutenant General George S. Patton, Jr., commanded the Army troops in the Casablanca area and took entire control as soon as his troops had secured their beachheads ashore.

The ocean crossing of the expeditionary force from the United States was uneventful. The transports and supply ships were protected from enemy surface raiders by battleships, including one of the newest, the *Massachusetts;* from U-boats and aircraft by the carrier *Ranger* and three escort carriers which furnished complete and continuous air patrol, and by numerous cruisers and destroyers that provided antiaircraft batteries and an antisubmarine screen throughout the voyage and during the landing. Included in the convoy was another carrier loaded with Army pursuit fighters primed to land as soon as an airfield had been captured.

For the expedition the Army had given its men a minimum of only three weeks' training in Chesapeake Bay. The crews of the landing boats had fared somewhat better, since they had had a few months' training. However, soldiers and sailors alike would have benefited if time had permitted additional exercises before landing through heavy surf on the coasts of Africa.

The French authorities were not alert; they failed to extinguish Casablanca light, and the American ships approached the landing places unopposed. Admiral Hewitt and General Patton first had to get the troops ashore, and then provide against counterattacks by French air and ground troops stationed in the vicinity. Thus airfields in the vicinity of Casablanca and roads and railways over which counterattacks could be launched constituted prime objectives of the carrier-based planes, and special arrangements had been made for the Army pursuit planes to take off from their carrier as soon as the airfields ashore were seized.

General Patton's plan for taking Casablanca included a main landing at Fedala, about 13 miles northeast of Casablanca, assisted by a pincer movement by means of a secondary landing at Port Lyautey, 65 miles north, where the principal objective was the near-by airfield, and at Safi, 125 miles south, where the port was the main objective. All landings were to be followed by a rapid advance on Casablanca. Four assault waves landed at Fedala about 6 A.M. on the 8th. They were supported by the fire of four destroyers, which soon dominated the fire of the French shore batteries. At 6.20 a general advance was ordered and by 2.30 P.M. Fedala surrendered. In spite of air attacks, mine sweepers cleared the channel on the 9th, and by the afternoon of the 10th the debarkation of troops and vehicles was complete. Roundly 20,000 men and 77 light tanks had been landed at Fedala with little or no loss, and were advancing on Casablanca when the French surrendered on the 10th.

Meanwhile, at about 7 A.M. on the 8th the *Massachusetts*, two heavy cruisers, and several destroyers had begun to bombard the forts at Casablanca and the French battleship, *Jean Bart*, anchored in the harbor. French submarines had already sortied; several escaped, and at least two fired torpedoes at the *Massachusetts*, which evaded them. French destroyers and torpedo boats, attempting to sortie, were practically annihilated, and the uncompleted *Jean Bart* was sunk inside the harbor by 16-inch shells from the *Massachusetts* and bombs from carrier planes. It is probable that some German U-boats participated in these attacks, for Doenitz asserts that as soon as news of the landing was received he concentrated all German submarines in the landing areas.

A secondary landing was made on the 8th at Mehdia, which is a small coastal village near the mouth of the Sebou River, to secure the harbor and adjacent airfields of Port Lyautey. Task Group "H-8," a detachment of Hewitt's

THE BATTLE OF THE ATLANTIC 173

task force (known as Task Force H), Rear Admiral Monroe Kelly commanding, gave fire support, and landed troops and equipment on five beaches on both sides of the harbor entrance. A regiment of the Ninth Division, a Ranger detachment, and a combat team of the Second Armored Division, aggregating 9,000 men and 65 light tanks, began landing at about 5 A.M. The *Texas*, the *Savannah*, five destroyers, and American planes countered the attacks of enemy shore batteries and aircraft, but after seven waves had been landed the batteries compelled the transports to retire temporarily. Sharp opposition was also encountered by troops landing near the mouth of the Sebou River, but by 10 A.M. a beachhead had been established south of that stream. Progress thereafter was arduous; enemy battery and air attacks increased. In the late forenoon the destroyer *Dallas* twice attempted to run past the batteries at the Sebou, but was driven off by the guns of the Kasba, the strongly fortified portion of the old native city. The fiercest fighting took place around the Kasba; it changed hands three times, finally falling to Army forces about midday on the 9th. Shortly afterward Army planes landed on Port Lyautey Airfield.

At 4.30 on the morning of the 10th the captain of the *Dallas*, assisted by a Free French pilot, navigated the narrow, shallow channel of the Sebou River, and at 7.40 disembarked the detachment of Rangers. Still the enemy refused to surrender. Reënforcements were spotted by Allied carrier aircraft, which strafed and bombed the columns as they converged on Port Lyautey. Carrier planes coördinated their attacks with the Army ground troops; a British observer declared that "the support given by naval aircraft was quite astounding." When General Truscott made the final attack on the citadel, naval dive bombers had so softened its defenses that it was taken without casualties. At 4 A.M. on the 11th Truscott ordered, "Cease firing." Word had come from Admiral Hewitt that hostilities had ceased in French Algeria. Meanwhile British and American ships were warned to watch for Axis U-boats.

The secondary landing to the south of Casablanca, at Safi, to secure its port facilities and airfield, and to stage one part of the pincer movement if Casablanca should hold out, was made without great trouble. Before 5 A.M. on the 8th the destroyers *Cole* and *Bernadou* rushed the harbor under cover of their own and the *Mervine's* fire and landed a detachment of Rangers, which captured the dock, and a special naval contingent, which was to operate the cranes. Between 5 and 7 A.M. ten assault waves landed, while the battleship *New York* and the cruiser *Philadelphia* kept down the shore batteries. Before noon Army troops had captured the shore batteries. By 3 P.M. the Army had occupied Safi and the *Lakehurst* was unloading heavy trucks alongside the dock. On the 9th planes from the escort carrier *Santee* bombed enemy troop concentrations and their airport at Marrakeech, about 75 miles inland, to cut off possible assistance by air from that source. On the 10th the landing field at Safi was occupied. That night the French surrendered locally. This operation around Safi went off practically on schedule, largely due to the skillful coördination of ships, planes, and troops.

General Patton had roundly 9,000 men, 65 light tanks in and around Port Lyautey and Mehdia; about 7,000 men, 54 light tanks, and 54 medium tanks at Safi; and about 20,000 men and 77 light tanks in the Fedala-Casablanca area. He had the port facilities at Port Lyautey and Safi and a shipload of pursuit planes ashore, in addition to the planes from the *Ranger* and three escort carriers. He was in a position to bomb any French formations that attempted to counterattack or come to the relief of Casablanca. Admiral Hewitt had made the landing possible, and had furnished both gun and air support until the Army was ready to take over. If the French in Morocco had not capitulated on the 11th, they could have delayed but not stopped Patton's advance.

The capitulation at Algiers facilitated the surrender of Oran and Morocco. The news was slow in reaching American commanders, and apparently never was sent to the French submarines, whose attacks continued. In spite of air coverage and an antisubmarine screen, seven transports were torpedoed off Casablanca between the 11th and the 13th; four of them sank. The submarines which had escaped from Casablanca on the 8th may have been responsible. For-

THE BATTLE OF THE ATLANTIC 175

tunately the troops had been disembarked from the transports and most of the cargo had been discharged. The majority of the survivors were rescued and personnel losses were small. By November 19 the remaining transports were en route to the United States. A naval base was in operation at Casablanca, and Task Force "H" was established as the sea frontier forces, preparatory to supporting the invasion of Sicily in the spring of 1943.

The British Navy was entirely responsible for the escort and naval support of the land forces that occupied Oran and Algiers. The British Army provided 23,000 men and the American Army 49,000 for this Expeditionary Force. The Algerian force was almost twice the size of that at Casablanca. Movements will not be described in detail because the composition of the naval escort, the amphibious tactics, and the operations of the Army units after landing followed the same pattern as at Casablanca. British battleships, aircraft carriers, cruisers, and destroyers performed the same duties for the troops coming from the United Kingdom that Admiral Hewitt's task force did for General Patton's command. Attempts were made to seize the port facilities intact by surprise landing. The main operations against Oran began with landings at Les Andalouses to the west and at Arzeu to the east; those against Algiers with landings at Sidi Ferruch to the west and near Surcouf to the east, with other forces ready to occupy the two ports when their adjacent airfields, roads, and railway net had been seized and their communications with the interior cut.

By the afternoon of the 8th the detachment coming from Les Andalouses had occupied the two airfields south of Oran and the road and rail net. Simultaneously in spite of severe resistance the port of Arzeu had been taken with its facilities intact, and American troops had advanced to St. Cloud, which lies somewhat inland, and toward Oran. The subsequent French capitulation included the surrender of Oran, which made its capture unnecessary; it was practically encircled and could not have resisted long in any event.

Resistance at Algiers was never as severe as at Oran; the landings at Sidi Ferruch and off Surcouf synchronized with those at Les Andalouses and Arzeu. Two American transports were disabled, the *Thomas Stone* by a submarine before she reached the disembarkation area, and the *Leedstown* by enemy planes during disembarkation on the 8th. Enemy planes concentrated their attacks on this most easterly landing, and their success indicated the additional hazard that would have been encountered had the landing been made still further east, nearer the Axis airfields in Sicily and Italy.

By 3 P.M. on the 8th, 12 hours after landing, British and Americans had occupied Blida Airfield and the high ground two miles west of Algiers. By 5 P.M. the local French forces had capitulated and the city and port were occupied without further resistance.

All landings were made during darkness or just after dawn. And it is most remarkable that Admiral Cunningham set his forces ashore in Algeria at almost the same time that Admiral Hewitt began disembarkation in Morocco. The entire operation had been surcharged with diplomatic drama which reached its climax in the capitulation of Admiral Darlan, the Anglophobe who had inspired the French Navy to resist Churchill's pleas in 1940 and who, when the landings occurred, was fortuitously present in Algiers, being on leave from France. Having decided to desert the Axis, Darlan had no difficulty in pursuading the Algerian officials to capitulate on November 10. The protocol had scarcely been signed when the admiral was assassinated. However, French officials loyally fulfilled its provisions and their armed forces cheerfully coöperated with the Anglo-Americans. Attacks continued by some unidentified aircraft and submarines, probably German, but which may have been manned by Frenchmen who did not get word of the surrender.

On November 11 the 36th Infantry Brigade landed at Bougie. General Eisenhower had started to move on Tunis. Uncertainty about the attitude of Generalissimo Franco, who had openly assisted the Axis, caused Eisenhower to leave a strong Allied force on the Moroccan border to observe the Spanish Colonial Army. Eisenhower's inability to use all his strength, and the prompt reënforcements sent

THE BATTLE OF THE ATLANTIC 177

to Tunisia by the German High Command, prevented prompt exploitation of the successful landing, delayed the Anglo-American advance, and at least indirectly brought on the sharp American reverse at Kasserine Pass. Not until the spring of 1943 was North Africa rid of the Nazi, and not until summer could the invasion of Sicily commence.

The occupation of North and West Africa finally removed the fear of an Axis invasion of Dakar, and opened the western Mediterranean to Allied convoys. The land operations in Africa, made possible by sea power, in turn facilitated future control of the sea. The occupation of North Africa gave the Anglo-American navies control of the Mediterranean, and Allied aircraft based on African ports made it difficult for U-boats to operate in the approaches to that sea.

It is obvious that Eisenhower could not have landed in Algiers, nor Patton in Morocco, without Anglo-American control of the sea. But it is equally true, although not so patent, that Montgomery's break-through at El Alamein was due to the reënforcements that filled the ranks of his ten divisions, supplying him with double Rommel's number of tanks, men, and planes, and that all these reënforcements came by sea. And it is unlikely that Marshal Chuikov could have closed the trap around the German Sixth Army and captured General von Paulus and 200,000 Germans around Stalingrad if British and American ships had not carried 3,000 planes and 4,000 tanks halfway around the world to replace heavy Soviet losses. These successes on land were possible only because the Anglo-American navies controlled the Atlantic and most of the Indian Ocean.

Supporting the landings in North Africa would have been child's play for Admiral King except for other Anglo-American naval commitments. He had simultaneously to supply and protect the American share of the tonnage needed to furnish the British and the Red Armies with munitions and supplies. Also, transports were proceeding around the Cape of Good Hope to Egypt with reënforcements for the British Army that Rommel had driven back to El Alamein. The maritime and industrial resources of the two great sea powers were strained to the utmost during the summer and autumn of 1942. U-boats and the Luftwaffe inflicted such heavy losses that escorting convoys to Murmansk had to be temporarily abandoned, but not, however, until plans had been made and a road and rail net constructed to deliver supplies to the Red Army via the Persian Gulf.

In the summer of 1942, while waging a major war in the Atlantic, Admiral King had ordered the invasion of the Solomons in the Pacific. Nimitz, Ghormley, Halsey, and Vandergrift launched an attack that brought on the struggle for the Solomons.

Perhaps never has a nation demanded so much from its naval forces as did the United States between August, 1942, and August, 1943. Certainly American sea power had never been put to such a test as during these months, as was to become even more evident in the campaign for the Solomons.

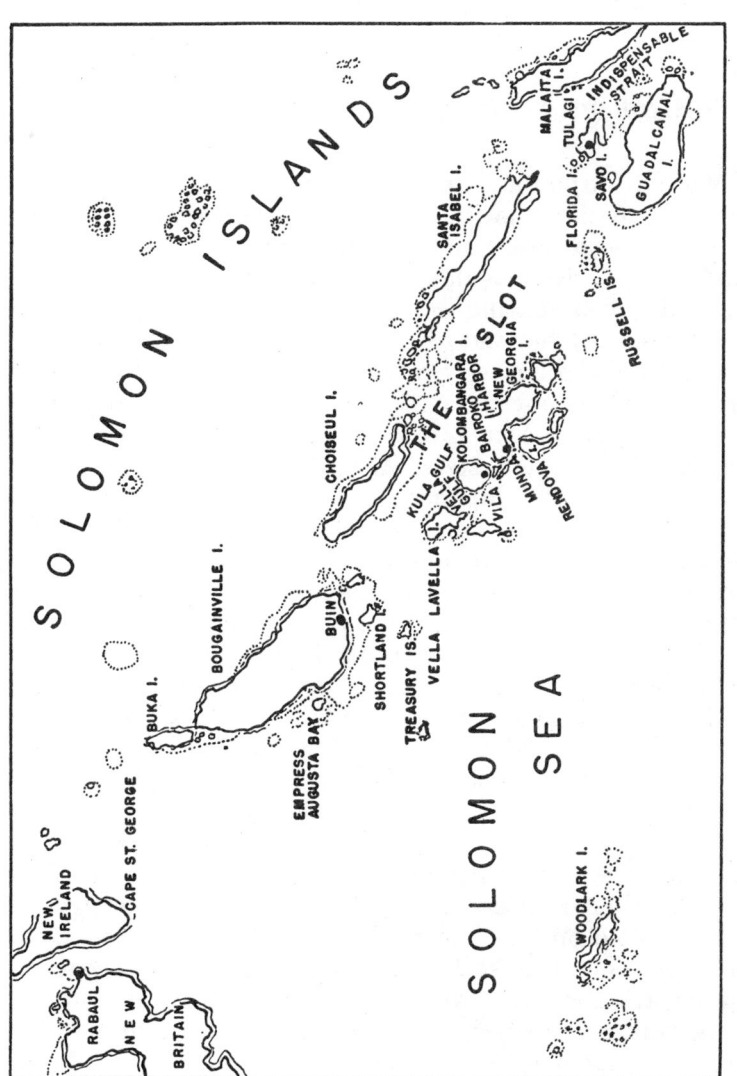

THE SOLOMON ISLANDS

XI

The Campaign for the Solomons and Aleutians

WHEN Japan and the United States entered the war it was evident that the Pacific would be the principal theater of naval operations, and that although the armed forces of Australia and New Zealand would give much assistance, the brunt of Allied fighting would fall on the much larger American forces. At the end of six months Japan controlled the western and the United States with its Anzac allies the eastern half of the north Pacific. The dividing line ran roughly from Kiska and Attu in the western Aleutians southward through Wake, the eastern Marshalls, the Gilberts, and the Solomon Islands. Japanese possession of the Solomons would menace American air and naval bases in the New Hebrides and New Caledonia, and if the enemy were to capture or neutralize these bases the line of communications between the United States and Australia would be cut.

Admiral King realized these dangers and in April directed Vice-Admiral Ghormley, Commander of the Southwest Pacific Fleet, to prepare plans to seize the southern Solomons. While Ghormley developed the plans, the battles of the Coral Sea and Midway were fought. Midway deprived the enemy of 60 to 70 per cent of their carrier pilots, killed or wounded, seriously reduced Japanese carrier strength, and made necessary a complete reorganization of the Japanese Third (Air) Fleet. When the enemy began construction of an airfield on Guadalcanal in July, King ordered the attack made on August 1 or as soon thereafter as possible, inaugurating the first American land, sea, and air offensive of the war, a campaign that continued a year and a half before the Solomons were retaken.

This long, bitter struggle for an almost unknown group of islands was the result of King's determination to remove the Japanese threat to the United States line of communi-

THE SOLOMONS AND ALEUTIANS 181

cations and the equally positive resolution of Admiral Yamamoto (according to Japanese sources) that the American offensive "must not be allowed to succeed . . . because Americans would gain confidence and push against other occupied areas." Yamamoto is described as being "willing to stake everything on a decisive fight in the Solomons area" to prevent the American advance.

Another reason influenced Yamamoto to hold the Solomons at all costs. The First and Second Air Fleets of land-based naval planes were training in Japan. The Admiral believed that when their program was completed these two air fleets based on fields in the Solomons could with occasional assistance from the Combined Fleet definitely halt the American advance. So, as a temporary operation, he was willing to employ the Combined Fleet with its air arm to delay Halsey's progress until the First and Second Air Fleets were ready for combat. With this plan of campaign in mind, Yamamoto concentrated the Combined Fleet at Truk, reënforced Vice-Admiral Kusaka's Southeast Area Fleet at Rabaul from time to time, and continually urged his army colleagues to provide ample land forces to eject the American troops from Guadalcanal.

Yamamoto's sudden decision to defend the Solomons represented an almost complete reversal of the strategy adopted when the Imperial General Staff had approved his proposal in April, 1942, to extend the original perimeter of conquest to include outposts in the Aleutians, Midway, and the Solomons. It had been agreed then that neither surface craft nor carrier aviation would be used to defend these outposts. Army garrisons and aviation, assisted by the navy's shore-based planes and submarines would wage a war of attrition against the American Fleet during its advance across the Pacific. Meanwhile the remainder of the Japanese Fleet would be concentrated and held ready for a decisive engagement in an area where both naval shore-based aviation and carrier planes could be employed to assist the surface fleet.

In their attempt to carry out this strategical concept and establish outposts in the Solomon Islands and the Bismarck Archipelago, the Japanese had placed army garrisons on numerous islands, which were entirely dependent upon the navy for munitions, troop replacements, and food. The navy understood that in the over-all strategy these garrisons would fight to the end to reduce the strength of the American Fleet, so that it could be attacked with a reasonable prospect of Japanese naval victory. Army representatives on the Imperial General Staff had agreed to this plan. When it became necessary, however, actually to withdraw navy ships and planes and to abandon these garrisons to starvation or surrender, the bulk of the army, not appreciating the importance of holding the Japanese Fleet intact and ready for a decisive engagement, insisted that the navy supply these marooned outposts. Even Japanese soldiers who were entirely willing to die for the Emperor in a banzai charge objected to being abandoned on a tropical island or left to freeze in Kiska or Attu. Yamamoto yielded to army pressure and at first used destroyers as fast transports and supply ships. As destroyer losses increased, it became necessary to employ submarines for the purpose. This diversion from the Combined Fleet of many of its destroyers and submarines weakened the combat strength of the fleet and prevented the Japanese Naval High Command from adhering to its strategic plan.

Admiral Yamamoto's decision to hold the Solomons was the second radical change he had sponsored in the original strategic plan of the Imperial Staff. Initial successes had inspired him to recommend enlarging the perimeter of the territorial acquisitions. Now the American invasion of the Solomons led to a second modification. Yamamoto was undoubtedly influenced here by pleas from his subordinates for assistance and an honorable reluctance to abandon army garrisons. It is easy to realize the appeal of these arguments, but they did not justify abandoning the sound strategical concept of keeping the fleet with its air arm intact ready to strike a heavy blow at the United States Pacific Fleet. During the Russo-Japanese War Admiral Togo resisted all arguments to change the carefully developed strategic plan. His army colleague, Field Marshal Nogi, well

THE SOLOMONS AND ALEUTIANS 183

knowing that ultimate victory depended primarily on control of the sea, sacrificed his troops in frontal attacks on Port Arthur so that Togo might husband his ships to fight Admiral Rozhestvenski's Baltic Fleet. Yamamoto allowed himself to be persuaded to use the Combined Fleet with its carrier force to defend the Solomon Islands and supply insular army garrisons. At his death he bequeathed a hopeless situation to his successor.

The Japanese Army, during the operations in the Solomons, overestimated its own strength and underestimated that of the Allies. The army was slow in carrying out its scheduled attacks, thus keeping the navy overlong in dangerous areas. It also dribbled men and supplies into the Solomons, each time believing that it was sending enough to overcome Allied resistance. Thus Japan failed to win decisively in the Solomons when she was potentially stronger there than her opponent, and the Allies were then able to bring in reënforcements and supplies and defeat the enemy decisively even though Japan eventually threw much stronger forces into the campaign.

The Solomons themselves were not as serious a loss to the Japanese as was the combat strength they expended in trying to hold the islands. Yamamoto and his successor Admiral Koga consented to send planes, pilots, and ships into the campaign; in the series of small but fiercely contested surface and air engagements, Japanese destroyers suffered heavily and their planes and experienced naval pilots were practically annihilated. The planes could be and were replaced, but after the Solomons campaign the Allies, who were moving from the defensive to the offensive, never allowed the Japanese sufficient time to train their carrier pilots properly, and consequently Japan's Air Force never regained its previous efficiency.

These losses in air strength were keenly felt a few weeks after Guadalcanal was evacuated, when the Japanese Fleet was unable to resist the American advance through the Gilbert and the Marshall Islands. As will be shown in the next chapter, lack of planes and trained pilots made adequate air coverage impossible and in turn forced Admiral Koga to abandon his plan to oppose Admiral Spruance's advance through the Gilberts and Marshalls.

By opening the campaign on August 7, before Yamamoto had completed the reorganization of the Third (Air) Fleet which had suffered such depletion at Midway, King deprived the Combined Fleet of an opportunity to recover from that defeat, and kept them "off balance." Also, by landing on Guadalcanal, which is 3,000 miles from Tokyo and 4,000 miles from Pearl Harbor, he compelled the enemy to fight at the terminus of a long line of communications and forced on them a supply problem comparable to that of the Americans.

Although the Solomons campaign was the first Allied offensive and the first campaign in which air, surface, and undersea craft were coördinated, American submarines had been on the offensive since Pearl Harbor. Those driven out of the Philippines had fallen back to Australia and operated as a part of the Seventh Fleet, under Vice-Admiral Carpender. Rear Admiral Fife was in immediate command. Submarines of the Pacific Fleet operated first under the direction of Rear Admiral English and later under Vice-Admiral Lockwood. In the Solomons campaign submarines of both fleets participated and at the same time the American submarines continued their war against the enemy merchant marine.

Vice-Admiral Ghormley, with headquarters in Nouméa, New Caledonia, planned and exercised operational control of the invasion. Vice-Admiral Fletcher commanded the two task forces; the air support force was under Rear Admiral Noyes; and the amphibious force (cruisers, destroyers, and transports) was under Rear Admiral Turner. Rear Admiral McCain commanded the Army, Navy, and Marine land-based planes operating from New Caledonia, the Fijis, and Samoa. General MacArthur's planes from Australia and New Guinea and a New Zealand squadron from Suva assisted by scouting certain areas and bombing enemy bases such as Rabaul. These naval and air forces escorted the ex-

THE SOLOMONS AND ALEUTIANS 185

peditionary forces to their landings and supported them with batteries and planes. General Vandergrift commanded the landing force which consisted of the First Marine Division less the Fifth Battalion plus the Second Regiment, the First Raider Battalion, and the Third Defense Battalion. After Guadalcanal the entire Pacific campaign was a succession of amphibious operations punctuated by a few decisive naval and air engagements, and in almost all of these landings the Fleet Marine Force made its own unique and invaluable contribution.

King's schedule barely allowed General Vandergrift time to finish loading his transports; however, he was able to report before sailing from New Zealand that "We have in each ship everything that is needed . . . and have practised disembarkment to see that things first needed—vehicles, gasoline, and ammunition—come out first." The full-dress rehearsal for the landing was carried out en route in the Fijis, and on August 7 Combat Group A of the Fifth Marine Regiment landed on Guadalcanal. Simultaneously other groups landed on Tulagi and Florida Islands, just across Sea Lark Channel. The enemy on Guadalcanal was taken by surprise and fled to the adjacent jungle. By sundown of the 8th, 11,000 Marines were ashore at Guadalcanal and had a fairly firm hold on the well-constructed Japanese camp and the northern shore of the island from Kukum to Koli Point.

The almost completed airfield, 3,600 feet long, was captured, with its hangars and machine shops and two radio stations intact, rechristened Henderson Field, and prepared for American fighters and dive bombers. The immediate objectives had all been taken within 36 hours, but for six months American and Allied soldiers, sailors, and marines fought in the air, on the ground, on the sea, and under the sea, resisting Japanese efforts to eject them.

The Battle of Savo Island, August 9

In the early evening of August 8 General Vandergrift had his first bad news. Admiral Fletcher withdrew the carriers for refueling and because their presence in the vicinity was known to the enemy whose shore-based planes were con-

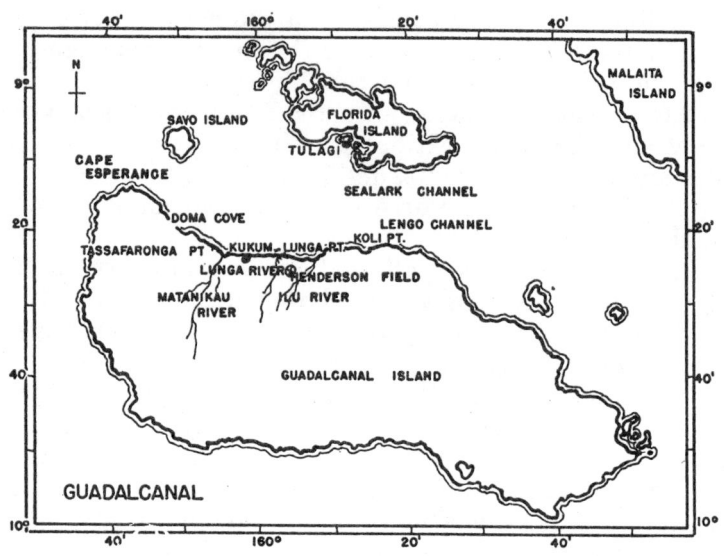

veniently placed to attack them. Rear Admiral Crutchley, R.N., senior Allied officer in the cruisers, and Rear Admiral Turner, commanding the transport forces, regrouped the heavy cruisers and destroyers to protect the transports and supply ships that had not been completely discharged. The *Vincennes,* the *Quincy,* and the *Astoria,* screened by two destroyers, patrolled the channel north of Savo Island; the *Canberra* and the *Chicago,* also screened by two destroyers, were south of the island.

Although the Japanese on Guadalcanal and Tulagi had been surprised, Admiral Inoue, as Commander of the Southeastern Defense Group at Rabaul, sent air squadrons to attack the invaders on the 7th and 8th. He also despatched Admiral Mikawa with the heavy cruisers *Chokai, Kinugasa, Kako, Furutaka,* and *Oaba,* and two light cruisers, the *Tenryu* and the *Tatsuta,* with one destroyer to make a night attack on the American transports. Mikawa arrived off Savo

THE SOLOMONS AND ALEUTIANS 187

Island about midnight on the 8th. His lookouts sighted the American destroyers on patrol before being observed. Next, the Japanese saw the American cruiser force steaming between Cape Esperance and Point Lunga, silhouetted by flares dropped from Japanese planes. Soon after passing Savo Island the enemy cruisers sighted the *Canberra* and the *Chicago* 2,000 to 3,000 yards away, launched torpedoes, and opened fire. Turning left to pass around Savo Island, the Japanese saw the *Vincennes,* the *Quincy,* and the *Astoria,* and deployed, the heavy cruisers passing to the east and the light cruisers to the west of the Americans. Both enemy groups steamed within 2,500 yards, easy machine-gun range, of the American ships and fired torpedoes and guns. During this 30-minute engagement the *Quincy, Vincennes, Astoria,* and *Canberra* were so severely damaged that they subsequently sank, and the *Chicago* and two destroyers were badly damaged.

The flagship *Chokai* used her searchlights and was the only Japanese ship hit, probably by the *Vincennes.* Her pilothouse was destroyed and all her charts damaged. Admiral Mikawa apparently did not realize the tremendous damage he had inflicted on the Allied cruisers, for he explained to his staff that he did not desire another night engagement with the American cruisers, nor to be within easy range of American aircraft and without air cover in daylight.[1] Accordingly he retired to Rabaul and Kavieng. On the way the heavy cruiser *Kako* was sunk by an American submarine off New Ireland.

Admiral King attributed this crushing defeat of the Allied forces to surprise, which in turn was due to poor communications, fatigue, and lack of war experience. The next day it was necessary for the American transports and escort ships to retire from the area. General Vandergrift, temporarily left without naval or air support, first centered the defenses around Henderson Field and Lunga Point, with trenches and guns placed to resist an enemy landing on the shore front. He then provided against attacks from the interior by

---

1. It was Japanese procedure to keep surface ships without air escort 250 miles from enemy planes.

fortifying an oblong position between the Lunga and Ilu Rivers that emptied into Sea Lark Channel. Beyond the entrenchments he established a few carefully chosen outposts, connected by small patrols. The sea front and two flanks along the rivers were fairly strong, but the side toward the interior was very lightly held, for the size of his force did not permit further dispersion. The almost impassable jungle was trusted to prevent mass attacks. The position was gradually strengthened and the airfield improved and enlarged by a construction battalion (Seabees), but during three critical months the Marines were open to attack from any direction.

On August 12 a destroyer returned to land à cargo of gasoline and bombs at Kukum, a small village west of the Lunga River, and a plane landed on Henderson Field to evacuate some of the wounded. The Marines were no longer isolated. By the 20th, when 19 fighters and 12 dive bombers landed on Henderson Field, the situation was visibly improving. Vandergrift had had other assistance; on the 8th, just south of Rabaul, the American submarine *S-38* had sunk a Japanese transport carrying 600 enemy marines, a crack outfit that had been selected to lead the expected landing on Midway in June, and which on August 8 had been on its way to Guadalcanal.

Vandergrift was also benefited by the erroneous report sent from the Japanese on Guadalcanal that his force numbered only about 1,000 men. When the Japanese Army made preparations to retake the island they began by sending the 28th Regiment, which landed just beyond the Ilu River. On the morning of August 21, 200 men of this detachment attempted to overrun the Marine position near the mouth of the Ilu, but were ejected by a swift counterattack. At daylight Colonel Cresswell with a reserve battalion first encircled the Japanese and then compressed them between the river and Sea Lark Channel. By 5 P.M. 900 of the 1,000 who had landed had been killed, a few badly wounded had been captured, and the remainder had escaped to the jungle.

The Battle of the Eastern Solomons, August 23–25

After the battle of Savo Island there was a lull in naval action for two weeks. Japanese aircraft bombed Vander-

THE SOLOMONS AND ALEUTIANS 189

grift's Marines and made the waters around Guadalcanal untenable for surface ships during daylight but could not prevent reënforcements and supplies from reaching the island. Aided by the Seabees, the Marines steadily improved Henderson Field by building additional landing strips, and strengthened their position. The Japanese also built up their forces on Guadalcanal. The Japanese Navy showed more interest than the Army in retaking the island, and on August 23 had assembled 2 battleships, the *Hiyei* and the *Kirishima*, 3 heavy cruisers, 1 light cruiser, and 10 destroyers from the Second Fleet. This was to support the Third (Air) Fleet, which had the large carriers *Zuikaku* and *Shokaku*. Meanwhile, west of this strong force, and just north of Guadalcanal, an enemy transport group consisting of 4 transports, the light cruiser *Jintsu* with Rear Admiral Tanaka, and 4 destroyers, was approaching. The transports contained special army and navy troops that were to be landed. Operating east of the transport group and between it and the larger carriers was the smaller carrier, the *Ryujo*, accompanied by the heavy cruiser *Tone* and several destroyers. The small number of transports is further proof that the Japanese had underestimated the strength and fighting caliber of the Marines on Guadalcanal.

To oppose the Japanese Ghormley organized his three carriers *Saratoga, Enterprise,* and *Wasp*, the new battleship *North Carolina*, and cruisers and destroyers into three task forces—F, K, and N—building each around one carrier. Only Task Force F, under Admiral Fletcher, and K, under Admiral Kinkaid, participated in the engagement of August 24–25. Task Force F included the *Saratoga*, the cruisers *Minneapolis* and *New Orleans*, and five destroyers. Task Force K included the *Enterprise*, the *North Carolina*, the cruisers *Portland* and *Atlanta*, and six destroyers.

The American and Japanese task forces were each striving to intercept and attack the other. Both were assisted by their submarines and land-based planes. The opposing commanders had a continuous flow of information, much of it inaccurate and most of it arriving too late to be useful. Erroneous information led American forces on the 24th to attack and sink the smaller carrier *Ryujo*, when they might have attacked the *Zuikaku* and the *Shokaku* and thus forestalled counterattacks on the *Enterprise* and the *North Carolina*. In spite of the heavy antiaircraft fire of the *North Carolina* and other ships comprising the escort, the *Enterprise* received three direct hits and several near misses. Damage control on the carrier was excellent, however, and fires were under control within an hour. She retired with the other ships at 24 knots.

At the same time American carrier planes and antiaircraft batteries, assisted by Marine and Army air attack groups, had sunk one of the transports and made hits on approximately a dozen other enemy vessels, including a battleship and several cruisers and destroyers. The most telling and important damage, however, was the extremely heavy loss inflicted on the enemy's carrier planes. The Americans estimated that two carrier groups, plus 20 planes which probably were from Rabaul, had been destroyed. Subsequent reports from Japan indicated that Yamamoto was now temporarily without carrier planes. These heavy losses caused the Japanese to defer further large attacks for seven weeks, during which time there were numerous minor clashes, usually at night, between light forces.

During this lull Ghormley's fleet maintained a continuous flow of replacements and supplies to the Marines and attempted to intercept replacements and supplies destined for enemy forces situated in the northern section of Guadalcanal. Yamamoto, with the Combined Fleet, operating from Truk, and Vice-Admiral Inoue, commanding the Southeastern Fleet, operating from Rabaul, were simultaneously attempting to reënforce their troops and intercept American reënforcements. During the many encounters of this period the American carrier *Wasp* and five destroyers were lost, without having inflicted commensurate damage on the enemy.

The first half of September was the grim period ashore. Vandergrift's supplies of ammunition and food ran low, and he was obliged to watch the expenditure of ammunition and for a while to reduce his men to two meals a day. The Japanese, having succeeded in increasing their forces somewhat

THE SOLOMONS AND ALEUTIANS   191

during August and the first ten days of September, attempted to exploit their advantage by another attack on Henderson Field on September 13. The issue was doubtful for several hours, but the Marines, with artillery and rifle fire, finally decimated the attackers.

The Battle of Cape Esperance, October 11–12

The Japanese Navy pressed their Army colleagues to greater exertions and by the end of September the equivalent of at least a new division had been landed on Guadalcanal, making it essential to reënforce General Vandergrift. The 164th Infantry Regiment was available; in support of its landing, American carrier planes first attacked enemy shipping in the north Solomons. Admiral Ghormley then deployed the *Hornet* task force to the west of Guadalcanal, the battleship task force to the northeast, and a cruiser and destroyer task force under Rear Admiral Scott on the *San Francisco* to the south.

The enemy immediately reacted. On the afternoon of October 11 planes attacked Henderson Field and simultaneously surface ships were reported in "the slot" (the inside route between Choiseul and New Georgia Islands), steaming rapidly toward Guadalcanal. Scott promptly turned north to intercept them, rounding the northwestern end of Guadalcanal about 10 P.M., and formed column, with three destroyers in the van followed by four cruisers, the *San Francisco,* the *Boise,* the *Salt Lake City,* and the *Helena,* and with two destroyers in the rear. Radar contacts with unknown ships were made as early as 11.25. The *Helena* opened fire 20 minutes later, the *Salt Lake City* followed, then the others. In less than five minutes four of the five targets disappeared.

Rear Admiral Goto commanded the enemy force, consisting of three heavy cruisers, the *Aoba* (flagship), the *Furutaka,* the *Kinugasa,* and two destroyers, with orders to bombard Henderson Field and cover the landing of Japanese reënforcements. He was leading the cruisers with a destroyer on each beam in a T formation, and steamed head on into Scott's formation. When the *Helena* opened fire Goto, completely surprised, at first thought his force was being fired on by other Japanese ships. Course was reversed promptly, the *Kinugasa* turning to the left, the others to the right. The *Aoba* was hit about 40 times, the admiral mortally wounded, and his flagship badly damaged. One destroyer, the *Fubuki*, was sunk before completing the turn, the cruiser *Furutaka* shortly after. A smoke screen laid by the *Aoba* saved the other destroyer, the *Murakumo*, but American carrier planes sank her off New Georgia Island on the 12th.

By turning to the left the cruiser *Kinugasa* avoided the congestion and the concentrated fire and maintained effective fire on the American ships, doing "most of the fighting." Captain Kijima consoled his dying admiral with the assurance that he "could die happy; we have sunk two enemy cruisers." The Japanese had not sunk a single ship. But the destroyer *Duncan,* steaming between the opposing forces in order to deliver a torpedo attack on an enemy cruiser, was probably hit by both friend and foe. She drifted helplessly astern, a mass of flames, and had to be abandoned; she sank the next day.

This victory was due first to surprise, next to superior gunfire; it prevented Admiral Goto from landing troops or bombarding Henderson Field, and safeguarded the landing of American reënforcements which were badly needed. On the next night the enemy artillery ashore laid a barrage on Henderson Field, followed by a bombardment by ships that stood off Savo Island to "lob" shells into the Marine position which they had illuminated by parachute flares. Heavy damage was done to Marine installations and numerous casualties were inflicted.

The Japanese Army was still content to dribble in reënforcements, but the Navy was getting more concerned. And in September Admiral Yamamoto called a conference of army officials and Admiral Kusaka, who had succeeded Inoue as Commander in Chief of the Southeastern Fleet. Arrangements were made for a combined assault on October 21, and the Second Fleet and the Third (Air) Fleet were made available to support the landing of Japanese reënforcements.

THE SOLOMONS AND ALEUTIANS 193

This led to three actions, culminating at sea in the battle of Santa Cruz, October 26; ashore in the decisive battle of October 25–26 on Guadalcanal; and in the air in the battle of Santa Cruz, October 26.

Battle of Santa Cruz, October 26

Vice-Admiral Nagumo, veteran commander of the air fleet at Pearl Harbor and Midway, commanded the Third (Air) Fleet, which included 3 carriers, the flagship *Shokaku*, the *Zuikaku*, and the *Zuiho*, with 160 aircraft; 2 fast battleships, the *Hiyei* and the *Kirishima*; 4 heavy cruisers; and 1 destroyer squadron with 12 destroyers. Vice-Admiral Kondo, whose Indian Ocean raid and participation in Midway have been mentioned, had the Second Fleet, with the carrier *Junyo* with 45 planes; 2 fast battleships, the *Kongo* and the *Haruna*; 6 heavy cruisers; and a destroyer squadron. The fleets operated about 60 to 100 miles apart, under the tactical command of Nagumo. The presence of 4 fast battleships and 4 carriers, with the cream of the Japanese naval pilots aboard, proved the determination of Yamamoto to retake Guadalcanal.

On October 18 Vice-Admiral Halsey relieved Vice-Admiral Ghormley, and organized his strength into two task forces, with one aircraft carrier each. Rear Admiral Kinkaid exercised command of all the forces, and had direct command of the *Enterprise* group, which was supported by the *South Dakota*, 1 heavy and 1 antiaircraft cruiser, and 8 destroyers. The other force, the *Hornet* group, was supported by 2 heavy cruisers, 2 antiaircraft cruisers, and 6 destroyers.

Kinkaid's orders were to intercept the Japanese forces known to be approaching Guadalcanal; Nagumo's orders were to support the landings, and to intercept Kinkaid's forces and any American convoys. An air battle was inevitable.

Commander Okuiya, on the air staff throughout these engagements, asserts, probably correctly, that Japanese carrier forces knew the position of Kinkaid's forces during the entire campaign and waited north of Guadalcanal for their approach. Not until the 25th did Kinkaid receive information of the position of an enemy force including two carriers. A search by carrier planes that afternoon had negative results, but land-based planes reported the Japanese were proceeding northwest.

While the surface fleets maneuvered, the Japanese ground troops on Guadalcanal launched an assault against Vandergrift's line which culminated in a fierce night attack on the 23d–24th. Four times the Marines repulsed the attacks, but during the forenoon of the 24th the assault was resumed. It was again beaten off, this time mainly by artillery and aircraft. Soon after, heavy rains turned Henderson Field into a quagmire, and for a day Marine planes could not take off. Meanwhile at dawn on the 25th the Japanese landed reenforcements on Guadalcanal under fire support of two cruisers and four destroyers. The rain had ceased and the field dried sufficiently to launch 25 bombers, which attacked enemy surface ships from noon until 5 o'clock.

After dark the Japanese resumed their attacks, and the Marines, worn down by incessant fighting, gave way along Lunga Ridge the night of the 25th. But the Marines gathered a group of headquarters troops, members of the band, and other special details and restored the position after a bitter hand-to-hand struggle in the darkness. The fighting ashore reached its peak during the night of the 25th–26th, but continued until the 28th. Thereafter it died down and never again did the enemy land enough troops on Guadalcanal to threaten the American position seriously.

During the struggle ashore Kinkaid had steamed northward to intercept the enemy fleet, and the fighting which ensued in the air was as savage as that on sea or land. By 8 A.M. on the 26th the entire Japanese force had been sighted, and in another half hour the small carrier *Zuiho* had been hit by two bombs from the search group. Attacks on the large, fast, and well-protected *Shokaku* and *Zuikaku* followed. Meanwhile 12 Zero fighters dived out of the sun to attack the *Enterprise* planes. The *Hornet's* pilots saw this attack but steered straight for the enemy carriers, and the torpedo planes barged through the middle of the melee. Japanese pilots were equally bold; their fighter patrol defending the

THE SOLOMONS AND ALEUTIANS 195

Shokaku pursued the first wave of the *Hornet's* bombers after they reached their "push-over" point and dived upon them in a desperate effort to protect their ship. The *Shokaku* was hit by six bombs in the Santa Cruz battle but still survived, a credit to her builders. The *Zuikaku* escaped unscathed and the *Zuiho* was only slightly damaged. The planes of the fourth carrier, the *Junyo*, attacked Guadalcanal and did not take part in this engagement.

Difficulties of all kinds, mainly faulty communications, prevented Admiral Kinkaid from taking a larger toll of the enemy, who launched planes against the *Enterprise* and the *Hornet* before the American planes could take off. The *Hornet's* combat air patrol had just been refueled and relaunched when, shortly after 10 o'clock, she was attacked by dive bombers and torpedo planes. A hit in the engine room rendered her helpless, and while repeated attempts were made by the *Northampton* to take her in tow, wounded and excess personnel were removed. Afternoon attacks made it necessary to abandon the *Hornet*. The enemy returned again to bomb the ship and delayed the rescue of personnel. The Japanese admitted the loss of 100 of the 160 planes that took part in the first attack.

The *Enterprise* fared better; she was hit by three bombs but evaded all torpedoes. The new battleship *South Dakota* received one bomb hit that disabled the forward turret and wounded Captain Gatch. A submarine torpedoed the destroyer *Porter* while she was recovering survivors. Thus ended the grim, three-day, four-dimensional, land, sea, air, and undersea battle.

Our naval forces were compelled to withdraw; some enemy ships pursued until they sighted the burning and abandoned *Hornet*, when they were ordered by Nagumo to withdraw lest they be attacked by American land-based planes. The enemy carriers *Shokaku* and *Zuiho* and the cruiser *Chikuma* were sent to Japan for repairs. This did not compensate for the loss of the *Hornet* and the *Porter* but did deprive the Japanese of these carriers during the next engagement.

The real compensation for the loss of the *Hornet*, not

realized at the time, was the heavy operational and combat losses inflicted on enemy carrier planes and pilots. Halsey was nearly running out of carriers; Yamamoto was running out of trained carrier pilots. The Japanese surface ships were exhausting their fuel; the need to refuel and the failure of the ground troops to break through the Marine positions were the probable reasons for their withdrawal. The surface ships had come to exploit a break-through that their infantry could not make, but the effort nearly succeeded and in November they were to make another attempt.

American surface losses again left the Japanese in temporary but not undisputed control of the waters around Guadalcanal; United States submarines moved in to attack the enemy supply line. On October 30 the light cruiser *Atlanta* and four destroyers bombarded Japanese positions near Point Cruz. On Guadalcanal American Marines, with naval support, crossed the Matanikau River on November 1 and by the 3d had advanced beyond Point Cruz. The next day a force of 1,500 Japanese with light artillery was landed on Koli Point but naval forces bombarded their beachheads, driving them into the jungle where the Marines gradually exterminated them.

Rear Admiral Nomura, who commanded the *Chikuma* at the battles of eastern Solomons and Santa Cruz, testifies that he considers the battle of Santa Cruz more decisive than Guadalcanal. He attributed the Japanese defeat ashore to the failure of the army to keep to its schedule. Repeated delays compelled the navy to remain in the combat area under observation of search planes. When the battle finally took place, Nomura asserts, fuel was low and at a critical time the carriers were damaged. After that battle the Americans were able to reënforce Guadalcanal and their own naval forces, whereas the Japanese naval strength in the November battle was less, and there was no proper air coverage, due to the heavy loss of pilots and damage to the carriers. After that time, Nomura states, the Japanese were never able to reënforce their troops on Guadalcanal so that they could retake the island. Nomura's opinion is supported by the absence of any carriers in the November 12–15 battle,

THE SOLOMONS AND ALEUTIANS 197

and the Japanese failure to reënforce their ground troops in November.

The Battle of Guadalcanal, November 12–15

In spite of the failure of the Japanese assault on the 25th and 26th of October Captain Omae, Chief of Staff of the Southeast (Eighth) Fleet of Admiral Kusaka, was sent to Guadalcanal to organize another general assault by land, sea, and air forces. This resulted in the battle of Guadalcanal, November 12–15. The Japanese Army had at last recognized the caliber of the American ground forces. The Hiroshima Division in the Rabaul-Shortland area, fully equipped and supplied, and scheduled for an attack on Port Moresby, was diverted to Guadalcanal. (Thus the Solomons campaign relieved MacArthur of fighting at least one additional division of the Japanese Army.) Japanese troops were present in strength on the western side of Guadalcanal. It was proposed to land the Hiroshima Division on the east side of Cape Esperance, and assault the Marines from the east and west simultaneously in an effort to split Vandergrift's forces and then defeat them.

Admiral Halsey had noticed increasing signs of Japanese activity in the Rabaul-Shortland Island-Buin area. It was estimated that the Japanese could supply 2 carriers, 4 battleships, 5 heavy cruisers, 30 destroyers, and sufficient transports to attempt a landing in force. Against these, Halsey could oppose 2 new battleships, the *Washington* and the *South Dakota,* 4 heavy and 4 light cruisers, and 22 destroyers. The *Enterprise* was not yet ready for action, and it was thought the available Japanese land-based planes exceeded the American. On November 6 American reënforcements had landed on Guadalcanal. More were needed, however, and Halsey, deciding to bring them in before the anticipated enemy attack, landed them on November 11 and 12.

Beginning November 10 Admiral Halsey increased the land-based planes in the Guadalcanal area. Dive bombers, torpedo planes, and fighters were flown from an auxiliary carrier or unloaded from cargo ships at Espiritu Santo. The Army B-26's in the Fijis were equipped with torpedoes, and General MacArthur sent pursuit planes and B-26's to Espiritu Santo on the 12th.

Repairs on the *Enterprise* were rushed and, accompanied by the *Washington* and the *South Dakota,* and cruisers and destroyers, Task Force K under Admiral Kinkaid left for Guadalcanal at noon on the 11th. The force was not in time, however, for the two battleships to take part in the night action of November 12–13.

The enemy launched heavy air attacks on the 11th; one plane dived into the *San Francisco,* flagship of Admiral Callaghan, doing considerable damage. But the Japanese lost heavily in fighters and bombers. On the 12th strong Japanese forces were located standing toward Guadalcanal. The battleship force under Vice-Admiral Lee was too far away to arrive in time, so it was decided to withdraw the transports from the combat area and to have Callaghan fight a delaying action with the oncoming Japanese.

The plan was executed successfully and just at midnight on Friday the 13th Callaghan and 13 ships, including 5 cruisers, entered Lengo Channel in search of the approaching enemy. The destroyer *Cushing* led the single column, followed by 3 other destroyers, then Scott in the *Atlanta* and Callaghan in the *San Francisco,* followed by the 3 other cruisers and 4 other destroyers. Callaghan had no trouble in finding the enemy, who was approaching in 5 groups, and he led his forces midway between them. The van of the American forces was mingled with the enemy before the Japanese searchlights illuminated the American ships and their guns opened fire.

The Japanese were skilled in using planes to drop parachute flares and destroyers to illuminate the enemy with searchlights, so that cruisers and destroyers could use their guns and torpedoes effectively. The Americans, less experienced, were learning. In the intense darkness the melee began before a gun was fired; within 15 minutes the *Atlanta* was burning, the *San Francisco* and the *Portland* were badly holed, the *Helena* was slightly damaged, and the *Juneau* was forced out of action. Of the destroyers the *Laffey* was sunk, the *Barton* blown up, the *Cushing* completely disabled, and

THE SOLOMONS AND ALEUTIANS 199

the *Sterrett* and the *O'Bannon* damaged. The uninjured destroyers *Aaron Ward, Monssen,* and *Fletcher* continued the action. The *Monssen* hit a damaged battleship with torpedoes; all fired torpedoes and guns at 2,000-yard range at enemy cruisers and destroyers. The *Monssen* was presently so badly damaged herself that she had to be abandoned. The *Sterrett* also had to retire. The *Fletcher* terminated the action by torpedoing a heavy cruiser. The battle lasted 24 minutes and was one of the most furious naval actions on record. After the firing ceased the *Helena,* the *San Francisco,* and the *Fletcher* joined up during their withdrawal and later fell in with the *Juneau,* the *O'Bannon,* and the *Sterrett.*

The assistant gunnery officer of the *Kirishima,* Lieutenant Commander Tokuno, reports that the Japanese force consisted of the 2 battleships *Hiyei* and *Kirishima,* 2 heavy cruisers, 1 light cruiser and 11 destroyers. While they were steaming toward their bombardment position off Henderson Field, the battle began. Both battleships turned left to reverse course; the *Hiyei* was leading and received most of the hits. The *Kirishima* was hit only once, and then only by a 6-inch shell. Many salvos landed close to both ships. The bombardment of Guadalcanal was abandoned.

Lieutenant Commander Yokuni, assistant fire control officer of the *Hiyei,* thought his ship sank several American ships but was not certain, for the *Hiyei* had high explosive ammunition but no armor-piercing shells aboard. When the battleship turned on her searchlights she received 85 hits above the waterline from the American cruisers and destroyers. She was not hit by torpedoes that night, and although several aerial torpedoes struck her the next day only three exploded. Dive bombers hit her several times, and about noon high-flying Boeing planes attacked but without harming her further. The *Hiyei* survived hits from guns, torpedoes, and bombs, but she had been so badly damaged that after dark her crew were transferred to destroyers and the ship was scuttled.

After the night engagement of the 12th–13th the enemy transports retired northward. The next night enemy cruisers and destroyers shelled Henderson Field for an hour and a half but were attacked and driven off by PT boats from Tulagi before they had inflicted serious damage on the field. The transports then turned about and headed for Guadalcanal.

In the forenoon of November 14 search planes from the *Enterprise* and from Guadalcanal attacked the retiring bombardment group, making hits on a heavy and a light cruiser. The heavy cruiser, the *Kinugasa,* which had fought well in the battle of Cape Esperance, was sunk by planes near Rendova Island.

About 10 A.M. on the 14th 2 search planes from the *Enterprise* located the 12 enemy transports which were approaching Guadalcanal. Carrier and land-based planes began attacks which practically annihilated the ships and their cargoes, the Hiroshima Division (see p. 197), reënforced with 1,500 sea infantry. Two search planes hit one transport, and at about 11 A.M. the *Enterprise* planes, operating with Marine planes, made another attack, with six hits. An hour later the Army B-17's added a hit. Between 3.30 and 4 the *Enterprise* planes from Henderson Field returned and added seven more hits, and next the attack group from the *Enterprise* made six 1,000-pound bomb hits on five ships. By 7 P.M. four transports had been sunk, four lay dead in the water burning, and four cripples were steaming slowly north, escorted by destroyers.

Captain Omae reports that of 11 transports 7 were sunk, and 4 were beached at Doma Cove, Guadalcanal Island, on November 15, because of damage received on the 14th. Admiral Halsey regarded this air attack as "an excellent example of the employment of carrier aircraft from an intermediate airfield," in this case, Henderson Field. It was also an excellent example of coördination of Army, Navy, and Marine aircraft.

In spite of these heavy losses, the Japanese commander with grim determination persisted in the attempt to bombard Henderson Field, land troops from the damaged transports, and attack Vandergrift's forces. In the afternoon of the 14th four enemy heavy cruisers and 11 destroyers were

THE SOLOMONS AND ALEUTIANS 201

sighted north of Florida Island closing Indispensable Strait. Other contacts included the battleship *Kirishima*, cruisers, and destroyers.

Late in the afternoon Halsey ordered Admiral Lee, commanding Task Force L, with the new battleships *Washington* and *South Dakota*, and four destroyers, *Preston, Benham, Walke,* and *Gwin*, to be in position southeast of Savo Island by midnight. Almost on the stroke of 12 Lee made contact with an enemy force consisting, according to Captain Omae's later testimony, of the *Kirishima*, two heavy cruisers, three light cruisers, and eight destroyers. The *Washington* opened fire on the leading enemy ship, the *South Dakota* on the third. The enemy was not idle; within the first few minutes, although neither of the battleships had been hit, the *Preston* and the *Walke* were sunk, and the *Benham* and the *Gwin* were hit and forced to retire. The *Washington* fired on the *Kirishima*, the *South Dakota* on a ship, probably a destroyer, using searchlights.

Then a Japanese destroyer illuminated the *South Dakota,* and the *Kirishima* opened fire and hit her. The battleship was already under concentrated fire from enemy heavy cruisers. The upper works were badly cut up and one turret was disabled but the armored hull was undamaged. Meanwhile projectiles from the *Washington* promptly disabled the *Kirishima's* steering gear so that she steamed in circles. Next her engines were damaged. The accurate and rapid fire of the *Washington* continued, and the captain of the *Kirishima* gave the order to scuttle the ship. About two and one-half hours after she received her first hit, the *Kirishima* sank.

The *Washington* and the *South Dakota* withdrew southward, the Japanese northward. On November 15, according to Admiral King, the destroyer *Meade* ". . . now exercised complete control in the area" and leisurely demolished the four transports that had beached themselves in Doma Cove to escape sinking. Ashore, General Vandergrift's forces had the situation in hand; they continued stamping out the Japanese. But the Marines were due for replacement and refit. They were gradually withdrawn and replaced by Army divisions and in December General Vandergrift turned over the command of Guadalcanal to General Patch, U.S.A.

The Battle of Tassafaronga, November 30

Toward the end of November Admiral Halsey suspected another attempt to retake Guadalcanal, and on November 29 he despatched Rear Admiral Wright, who had relieved Admiral Kinkaid only a few days earlier, with five cruisers and four destroyers, from Espiritu Santo to intercept a Japanese force reported attempting to reënforce enemy ground troops on Guadalcanal. About 9 P.M. on November 30, just before the engagement, two more destroyers joined Wright in Lengo Channel. With four destroyers in the van and two in the rear, the cruisers stood westward in line of bearing until the *Minneapolis* picked up two targets, when all ships turned and formed column on a northwesterly course.

At about 11.20 the van destroyers launched torpedoes on five enemy ships, and followed with gunfire and illuminating shells. The enemy craft were eight destroyers of Squadron Two that had been commanded by Rear Admiral Tanaka throughout the war. They were in three groups on a southeasterly course between Cape Esperance and Tassafaronga, and were preparing to land supplies and troops at the latter place. Two American torpedoes passing ahead of the column was the first intimation the Japanese had of the approach. Tanaka immediately signaled full speed and a simultaneous change of course. He ordered all torpedoes fired, and no gunfire while turning away. According to his Chief of Staff, Captain Toyami, the squadrons had practiced this maneuver at night for the past 18 months. It was very successful. At about 11.30 torpedoes blew the bows off the *Minneapolis* and the *New Orleans,* and ten minutes later the *Pensacola* was so badly hit that the fires could not be controlled for four hours. In another ten minutes the *Northampton* was hit by two torpedoes, and later had to be abandoned. The action was over in 20 minutes. The *Takanami* was the only destroyer to use guns; she fired about 70 rounds and was sunk by American gunfire.

THE SOLOMONS AND ALEUTIANS

The destroyer *Naganami* flying Admiral Tanaka's flag was hit twice but not seriously damaged. Fearing pursuit and interception, the entire Japanese force retired northwest to Buin at full speed. The effort of the Japanese to reënforce Guadalcanal had been frustrated, but at a heavy cost. However, by temporary repairs and skillful seamanship the *Minneapolis*, the *New Orleans*, and the *Pensacola* reached port and were repaired. In this final surface engagement before their evacuation of Guadalcanal the Japanese again showed their proficiency in night tactics and the destructive effect of their large 24-inch torpedoes.

Guadalcanal Campaign Losses

Japanese*	Allied
2 Battleships	
Hiyei, Kirishima	
1 Aircraft carrier	2 Aircraft carriers
Ryujo	*Hornet, Wasp*
5 Cruisers	8 Cruisers
Furutaka, Kinugasa, Tenryu,	*Chicago, Vincennes, Quincy,*
Yura, Kako	*Astoria, Canberra, Northampton, Juneau, Atlanta*
13 Destroyers	17 Destroyers (including those used as transports)
7 Submarines	1 Submarine

Until the battles of November 12, 13, and 14, both the Japanese Army and Navy had been determined to retake Guadalcanal, although American aviation had caused the Japanese Navy great difficulty in its attempts to supply and reënforce the garrison. After the battle, only destroyers and barges protected by aircraft were used to support the garrison on Guadalcanal. Enemy losses in destroyers were severe during the August-November period but losses in aircraft and pilots were prohibitive. According to Captain Omae, three or four air squadrons had at one time been concentrated at Rabaul but all had eventually been lost. And in

* Enemy losses include those due to submarine attacks in the Solomons-Bismarck areas and air attacks on shipping in the Rabaul-Buin area by southwest Pacific aircraft.

addition to these losses in carrier planes, the 21st, 24th, 25th, and 26th Air Groups of navy land-based planes had been destroyed. Almost all the first-class naval pilots had been killed. The Japanese therefore determined to evacuate Guadalcanal, and for this purpose, late in January, 1943, assembled 20 detroyers with a covering force from the Combined Fleet. The evacuation was completed on the night of February 7–8.

The occupation of Guadalcanal was costly to the United States Navy. The Japanese, however, also lost heavily, as revealed in the table on page 203, which shows losses of both sides in the Solomons and adjacent areas during that campaign, through the date of the Japanese evacuation of Guadalcanal, February 8, 1943.

Struggle for Central Solomons

After evacuating Guadalcanal, Admiral Yamamoto continued his efforts to hold the central Solomons. He had the airfield at Munda on New Georgia Island improved and secondary fields constructed on Kolombangara Island. He had regarded the Rabaul-Solomons area as very important and at one time had personally directed the Japanese offensive from Rabaul. But after February Yamamoto sent no battleships or carriers to the Solomons, and only used destroyers as escort ships.

Halsey, on the other hand, planning the invasion of the central Solomons, seized and fortified the Russell Islands, 60 miles northwest of Guadalcanal, on February 21, and constructed airfields. In the almost continuous exchange of air strikes which ensued, the Russells proved very useful. Occasional destroyer engagements occurred as both sides endeavored to supply and increase their own forces and simultaneously intercept enemy reënforcements. Airfields were bombarded by surface ships as well as planes, but both sides discovered that damage to airfields could be quickly and easily repaired. Only in preparation for an invasion or to neutralize the planes operating from the fields during a major operation, or if enemy planes were caught on the ground, were bombardments of airfields profitable.

THE SOLOMONS AND ALEUTIANS 205

In June, 1943, as Halsey intensified his preparations to invade New Georgia Island, northwest of Guadalcanal, the number of air strikes increased. The Japanese sent 60 bombers, escorted by as many fighters, over Guadalcanal on the 16th; 100 American planes flown by Army, Navy, ánd Marine pilots intercepted them and, in one of the most furious air battles of the Pacific war, shot down 107 enemy planes at the cost of six American fighters. These air battles continued to consume Japanese naval pilots faster than replacements could be trained.

Halsey despatched Rear Admiral Merrill with a task force of cruisers and destroyers to bombard Kolombangara and the Shortland Islands on June 29 and 30, preparatory to the invasion of New Georgia on the 30th, and followed the bombardments with air strikes. While Halsey landed Navy and Marine forces on New Georgia, MacArthur, between June 22 and August 5, put troops ashore at the Woodlark Islands, lying between New Guinea and the Solomons, and at Nassau Bay in New Guinea. Throughout the Solomons-New Guinea campaign Halsey and MacArthur had often synchronized their blows at the enemy; now they were advancing and were to encircle the Bismarck Archipelago in a series of coördinated movements.

New Georgia is a large island and it was not until October 6 that it was captured with its outlying islands. Its invasion brought on various naval engagements, usually at night between opposing forces of cruisers and destroyers which were attempting either to land supplies or reënforcements or to stop them. Rear Admiral Merrill, in command of three light cruisers en route to bombard Vela, in March had sunk two enemy destroyers, the *Minegumo* and the *Murasame,* that had just delivered supplies to Vela. A surviving enemy officer reported the ships were sunk so quickly they were able to fire only a few rounds. And on May 12–13 Rear Admiral Ainsworth combined a successful mine-laying expedition with a bombardment of Munda and Vela Airfields. In July he fought two sharp night engagements with enemy forces in Kula Gulf. These battles were costly, the cruiser *Helena* and the destroyer *Gwin* being lost and two other cruisers damaged by torpedoes, but Ainsworth sank four enemy destroyers and prevented the Japanese from reenforcing their garrisons in New Georgia. On the night of August 6 Commander Frederick Moosbrugger with six destroyers surprised an enemy force of four destroyers escorting troops and supply barges into Vella Lavella Gulf. Three of the enemy ships were sunk without loss to the American forces. On August 9–10 Commander Moosbrugger returned to the Gulf. He encountered no enemy destroyers but sank several barges carrying troops and supplies. The failure of the barges to reach the ground troops on Georgia Island undoubtedly influenced the subsequent Japanese decision to evacuate. On August 15 American ground troops landed on Vella Lavella; and on August 25 Bairoko Harbor on New Georgia was occupied.

The Death of Yamamoto; Koga's Succession

While Admiral Halsey was taking the central Solomons, a change occurred in the Japanese High Command. Admiral Yamamoto was killed in an airplane crash and Admiral Koga became Commander in Chief of the Combined Fleet in Truk on April 23, with Rear Admiral Fukudome as Chief of Staff. According to Fukudome, Koga was convinced that the only hope of winning the war was by a decisive naval battle; further, he believed that he had even chances of a victory if he could preserve the Combined Fleet and bring on the engagement in an area where land-based Japanese planes could be employed. For that reason Koga did not intend to intervene with the fleet in the defense of the Solomons or Rabaul, and directed that only enough reënforcements to be of "nuisance value" be sent to Vice-Admiral Kusaka, who as Commander of the Southeastern Area Fleet at Rabaul was in immediate charge of naval operations in the Solomons. However, Koga went to Japan a month after taking command and left Vice-Admiral Ozawa in temporary command over the Combined Fleet at Truk. Ozawa, whose permanent command was the Third (Air) Fleet, had served for a short time under Yamamoto, and in Koga's absence in June and July he seems to have operated much as Yamamoto had after evacuating Guadalcanal. Certainly air reenforcements from the Combined Fleet participated in the 1943 summer campaign.

The purpose of Koga's visit to Japan was to direct the operations which were to occur shortly in the Aleutians, and to get the approval of the Imperial General Staff for his plan of operations in the central and south Pacific. He had no difficulty in getting approval of his plan, which was to remain with the Combined Fleet in Truk in readiness to attack either Halsey, advancing through the Solomons, or Spruance, if he attacked the Gilberts or the Marshalls.

Reëstablishment of the American Forces in the Aleutians

It had become apparent to the Japanese High Command, before Koga's visit in May, that some action in regard to the Aleutians was imperative. Supply lines to the Japanese garrisons there were being cut so regularly by the Americans that either much greater strength would have to be used to hold these points successfully or the plan of maintaining the garrisons at all would have to be abandoned. Late in March this fact had been further emphasized by the battle of the Komandorski Islands.

When Koga reached Tokyo the decision to evacuate the Aleutians had already been made. It was a wise one. Vice-Admiral Hosogaya, who had persuaded Yamamoto to occupy Attu and Kiska after the defeat at Midway, had remained with the Fifth Fleet in the Kuriles. Maintaining communications between the Aleutian garrisons and Japan had been his responsibility, but he had found it impossible to furnish personnel replacements, munitions, and supplies to the garrisons he had established in those stormy fog-bound islands in June, 1942. American submarines and aircraft, assisted by planes of the Royal Canadian Air Force, had sunk so many Japanese supply ships that the dwindling garrisons were on half rations much of the time.

On August 7, 1942, as a diversion for the Guadalcanal attack, American forces had bombarded Kiska, and late in the same month had occupied Amchitka, the island to the east of Kiska. In February, 1943, Attu, the westernmost island, was

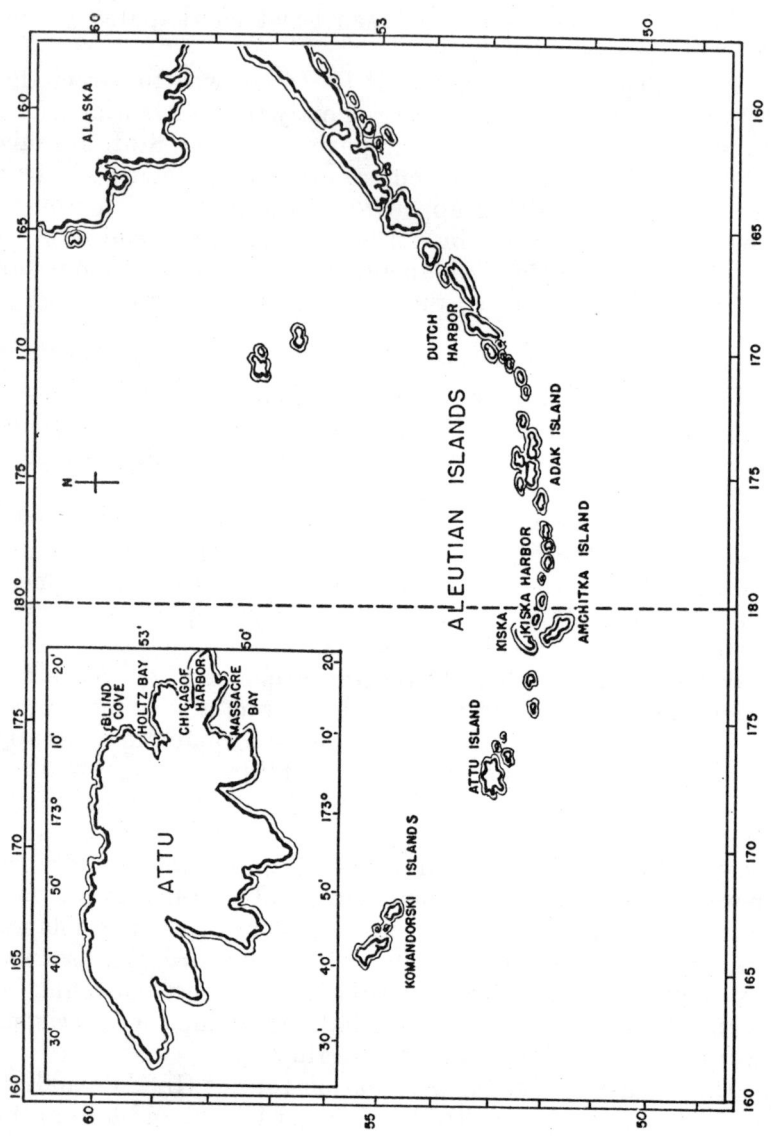

THE SOLOMONS AND ALEUTIANS 209

bombarded. Late in March Rear Admiral McMorris in the light cruiser *Richmond*, with the heavy cruiser *Salt Lake City* and four destroyers, deployed his forces on a scouting line seeking to intercept enemy convoys. One of his destroyers encountered an enemy force of unknown strength. McMorris concentrated his vessels and was anticipating a "Roman holiday" destroying enemy supply ships or transports. The situation clarified and changed "radically and unpleasantly," for the enemy force proved to be Hosogaya's Fifth Fleet plus the *Nachi* and the *Maya*, a total of two heavy and two light cruisers and five destroyers escorting a fast convoy to Attu. The battle of the Komandorski Islands ensued, for Hosogaya was aware of the proximity of McMorris and knew his approximate strength; the Japanese commander detached the convoy on a northwest course while he headed southeast and, interposing his force between McMorris' ships and their base, attained the better tactical position. Using his superior fire power, he opened the engagement. After a brief gun duel McMorris retired under cover of a very smart destroyer attack carried out under a smoke screen. Gradually McMorris worked his way eastward, out of effective range. In answer to his signals Admiral Kinkaid, who after leaving the Solomons had taken command of naval forces in the Aleutians, despatched air assistance. Japanese transports reported being attacked by heavy bombers and Kiska informed Hosogaya that American planes were on the way to attack him. Accordingly he broke off the engagement.

During the fight American ships suffered and inflicted light damage. Both sides fired torpedoes but neither made hits. In endeavoring to cut off an enemy convoy, McMorris had found a superior enemy force between himself and his base, but by skillful maneuvers he extricated his ships and avoided close action until the reported approach of American planes caused the enemy to break off the action. McMorris had saved his own force and prevented the enemy convoy from reaching Attu. Hosogaya explains that he quit fighting because first, he was warned by Kiska of the approach of an American bombing squadron; second, his remaining ammunition was below the minimum prescribed, and would not have sufficed for defense against a combined air and surface attack; and finally, the ships had been steaming at high speed and the remaining fuel would not have been sufficient to get them back to base if they had continued the fight. Several Japanese officers praised the American destroyer gunfire, saying the 5-inch shells fell like rain in the upper works.

At that very time Admiral Kinkaid and Lieutenant General De Witt were preparing to retake Attu. Rear Admiral Rockwell, who had begun the war in Cavite, commanded the attack force, including three battleships, one auxiliary carrier, and destroyers. Admiral McMorris and Admiral Giffen commanded the supporting force of cruisers and destroyers; the Army air forces that participated were under Major General A. E. Brown.

On May 11 landings were made at Massacre Bay on the southeast and Holtz Bay on the northeast coast, with a reconnaissance group put ashore at Blind Cove, northwest of Holtz Bay. The three groups were to encircle and capture Chichagof Harbor, the enemy's naval base, using the same pincer tactics successfully employed in the African landings. A total of 11,000 troops were employed, 8,000 of whom landed at Massacre Bay. The effective work of McMorris' force had prevented reënforcements and supplies from reaching Attu and had placed the small garrison of less than 3,000 on even shorter rations than before. The main obstacle was the fog which delayed the landings, hampered the ships, and caused two destroyer collisions. Since the ships could give no direct artillery support in the fog, they attacked Chichagof Harbor instead.

By 10 P.M. of D-Day 400 men were ashore in Blind Cove, 1,100 at Holtz Bay, and 2,000 at Massacre Bay. The fog prevented the Japanese from interfering with the landings but did not entirely keep them from delaying the American advance from Massacre Bay. Whenever the fog lifted battleships, cruisers, and destroyers would open fire on enemy installations ashore. The ships' fire had a good moral effect, but the hits were few. At a critical period in the advance

THE SOLOMONS AND ALEUTIANS 211

from Holtz Bay on the 12th the destroyer *Phelps* and the battleship *Idaho* were able to give effective support, but it was temporary. Not until the morning of May 18 did the Holtz Bay and Massacre Bay forces effect a junction. The command of the ground troops then passed from Major General Brown to Major General Landrum.

On May 29 the Japanese commander at Chichagof reported to Tokyo that the Attu garrison (of some 250) was about to make the final banzai charge. The charge overran a portion of the American Third Battalion of the 17th Infantry, but was intercepted by the force reserve. More than 100 Japanese were killed; the rest were dispersed. Some holed themselves in groups and continued to fight. On the 30th these remnants made a last weak attack, but on the 31st Chichagof Harbor was occupied and the American conquest of Attu was complete. Losses ashore included 550 Americans killed and 1,140 wounded; 2,350 Japanese had been killed and 24 taken prisoner.

Plans for the seizure of Kiska were begun as soon as Attu was taken, but the Japanese were simultaneously making plans for its evacuation. Between the end of May and June 10, 15 submarines of the I-78 class evacuated 700 persons, but Commander Hashimoto on Hosogaya's staff reports that whenever a submarine surfaced it was exposed to attack. Four of the 15 submarines were sunk. A plan to employ 12 destroyers and 3 light cruisers in a dash from Paramushiro to Kiska during fog was substituted, but attempts on June 20 and 30 failed. The third, on July 28, succeeded, thanks to several days of dense fog. The light cruiser *Tama* lay to, about 30 miles southwest of Kiska, while 2 light cruisers and 8 or 9 destroyers, concealed by the fog, entered Kiska Harbor. Approximately 3,100 Navy and 3,000 Army personnel, waiting on the beach, were brought off in 18 landing boats. The entire orderly operation was completed in less than an hour. The Japanese left time bombs to destroy shore installations, disabled their guns by removing essential parts, and sank their landing boats after the last trip. The évacués were taken to Paramushiro to reënforce that island.

When Admiral Kinkaid landed the Expeditionary Force on Kiska August 15 there was no opposition, and as the troops advanced inland evidences of hasty although well-planned departure were found. The visibility was low and three days were required to ascertain that the enemy had actually departed.

Retaking Attu and reoccupying Kiska gave a new base to attack the Japanese Kuriles. But the Aleutians were a threat only on the map. The stormy weather and the almost continuous fog had limited Japanese and American operations between June, 1942, and July, 1943, to the capture of Attu, the bombardment of Japanese-held islands by American forces, and the battle of the Komandorski Islands. The other activities of both forces consisted solely of occupying undefended islands. The predominant factor in the campaign was the continuous submarine and air attacks by American forces on Japanese supply ships.

Anglo-American Landings in Sicily

Meanwhile America's increased war potential permitted Halsey's operations to continue in New Georgia, as well as Kinkaid's in the Aleutians, without interfering with Hewitt's support of the landing in Sicily on July 10. General Eisenhower was in command of the Anglo-American Expeditionary Force, while Admiral Cunningham, in charge of the British Mediterranean Fleet, commanded all the naval forces; Admiral Hewitt and General Patton again commanded the American Expeditionary Force, Brigadier General Spaatz commanded the Army Air Force.

The immediate territorial objectives of the American forces, Scoglitti, Gela, and Licata, all lay on the south coast of Sicily. At daylight on the 10th Hewitt prepared the way for Patton by bombarding shore batteries and enemy trenches on and near the beaches. At Gela the first wave met little resistance, but the second encountered stiff opposition until the light cruisers *Savannah* and *Boise* silenced the shore batteries. At Licata there was comparatively heavy opposition from the time the troops landed, and the forces were subjected to intense enemy air attacks. By early fore-

THE SOLOMONS AND ALEUTIANS 213

noon, however, all three beaches had been captured, all troops were ashore, and unloading of supplies had begun. Enemy aircraft sank a mine sweeper, the *Sentinel*, and a destroyer, the *Maddox*. Ships' batteries, however, broke up a German tank attack which developed during the three-day battle before Patton's antitank guns had been landed.

By July 13 most American auxiliary ships had completed discharging their cargoes and departed. Hewitt's men-of-war remained and throughout July and August, with Patton's tanks and motorized forces, capitalized on their joint sea and land mobility and comprised an invincible combination. Hewitt gave artillery and naval air support to Patton, who moved across and around the west and north coasts of Sicily until he reached Messina where he was eventually joined by Montgomery's forces approaching from the south and east.

The Anglo-Americans scarcely paused in Sicily before they jumped across to Italy, where they landed on September 9, only to meet strong counterattacks by German ground troops supported by the Luftwaffe. The enemy artillery fire was intense. Naval batteries, as they had done at Licata, broke up these counterattacks on the 11th and 12th in the vicinity of Salerno. The Germans renewed their attacks on the 13th and 14th, but Allied battleships, cruisers, and destroyers continued to bombard enemy positions while store ships and landing craft poured a steady stream of supplies and reënforcements ashore and ships' batteries helped to repel the repeated enemy attacks. On October 1 Naples was occupied, and the American Army began its long, hard campaign against the miscalled "soft underbelly of the Axis."

The landings in southern Italy were the first test of Allied amphibious forces against German troops entrenched ashore and supported by field artillery and the Luftwaffe, whose planes operated from long-established and well-serviced airfields. The Allied success was in strong contrast to the failure of Hitler's army and air force to invade England in the autumn of 1940 and it was the surface navy that made the difference.

XII

Sea Power and Amphibious Warfare

A NATION or an alliance can be said to possess sea power fully only if its fleets can transport armed forces overseas, support their landings until the ground troops are firmly established on enemy soil, and thereafter maintain lines of communication for forwarding personnel and supplies.

As has been said in Chapter VII, some military circles during the period following the first World War held the results of the Antwerp, Dardanelles, and other campaigns to show that the new weapons made successful amphibious warfare next to impossible; but the Marine Corps did not share this point of view. During those years the Marines, and to a lesser degree the United States Army and Navy, had experimented with new amphibious weapons and techniques to as great an extent as their limited funds would allow.

During the first months of the United States-Japanese participation in World War II it was the Japanese, however, who demonstrated what modern amphibious warfare can achieve. Within three months of their entry into the war, they had proved that if properly used the new weapons, particularly aviation, facilitated landings on a hostile shore and actually increased the value of sea power.

Not until the United States entered the war were the Marines allowed sufficient funds to develop the special equipment they needed and to adapt it and the new weapons to amphibious operations. Thus it was fortunate that the American landings on Guadalcanal were against newly established Japanese positions, for the Navy obviously lacked the skill and experience that the enemy had acquired in this type of warfare. Furthermore, American industry was only beginning to supply the special weapons, boats, landing craft, and attack transports that were to be employed so

SEA POWER AND AMPHIBIOUS WAR 215

effectively in subsequent campaigns. The military significance of the Guadalcanal campaign arose from the Americans' stubborn resistance to the continuous Japanese counterattacks rather than from the skill and success of the initial operations.

After the landings in Guadalcanal and North Africa, the Joint Chiefs of Staff greatly expanded and intensified the training program for amphibious warfare, for it was evident that the shortest road to victory was by landing a superior force in Hitler's Europe and, by "leap-frog" tactics in the Pacific, penetrating to Japan itself. From Chesapeake Bay to the Caribbean, from the West Coast to the Aleutian, Hawaiian, and south Pacific islands and Australasia, American marines, sailors, and soldiers were drilled in all the elementary exercises necessary to a successful landing, and subsequent training in higher echelons embodied all the experience thus far gained in the war. Preparations for amphibious war on a titanic scale continued in 1942 and through 1943, as Halsey's command recovered the Solomons and Allied forces landed in Sicily and Italy. In every fleet there was an amphibious force commander. In each successive landing the technique and effectiveness of amphibious warfare were improved. The success of these landings showed definitely that amphibious operations had regained all their previous potency. Task forces of the Anglo-American Allies were also growing and becoming expert in escorting transports, landing troops, and lending artillery support for the invasion of enemy territory.

The sea powers were learning amphibious war the hard way, in the school of experience. They learned it when Eisenhower and Hewitt invaded North Africa, and they continued to learn it as Nimitz, MacArthur, Halsey, and Spruance landed on islands of every size and description, from tiny mid-Pacific atolls fringed with coral sea walls to the huge semicontinental New Guinea and the Bismarck and Philippine Archipelagoes. The wide variety of Pacific islands offered a different setting for each new combination of land, sea, and air components of the amphibious forces as they marched toward Japan in 300-league sea boots.

The staging points for the landing in Saipan were in the Marshalls, 1,000 miles away, while the rehearsal areas were the Hawaiian and Solomon Islands, 3,000 to 4,000 miles distant. The landings in southern France were made from Sicily and adjacent islands in the Mediterranean; the United Kingdom was the base and forwarding point for Eisenhower's invasion of Europe and offered ideal facilities for assembling planes, ships, and personnel and launching them across the Channel. The experience gained in the earlier landings by Hewitt and his staff, by the British Naval Command in the African landings, and by Spruance, Halsey, Turner, Vandergrift, MacArthur, and Barbey in seizing Japanese outposts in the Pacific had all been made available to Eisenhower, his staff, and amphibious commanders.

Amphibious operations could not be standardized, but an over-all technique was evolved which could be adapted to each landing, to overcome enemy air, naval, and finally, army opposition. It first involved air strikes by carrier forces assisted wherever possible by land-based planes of the Army, Navy, and Marines, to destroy enemy planes and damage air facilities. Air strikes would be accompanied by air and submarine reconnaissance of the theater of operations, and particularly of the primary objective, and were followed with further "softening-up" bombardments by battleships, cruisers, and destroyers, depending upon the importance and expected resistance of the objective. The rapidity with which enemy airfields could be repaired and replacement planes flown in made it mandatory to continue the air strikes at regular intervals until the troops were established ashore, with their own airfields completed and occupied by their land-based planes to furnish air cover. The necessity for retaining carrier planes to support the ground troops until their own airfields were in full commission was emphasized during the Leyte-Samar landings, when torrential rains delayed setting up airfields ashore.

In short "hops" over the Pacific, such as that from Tarawa to Kwajalein, land-based planes could assist materially. In other amphibious operations where great distances

SEA POWER AND AMPHIBIOUS WAR 217

lay between the staging point and the landings, like the 1,000-mile hop from Eniwetok to Saipan, land-based planes could help only by keeping down enemy aircraft in their own neighborhood, while carrier-based planes were required to neutralize enemy airfields on and adjacent to Saipan and keep them neutralized. Neutralization was essential; otherwise, during the time required to take Saipan, the Japanese could have despatched planes from any Japanese airport in the western Pacific. Even with the heavy strikes made by Admiral Mitscher preparatory to the Saipan landing, the Japanese, as will be seen, claim to have flown planes to the Marianas on June 15, the day of the invasion.

Every effort was made during carrier air and naval bombardments to gain and maintain control of the sea and the air over the sea in the area of operations. As this usually required attacks on adjacent islands, such bombardments often served the additional purpose of confusing and sometimes surprising the enemy.

It was usually necessary to sweep for enemy mines in the waters adjacent to the landing beaches; and for important landings special underwater demolition parties reconnoitered in advance of the landing to blast away underwater barriers. The "tip-off" to an alert enemy of the time and place of a landing was the appearance of the mine sweepers and the beginning of the bombardment of shore installations and defenses by heavy surface ships, frequently accompanied by air attacks. These operations were usually synchronized to permit the surface ships and aircraft to protect the mine sweepers. The invasion by the ground troops followed as soon as possible in order to prevent the enemy from repairing the damage done by bombardment ashore and to stop the planting of new mines and other underwater obstructions

While these operations softened up enemy defenses the amphibious forces were on their way, embarked in various types of specially designed landing ships, including slow (nine knots), small (3,000-ton) landing ships carrying the amphibious tanks, called "alligators." Alligators could be launched easily and, when water borne, they would clamber over reefs through fairly heavy seas and scramble up the beach.

There were two types of these amphibious tanks. One, armed with 3-inch howitzers, was intended primarily to give artillery support during the critical period when the naval gunners lifted their gunfire from the beaches to avoid hitting their own men. This type of alligator also carried 20 to 30 heavily equipped ground troops which comprised a ground escort as the alligators formed ashore into a covering force of tanks to assist the troops in taking the first—and usually the hardest—few hundred yards. The other type of alligator was primarily a troop carrier with one or two machine guns for use against enemy aircraft that attempted strafing attacks. The troop-carrying alligators, following closely behind the first type during the initial assault across the beach, were covered by the howitzers in the artillery alligators.

The ships that carried combat teams were larger and faster than those bringing the alligators, and carried their own landing craft. These craft would be hoisted out on arrival at the transport area, usually five to eight miles off the beach, depending upon the range of the enemy shore artillery. When the combat team troops had been embarked, the landing craft would be formed in column and proceed under their own control officer to join their "attack wave" at the line of departure, which was usually about half an hour's run from the beach. Each of these boats carried machine guns to use against strafing planes, and often they would also be provided with rocket launchers to use against enemy troops entrenched ashore.

In large expeditionary forces, transports, whose interiors resembled a floating dry dock, carried about 16 tank lighters. Each of these 56-foot lighters held a medium tank. The transport would launch a lighter, the lighter carried the tank to the beach, often over a reef, and the tank waddled down a ramp to join the assault formation. In addition to these specially designed landing craft and tanks, gunboats and smaller craft armed with rocket launchers and mortars

SEA POWER AND AMPHIBIOUS WAR 219

stood close inshore to give immediate fire support during the landing.

In these amphibious landings the attack transports were in reality combat ships, comparable in many respects to aircraft carriers. The attack transports would launch their assault troops to take a beachhead just as the carriers launched planes for air combat. Both types of ships carried the means of delivering deadly blows but had to be protected from enemy submarine, surface, and air attacks.

The squadron commander of transports provided a squadron control officer in a fast patrol boat, to control the whole formation through division control officers much as motorcycle policemen form a parade in a city. In this way any desired number of battalion combat teams could be lined up in their infantry landing craft in a succession of waves that would follow closely behind two or three waves of alligators. While the troops were forming, both air and ship bombardments would continue to dominate shore artillery, destroy the beach defenses, and disorganize the rear areas from which counterattacks could be launched. Simultaneously an air and submarine patrol was usually furnished by the escort carriers and destroyers that accompanied the amphibious force, to protect the troops and transports from air and submarine attacks. And, depending upon the reported strength and position of the enemy combat fleet, the task force of battleships, carriers, cruisers, and destroyers would take station to intercept any attack on the amphibious forces.

In addition to the fire support given by tanks and alligators, tanks were frequently equipped with flame throwers, while in every battalion combat team a special weapon section would furnish portable flame throwers, hand grenades, and other weapons specially designed to force Germans out of pill boxes and Japanese out of caves.

It requires no little imagination to conceive the amount of preliminary planning necessary to accomplish an amphibious operation. The problem of supply was difficult; fuel oil represented the greatest tonnage, the bulk of it coming from the Caribbean oil fields in War Shipping Administration tankers to the Marshalls where it was transferred to fleet tankers or barges. Heavy ammunition also presented a problem because of the difficulty, for example, of handling 16-inch shells. Until special equipment was provided by Mobile Service Squadron Ten, battleships had been sent to Pearl Harbor for ammunition. Under Commodore Carter, Squadron Ten with its floating dry docks, various repair ships, and supply ships, followed the American forces closely as they advanced across the Pacific, and its salvage tugs hovered at the edge of battle areas ready to tow disabled ships to the floating docks for emergency repairs. Consequently, in the last stages of the war, United States fleets cruised in the western Pacific for months at a time, and for the first time since steam supplanted sails, fueling at sea made it possible for men-of-war to operate almost indefinitely. The need for the service squadron had been anticipated by Admiral Nimitz, the Navy had provided the necessary ships and equipment to bring it into being, and throughout the final phases of the war it provided the Pacific Fleet with what appeared to the enemy to be a sea-going magic carpet.

After all preparations for a landing were made, a crucial test of the plan came in its over-all direction by the commander of the fleet. For the later and larger expeditions that commander was usually Spruance, Halsey, or Kinkaid. One of these admirals would be responsible for synchronizing the movements of an entire operation. In the taking of Saipan, for instance, transports came from the Hawaiian and Solomon Islands to converge at exactly the right time at Eniwetok and, with other units of the amphibious force, be regrouped for the final run to Saipan. The first Moltke made his reputation by concentrating his forces on the battlefield of Sadowa. The forces of Halsey, Kinkaid, and MacArthur that converged on the Leyte battle areas make Moltke's feat of arms appear Lilliputian.

To help American marines and infantrymen get ashore successfully in amphibious landings, it was the function of all parts of the fleet and the High Command to coördinate all the weapons and equipment that America could build.

SEA POWER AND AMPHIBIOUS WAR 221

The Japanese and Germans also had aviation, artillery, and machine guns; they had prepared themselves to repel the landings. The first waves of Allied combat troops had to leave the comparative shelter of their landing craft, weighted down with essential weapons, wade or swim ashore through smooth or choppy seas which might prove to be ankle or neck deep, and, following close behind their tanks, assault the first line of beach defenses. Crossing a "no man's land" on shore to attack an entrenched enemy bristling with field artillery, high explosive mortars, machine guns, and automatic rifles, is an ordeal. But to scramble through unfamiliar seas, often through a pounding surf, where the mines may not have been entirely swept or the submerged obstructions entirely removed, and at the end to find the necessary strength and courage to charge the enemy who are firing from the rubble of their pill boxes, or to bayonet them as they emerge from their fox holes—these are the demands that amphibious warfare makes on ground troops. In the end the success of amphibious war depends upon the battalion, company, platoon, and squad leaders, and upon the individual marine and infantryman who can take it—and give it.

Three-pronged Allied Thrust, Fall, 1943–Spring, 1944 *

The experience gained by the High Command in amphibious warfare in Guadalcanal and Africa and the vastly enlarged amphibious forces created under the direction of the Joint Chiefs of Staff in 1942 and 1943 enabled the Americans and their Anzac allies to launch a powerful thrust against Japan beginning in November, 1943, and continuing throughout the spring of 1944. The outposts Japan had established in the western Pacific were subjected to an irresistible, synchronized, three-pronged attack which overtaxed Japan's defensive strength and foreshadowed the ultimate conquest of the Japanese Empire. The advance of Admiral Spruance through the Gilbert and the Marshall Islands to Eniwetok constituted the northern prong of this great thrust; that of

* See map, p. 102–103.

Halsey from the Solomons to St. Matthias the central prong; and that of MacArthur, sometimes reënforced by task forces from Nimitz, to the Admiralty Islands the southern prong.

The movements of these three forces, coördinated by the Joint Chiefs of Staff in Washington, forced Admiral Koga, between November, 1943, and June, 1944, to withdraw the Combined Fleet from Truk to Palau, and then from Palau to Mindanao in the Philippines, and to leave thousands of Japanese soldiers marooned throughout eastern New Guinea, the Bismarck Archipelago, and the Solomon, Caroline, Gilbert, and Marshall Islands. This powerful offensive set the stage for the invasion of the Marianas and the Philippines in June and October of 1944, with the accompanying decisive air and naval actions that destroyed the Japanese Navy and the trained airmen of both the army and the navy.

Movements of Japanese Forces, August, 1943–June, 1944

When Koga returned to Truk in August, 1943, he was still convinced that the only chance of a Japanese victory was in a decisive engagement with the American Fleet in an area where he could employ land-based planes to compensate for the inferiority of his surface fleet. He knew the Solomon Islands were lost, and while he believed Rabaul could and should be held for some time by local forces alone, he was determined not to employ the Combined Fleet or carrier aviation in its defense. During September and October Koga kept the fleet concentrated at Truk and twice advanced to Eniwetok in the northern Marshalls in anticipation of a forward movement by Spruance, during which he hoped to get an opportunity to attack under favorable conditions. But the anticipated American landings in the Marshalls did not occur. Instead, during October a series of air and surface bombardments of the northern Solomons and the Gilbert and eastern Marshall Islands warned Koga that hostile landings might occur in any of these areas. Meanwhile MacArthur's advance to Finschafen on October 2 emphasized the increasing peril to Japanese Army garrisons in New Guinea and added to the difficulties of defending Rabaul.

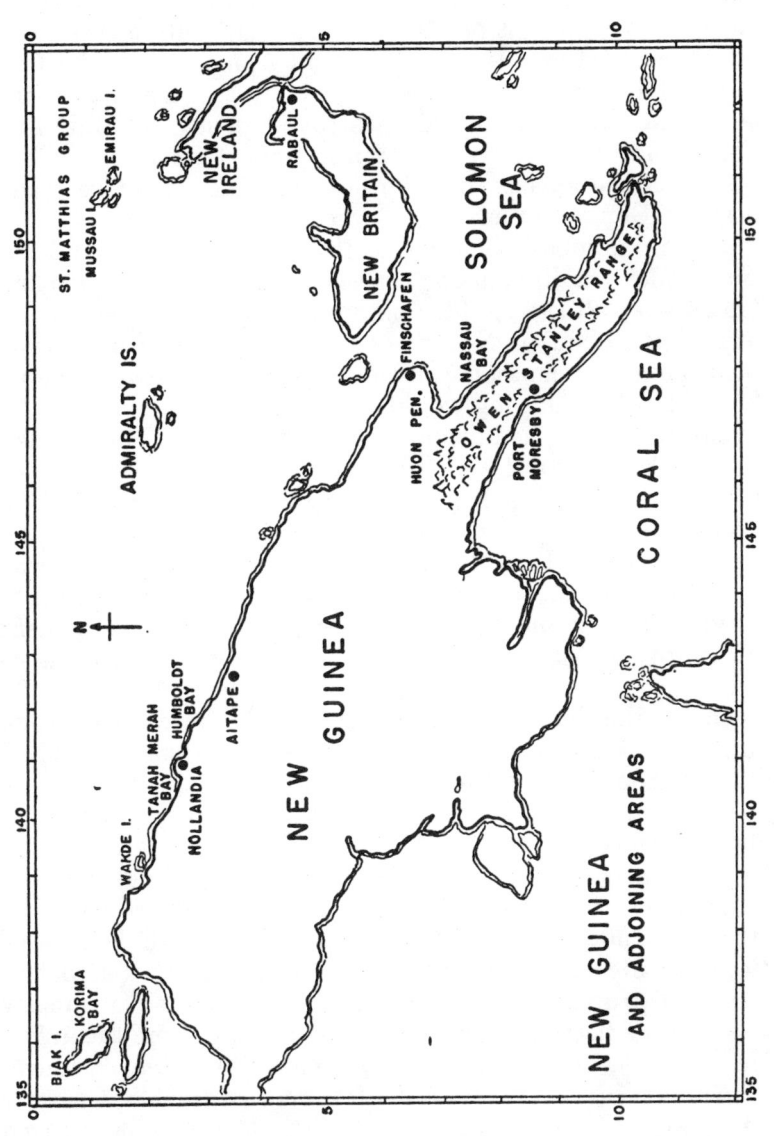

Between October 26 and 28 Halsey landed New Zealand and American troops on Treasury Island, south of the Bougainville-Shortland Islands area and American Marines on Choiseul Island, southeast of the same area. The bombardments and landings not only destroyed enemy shipping and planes and temporarily neutralized important air bases but convinced the enemy that the next landing would be made in south Bougainville.

Late in October, yielding to the repeated pleas of local commanders at Rabaul for air assistance, Koga despatched Ozawa with all the fighting planes of the Third Fleet. They arrived at Rabaul on November 1 and 2, and at the same time the Japanese commander on Bougainville, who had expected the next Allied landing would be in the southern part of the island, was surprised when Vice-Admiral Wilkinson landed General Vandergrift's Third Amphibious Corps of Marines in Empress Augusta Bay in west-central Bougainville. The attempt of Vice-Admiral Omori, commanding the naval forces at Rabaul, to attack the American transports was frustrated by Rear Admiral Merrill who turned back a heavier cruiser and destroyer force in a brisk engagement off Empress Augusta Bay during the night of November 1–2.

Under the impact of these American successes, Koga authorized his jealously guarded carrier pilots, whom he had already allowed to go to Rabaul, to be used in the defense of the northern Solomons, the eventual loss of which he had already conceded. And, having departed from his resolve to keep the air fleet intact and with the surface fleet, he next despatched to Rabaul the pick of the cruisers and destroyers, under Admiral Kurita, to assist in the defense of Bougainville. The fleet was being consumed in a hopeless effort to protect islands that had been occupied originally to serve the fleet. Kurita's force was sighted from the air on November 4, and was struck by planes from Rear Admiral Sherman's carrier force on the forenoon of the 5th. Ozawa's newly arrived fighter planes joined the Japanese land-based planes on Rabaul in an intercepting air battle, during which Sherman's fighters cleared the air for the bombing squad-

SEA POWER AND AMPHIBIOUS WAR 225

rons. The bombers caught Kurita's cruisers and destroyers as they were trying to escape from Rabaul, inflicted heavy damage on them and also on shipping at anchor in the harbor.

The Japanese state that only one or two destroyers were sunk, but admit that the heavy cruisers *Haguro* and *Myoko* were seriously damaged and most of the remaining cruisers and destroyers damaged. All of Kurita's ships which could steam were compelled to return to Truk for temporary repairs and several had to return to Japan for major overhaul. Sherman's victory was opportune. Merrill's small force of light cruisers and destroyers would have had great difficulty in boxing off Kurita's heavy cruisers which had been given orders to destroy the amphibious force in Empress Augusta Bay.

Ozawa remained at Rabaul until November 20, assisting the local air forces in their attacks on American ships in Empress Augusta Bay and on convoys reënforcing the Americans on Bougainville. By that time his air force was consumed.

Japanese surface forces were also suffering. On November 25 five American destroyers under Captain A. A. Burke intercepted an equal number of Japanese destroyers between Buka and Cape St. George. By Japanese admission, three of their ships were sunk, one was badly damaged, and the other slightly damaged. No damage was inflicted on Burke's command. The night tactics of the American cruisers and destroyers had improved during the Solomons campaign.

On November 20, the day Ozawa left Rabaul, Spruance's forces landed on Tarawa and Makin in the Gilberts. As has been said, Koga intended to strike at Spruance in an area where Japanese land-based planes could coöperate with the fleet. On November 22, with a view to attacking Spruance, he sent all available units of the Second Fleet to reënforce the commander of the Fourth Fleet, which was charged with local defense of the Inner South Sea area, including the Gilbert and the Marshall Islands. At a conference the admirals of the Second and Fourth Fleets asked Koga to send

Ozawa's Third (Air) Fleet. Koga had to refuse this request because the carrier fighters of the Third Fleet had been expended defending Bougainville; it was this circumstance that forced Koga to abandon his plan to oppose the advance of Spruance.

The American amphibious forces easily captured Makin on November 22. Tarawa, held by 3,500 well-entrenched enemy infantry, could be taken only by a frontal assault. Its capture by American Marines, under command of Lieutenant General Howland Smith, was necessarily costly. After the naval barrage was lifted, the landing on the beach was delayed a few minutes, long enough for the enemy ground troops to emerge from their fox holes and the rubble of their pill boxes; their artillery and machine guns added to the cost to the American invaders. With characteristic determination, however, the Marines secured their beachhead on November 20 and by the 24th had taken complete possession of Tarawa.

The enemy's loss of their carrier pilots in futile efforts to hold Bougainville and to protect Rabaul facilitated the American occupation of the Gilbert Islands and made it practically impossible for the Japanese Combined Fleet to fight a decisive action until the pilots could be replaced. Koga, at Truk with the immobilized Combined Fleet, could only look on helplessly while Spruance, with Smith's Marines reënforced by Army divisions, occupied Majuro, Kwajalein, Roi, and Namur in the Marshalls during late January and early February, 1944.

On February 10 Koga became convinced that the Combined Fleet would risk destruction by remaining at Truk without its carrier fighters. He ordered Ozawa with the air fleet to Singapore to train replacement pilots for the carriers, and Kurita with the Second Fleet to Palau, while he himself proceeded to Tokyo to consult with the Imperial General Staff. This exodus enabled the Japanese Fleet to escape the strike made by Spruance against Truk on February 17 and 18.

On his arrival in Tokyo Koga had no difficulty in getting the Imperial General Staff's approval of his recommendation

SEA POWER AND AMPHIBIOUS WAR 227

to abandon all attempts to hold any territory beyond the Marianas and Palau in the western Carolines. The Japanese Army long before (May, 1943) had decided to abandon further attempts to reënforce eastern New Guinea. Koga hoped the garrisons already there, assisted by land-based aviation, could hold up the American advance until completion of the training of his carrier pilots. Members of Koga's staff hoped that the Japanese Navy would be called upon only to maintain the line of communication between Japan and the army and air forces in the Marianas, the Philippines, and the East Indies.

Measures were immediately taken in Tokyo to send the new 31st Army of three divisions to the Marianas to build necessary airfields and coastal defense works. Koga urged that the army send all its air force to the area to assist the navy in holding that line. To emphasize Koga's request, the American air strike on Truk on February 17, destroying an air combat unit of 50 planes and numerous supply ships, occurred during the conference and revealed the inferiority of Japanese air power in the central Pacific. However, in view of its other commitments, mainly in Asia, the army refused, but promised to despatch the remainder of its air force if subsequent developments proved its presence necessary.

When Koga returned to Palau at the end of February, he was still contemplating a decisive fleet engagement, near Saipan if the advance came through the central Pacific, or near Palau if it came from New Guinea, but in either case with aircraft taking the *major,* and ships the *minor* part. Accordingly the naval land-based planes in the Rabaul-Solomons area were withdrawn to Truk, and those in Malaya and the East Indies were shifted to the Philippines, western New Guinea, and the Celebes, while the First Air Fleet of the land-based naval planes, just completing its training, was sent from Japan to the Marianas. With this distribution of planes Koga had surrounded the prospective combat area with 2,000 planes in easy flying distance. He was ready for an engagement anywhere in the waters between the eastern Philippines, western New Guinea, and the Marianas. Koga prepared two headquarters, one ashore at Saipan to direct operations against an advance from the central Pacific, and another at Davao in case the advance should come from New Guinea.

Convinced that the war would be lost if the Marianas-Palau line were penetrated, Koga had determined to fight for that line. But on March 30–31 his force at Palau underwent a severe air attack. According to Japanese accounts, 3 destroyers, 20 merchant ships, and about 160 planes were destroyed, and many additional merchantmen beached. Simultaneously information reached Koga that an American amphibious force was proceeding west from the Admiralty Islands. The air attack convinced Koga that Palau could no longer be used as a naval base, and the report of the amphibious force persuaded him that the first American advance would come from New Guinea toward the Philippines. To meet it, he ordered the First Air Fleet from the Marianas to Palau, and Admiral Ozawa's Third Air Fleet, whose new carrier pilots had not completed their training program in the Singapore area, to arrive at Davao by April 2. Having issued these orders, he assigned the flagship *Musashi* to the Second Fleet, and on March 31 left by plane for his shore headquarters at Davao, from which he planned to direct the attack on the American forces. The plane never arrived, and Admiral Koga was presumably lost at sea.

Admiral Toyoda succeeded Koga in May. His staff was organized about April 20. During the interim the Commander in Chief of the Southwest Area, Vice-Admiral Okochi, with headquarters in Soerabaja, was the senior officer in the Philippines-East Indies area. Captain Fuchida, a senior officer on Koga's staff, states that Admiral Okochi ordered the planes from Saipan to Palau, but Admiral Fukudome, Koga's Chief of Staff, states positively that Koga gave the order before he left Palau on March 31. Whoever gave it, the outcome was bad for Japan.

Toyoda accepted the strategical concept of his predecessor. Until his death Koga had professed his determination to attack the American Fleet, but after being forced from Palau he was convinced that the Combined Fleet could no

SEA POWER AND AMPHIBIOUS WAR 229

longer take a predominant part in the defense of Japan. He thought the "land-based air force would constitute the main strength, with the surface ships coöperating as fully as possible." In accordance with this strategy Toyoda disposed the fleet and land-based planes for the last phase of Japan's naval defense. This was the basis for the so-called AGO Plan for defense of the Philippines and the Marianas.

But Toyoda, like Koga, dispersed some of his forces. When MacArthur landed on Biak Island on May 27 the Staff of the Combined Fleet, contrary to the plan to husband Japan's strength for a decisive blow, ordered the 16th Cruiser Division to embark the Second Amphibious Brigade at Zamboanga to reënforce the garrison and give naval support if the situation permitted. On June 2 the expedition was halted because a strong American force had been reported east of Biak. On June 8 another attempt was made, but in spite of air cover provided by the 23d Air Flotilla the Japanese ships were again attacked. Two destroyers carrying troops were sunk. About midnight, June 8–9, as the force was entering Korima Bay, Biak Island, they sighted an Allied force and withdrew rapidly. They were pursued and heavily shelled, the destroyer *Harusame* being sunk. For some reason Toyoda ordered a third attempt, sending the battleships *Yamato* and *Musashi*, two heavy cruisers, and four destroyers. They arrived at Batjan on June 11, but were immediately recalled to Tawi Tawi and joined the Second Fleet en route to the Marianas. On June 9 planes operating from Woleai Island in the western Carolines had sighted Spruance's force headed for the Marianas.

Movement of American Forces, November, 1943–June, 1944

Admiral Spruance commanded the northern prong of the three-pronged American offensive that consumed the Japanese armed forces and prevented the naval commanders from anticipating the direction of the main assault. Under the orders of Admiral Nimitz Spruance advanced with a combined Army, Navy, and Marine force from Funafuti in the Ellice Islands, overran the Gilberts in November, then took the Marshall Islands, occupying Eniwetok by the end of February, and finally invaded the eastern Carolines. Until early June Spruance continued the preparations to invade the Marianas. Admiral Mitscher with the fast carriers opened the campaign with heavy air strikes at enemy airfields in the Caroline, Marianas, Wake, and Marcus Islands.

Meanwhile the southern prong, under General MacArthur, had moved forward in New Guinea. In mid-February, a few days before Spruance reached Eniwetok, Australian and American troops had effected a junction and nipped off Huon Peninsula on the northwest coast of New Guinea. And on February 29, in a brilliant feat of arms, MacArthur's amphibious forces, operating under Rear Admiral Fechteler and covered by Vice-Admiral Barbey's escort fleet, landed the dismounted First Cavalry on the Admiralty Islands in a reconnaissance in force. Encountering little opposition, they seized the island without further delay.

As these operations proceeded Admiral Halsey, commanding the central prong of the synchronized movement, had isolated enemy garrisons in the north and south of Bougainville by landing forces in Empress Augusta Bay. On March 20 Halsey's forces occupied the small island of Emirau in the St. Matthias group. American holdings in Bougainville, New Guinea, and the Admiralty Islands now encircled the Bismarck Archipelago. By-passing the Bismarck Islands deprived the Japanese Imperial General Staff of any hope that the American Navy would waste ships attacking strong points such as Rabaul and the south Bougainville-Shortland Islands area. Admiral Halsey had now completed the mission assigned him in October, 1942, and on June 15, 1944, turned over his territorial command to Vice-Admiral J. H. Newton in order to give his undivided attention to command of the Third Fleet.

In the region of the southern prong, on northern New Guinea, there was much activity up to and during the Marianas campaign. The purpose was to capture the New Guinea area and deny the enemy any opportunity to act aggressively or threaten Allied lines of communication in that section of the Pacific, thus protecting and securing the Allied

SEA POWER AND AMPHIBIOUS WAR   231

flank for the Marianas operations and ensuing actions. Admiral Mitscher with the fast carrier forces, which had been operating in the Caroline Islands, was sent to support the first of these northern New Guinea actions, the landings at Hollandia and Aitape, on April 22. This was the largest amphibious operation undertaken in the southwest Pacific to that date. Mitscher's forces gave support to Admiral Barbey's surface fleet, which in turn escorted and protected the landings of Krueger's Sixth Army. The presence of these powerful naval forces, composed of carriers, battleships, cruisers, and destroyers, enabled MacArthur to strike far beyond the radius of his shore-based planes and expedited his return to Manila. Throughout this period and until the end of the war the strength and mobility of the Pacific Fleet, with its integrated aviation, permitted the rapid advance of the Sixth Army which repeatedly surprised the Japanese High Command.

After nine days of heavy preliminary bombardment, simultaneous landings were made on the 22d at Tanah Meroh Bay, under direct command of Admiral Barbey, at Humboldt Bay, under Admiral Fechteler, and 90 miles to the eastward, at Aitape, under Rear Admiral Noble. The first two landings trapped enemy troops and planes on the Hollandia airstrip, 12 miles inland. The landing at Aitape took an enemy strong point and gained another airstrip. The three landings cut off a total of 50,000 Japanese soldiers. Airstrips and port facilities were rapidly improved and promptly put to Allied use.

The Allies could now move up the New Guinea coast. The Wakde Island area was taken May 17–19 against light enemy resistance, paving the way for the important seizure of Biak Island, off the northwest coast of New Guinea, by amphibious assault, beginning May 27. Enemy resistance was light at first, but stiffened, and as has been described earlier in the chapter, the Japanese made three successive attempts to come to the rescue of Biak with strong naval reënforcements. Mitscher's fast carriers were not present during this operation, no ships larger than heavy cruisers being used. The same naval commanders who had conducted the Hol-

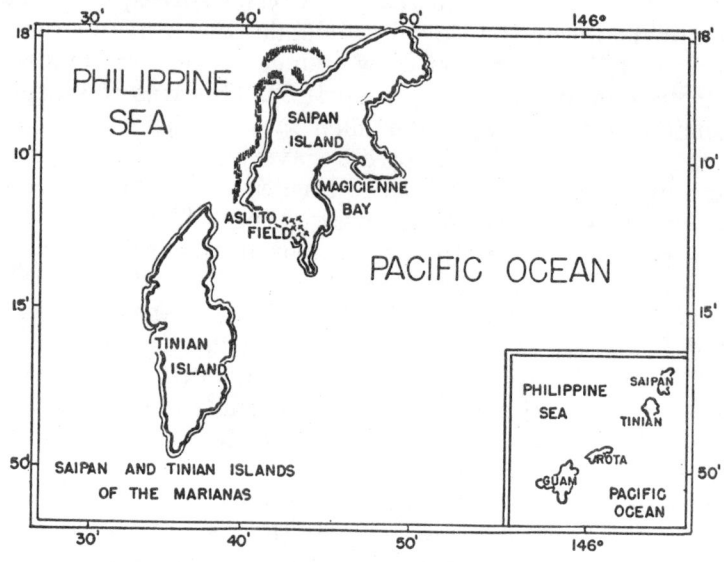

THE MARIANAS

landia landings, Admirals Fechteler and Noble, supported the Biak landing, while Vice-Admiral Crutchley of the Royal Australian Navy, who had served in the Solomons campaign, with a force of cruisers and destroyers intercepted and routed the Japanese Fleet trying to reënforce the island.

The movement which culminated in the Allied seizure of Biak had important strategic consequences, as has been related. It convinced first Koga and then Toyoda that the first American attack would fall on Mindanao or Palau. It caused Koga to order approximately half of the First Air Fleet from the Marianas to Palau, where Toyoda permitted them to remain until they were practically all lost, either in air combat or on the ground, or from operational accidents, thus reducing air opposition to American attacks on the Marianas in June.

SEA POWER AND AMPHIBIOUS WAR   233

Beginning of Marianas Campaign—Taking of Saipan

While Koga and Toyoda concentrated the Imperial Navy's planes and ships for the defense of the Philippines and the Marianas, Spruance's forces were assembling in Kwajalein, Majuro, and Eniwetok in the Marshalls. Here the harbors furnished secure and spacious anchorage for the combat ships of the Pacific armada and Mobile Service Squadron Ten which continued to provide the necessary services and supplies.

Admiral Spruance was in over-all command of the campaign to take the Marianas, with Vice-Admiral Marc Mitscher commanding Carrier Task Force 58, while Lieutenant General Howland Smith, whose Marines had taken Tarawa, commanded the assault troops. In strategic support, General MacArthur's air force scouted the New Guinea-Southern Philippines area, while in the battle area Vice-Admiral Lockwood deployed 28 submarines that contributed greatly to the American triumph.

Admiral Mitscher with Task Force 58 opened the campaign on June 11, four days before the landing, by destroying enemy aircraft and air facilities at Saipan, Tinian, Guam, and Rota by air and gun bombardments. Two days before the attack he began to destroy enemy aircraft, facilities, and shipping at Iwo Jima and Chichi Jima in a vigorous effort to prevent planes from being flown in to replace those already destroyed on Guam and Rota. In spite of Mitscher's persistent attacks, which continued until the day of the landing, the Japanese claim that 200 to 250 planes were flown into the Marianas by way of Iwo Jima on June 15.

Air strikes by the land-based planes in the rear areas, mine-sweeping operations and day bombardments by surface ships were begun on June 13. Destroyers continued harassing fire during the two intervening nights. The fast battleships and destroyers bombarded both Tinian and Saipan on the 14th, and on the 15th ground troops landed in the southern part of the west coast of Saipan. The initial assault was led by Marines from the Second and Fourth Divisions abreast, each division providing two regimental combat teams so that there was a simultaneous assault by eight battalion landing teams.

Within 15 minutes of the signal to begin the landing the first wave was under way for the shore, protected by an intense bombardment from surface ships that lifted as the boats approached the beaches. Resistance on landing was light; the Japanese had learned that naval bombardments would destroy forces on the beachheads. But opposition increased as the troops pressed inland, and ships and planes answered calls from advancing ground troops to knock out enemy strong points. By evening narrow bridgeheads had been established by both Marine divisions, who had no difficulty in beating off Japanese counterattacks during the night, although enemy mortar and artillery fire inflicted numerous casualties.

On the 15th and 16th all the combat troops and part of the service troops were landed, and during those two days the most severe fighting ashore occurred. On the 17th General Smith established his command post ashore and the 27th Infantry Division landed. As the marines and infantrymen advanced inland the Japanese reacted vigorously, but the advance continued. On the 18th the principal airfield, Aslito, was captured, and by the next day the ground troops were across the island and had a foothold on Magicienne Bay on the southeast coast. General Smith felt he had the situation in hand and assumed control of operations on the island on the 20th. Aslito Field was ready for emergency landings that same day, and two days later an entire squadron of American planes landed there.

The Battle of the Philippine Sea

Simultaneously with the ground fighting on Saipan, the naval-air engagement known as the battle of the Philippine Sea was being fought in the waters west of the islands to defeat the efforts of the Japanese Fleet to break up the Marianas landings.

When Admiral Toyoda had learned, about June 9, that Spruance's Fifth Fleet was advancing toward Guam, he had ordered the execution of the AGO Plan. The plan provided for a combined attack by Rear Admiral Kakuda's land-based planes and Ozawa's carrier-based planes to destroy Spruance's fleet covering the amphibious force, while Kurita's battleships, cruisers, and destroyers assaulted the amphibious force itself.

The land-based planes were stationed at Palau, Yap, and Guam; the headquarters of their commander, Rear Admiral Kakuda, were at Saipan. Kakuda was under direct command of Admiral Toyoda, who had established headquarters in the Inland Sea. Kakuda had about 500 planes (some Japanese officers reported 600); Ozawa's carriers had about 450.

On June 10 Ozawa heard from Saipan that the American force was headed for the Marianas. Hastily recalling the battleships *Yamato* and *Musashi* and some cruisers and destroyers which, as mentioned earlier, he had sent to reenforce Biak, he departed with the entire Second and Third Fleets to carry out his part of Toyoda's plan.

Admiral Toyoda had decided to use every plane and ship he had "in one big operation." He looked forward without any particular apprehension to an engagement with the American forces. His land planes were distributed around the rim of the probable battle area. His sea and air forces were "in readiness and waiting" for the American forces. He and many of his staff officers felt confident that if the attack on the Marianas came from only one direction the Imperial Navy and Air Forces could smash it. Thus as the campaign for the Marianas opened Toyoda anticipated the outcome with growing confidence.

Spruance's Fifth Fleet, including 15 large and small carriers, with accompanying cruisers and destroyers, and 7 fast battleships and 14 destroyers, was about to be subjected to the largest air attack yet delivered on surface ships. But the enemy strikes were poorly coördinated, due to the remote control by Admiral Toyoda from the Inland Sea and the lack of practice in coördination between Kakuda's land-based and Ozawa's carrier-based planes. However, it was not Japanese failure but American skill and teamwork that turned the air assault into a rout.

Admiral Lockwood's submarines had begun their patrols at approximately the same time that the "softening up" process against Saipan, Guam, and Tinian had started, and on the 13th of June the *Red Fin* had reported Ozawa's Second and Third Fleets as they sortied from Tawi Tawi. On the 15th the *Flying Fish* sent a message that a large force of battleships, carriers, cruisers, and destroyers had passed through San Bernardino Strait and was proceeding northeast. Receipt of the *Red Fin's* information caused Spruance on the night of the 15th to delay the projected landing on Guam.

Two days passed without further information. On the 17th the American submarine *Cavalla* sighted two large tankers with three escorting vessels, and later, about 10 P.M. she sighted Ozawa's force with 15 or more combat ships. This information did not reach Spruance until 3 P.M. of the 18th. Later, on the 18th, several small enemy planes were sighted, a radio report from a submarine was jammed, apparently by the enemy, and Nimitz also forwarded information indicating the enemy's approach toward Saipan. The searches by American land-based planes being conducted at the same time just missed discovering the enemy. In the early morning of the 19th an American flying boat from Saipan sighted Ozawa's force about 470 miles west of Guam. Again there was a delay in transmission, and this very important message did not reach Spruance until after the Japanese planes had attacked.

On the night of the 18th Ozawa had broken radio silence to tell Kakuda his very simple plan for attack. It was to strike the first blow at the American carriers on the 19th by launching his planes at a greater distance than usual and instructing them to land on Guam afterward and refuel there.

About 7 A.M. on June 19 fighters from the carrier *Belleau Wood,* patrolling over Guam, reported many enemy planes were taking off, and requested reënforcements. Other carriers despatched planes and control of the air over Guam was reëstablished. In the process 33 American fighters mixed with a slightly larger number of enemy fighters, resulting in 36 enemy planes shot down and one American

SEA POWER AND AMPHIBIOUS WAR 237

fighter lost. This early air victory had important results. The fighter group over Guam had probably been intended to act as an "air cap" to protect Ozawa's homing planes that would have to land and refuel before they could get back to their carriers. With the air cap destroyed, Guam became a graveyard instead of a haven for Ozawa's planes.

The submarines *Albacore* and *Cavalla* delivered the first blow against enemy surface ships at 9 A.M. on the 19th by sinking Ozawa's flagship, the carrier *Taiho,* and thus forcing the admiral to shift his flag in the midst of flight operations. This initial success was fully exploited by American planes and pilots.

Between 10 A.M. and 2.30 P.M. Japanese planes attacked Spruance's carriers and battleships. About 10.30 the first large wave, estimated at between 50 and 70 planes, was intercepted 60 miles away by combat patrol planes (F6F's). Most of the Japanese planes were shot down. A few broke through the air patrol and the *South Dakota* was hit by a small bomb with minor damage. A near miss on the *Minneapolis* and a suicide crash at the waterline of the *Indiana* caused superficial damage to both ships. Shortly after 11 a second wave from the same general direction, consisting of about 60 planes, was intercepted about 60 miles away and most of the aircraft destroyed. Four dive bombers broke through to make near misses, close to the *Bunker Hill* and the *Wasp.* These carriers were slightly damaged. From 11.30 to 2.30 isolated groups of from 15 to 20 planes attempted to attack. They were intercepted at from 2 to 60 miles distance, and most of them were destroyed. Six to eight glide bombers broke through and made unsuccessful attempts to bomb the *Wasp* and the *Bunker Hill.* At this time the carriers estimated that 300 enemy planes had been sighted and 220 destroyed, at a cost of 10 of the 171 American interceptors.

As the fighting ceased, carrier planes were taken aboard and refueled. About 2.30 radars and planes again reported enemy aircraft over Guam. Air patrols were despatched, and during the remainder of the afternoon about 75 of 130 enemy planes sighted near Guam were destroyed. In spite of their heavy losses a few enemy planes hovered around Task Force 58 until 10 o'clock that night.

Ozawa admits that he did not get any word on the 19th from Admiral Kakuda, who was directing the land-based planes from his headquarters on Saipan, or from the operating fields on Guam. His only information of the battle came from the incomplete reports of a very few pilots who succeeded in returning to the carriers. He did receive a report, his testimony shows, that "a considerable number" of his planes had gone to Guam. The admiral had other troubles. Not only did he lose his flagship, the carrier *Taiho,* on the morning of the 19th, but shortly after noon, while the *Shokaku* was recovering some of her planes of the first wave, she was torpedoed by the *Cavalla* and sank about three hours later. On account of the loss of the two carriers, only 100 planes took off in the second wave, and in the meantime Ozawa did not know what damage, if any, had been done by the combined land and carrier planes in their first attack.

Of the 301 American planes, practically all fighters, engaged in the air battles of the 19th, only 17 were shot down. Ozawa reports that his carriers had 400 to 450 planes and estimates that 500 shore-based planes were available, a total of 950 for the battle. Only 545 were sighted by American ships and planes, and of these 402 were shot down. Ozawa confirms the heavy Japanese plane losses. He says that of the 400 planes his carriers launched "very few returned." And on the 20th he had only 60 planes left in the entire carrier fleet, 40 of these on the *Zuikaku.*

Ozawa had ordered his planes to attack carriers in conjunction with the land-based planes in order that the way might be cleared for Kurita's battleships and cruisers to attack the amphibious force and thus prevent the landings in the Marianas. Instead of destroying the carriers, Ozawa's carrier planes and Kakuda's land-based planes had themselves been destroyed by American carrier planes and antiaircraft batteries. And Kurita now did not dare to approach the amphibious force.

Despite the great damage that had been inflicted on them by the combined forces of the American Fleet, the Japanese

SEA POWER AND AMPHIBIOUS WAR 239

did not change their plan; during the night of the 19th they steamed westward and on the 20th began refueling and keeping watch against American submarines, intending to resume the engagement.

After destroying the enemy's planes on the 19th Admiral Spruance headed west at 23 knots, hoping to close the enemy surface ships. On the 20th the morning searches were negative; not until 3.20 P.M. did the scout planes find the enemy. Mitscher informed Spruance that he intended to launch all the planes he had, although a night recovery would probably result. All air groups made contact with the enemy just before sunset; the Japanese ships were in three groups, and their evasive tactics confused an already complicated formation. Ozawa states that only the carrier *Hiyo* was sunk and the carrier *Junyo* and two or three tankers seriously damaged, although American sources indicate that much greater damage was inflicted. At any rate, the interruption in the fueling and the damage were sufficient to cause Toyoda to order Ozawa to abandon the attack; Ozawa headed for Okinawa where he refueled his ships and proceeded to the Inland Sea.

The American planes, many of them short of fuel, returned to their carriers after dark. About 90 planes landed in the water, but 143 of their 185 personnel were rescued. The recovery of planes and crews lasted until 11 P.M., when the pursuit of the enemy was resumed. During the night a long-range flying boat located the Japanese ships. And twice on the morning of the 21st, at about 6 and 7, the enemy was located anew, 340 miles distant. Two task groups, best off for fuel, were sent in pursuit of damaged ships, but the searches had negative results and the groups rejoined Task Force 58. Admiral Spruance then resumed his task of occupying Saipan.

In addition to the loss of carrier pilots and planes in the battle of the Philippine Sea, Ozawa had lost the carriers *Shokaku, Taiho,* and *Hiyo.* The *Junyo* was badly damaged, and four or five other carriers were damaged enough to require repairs in Japan. The loss of the carrier pilots, however, had the most serious effect on future Japanese plans.

Training programs were immediately established to provide replacements, but as will be seen, it was impossible to complete the training before the American offensive struck again.

In the battle of June 19–20 Toyoda had placed his main reliance on land and carrier planes. The practical annihilation of carrier pilots in this battle and the failure of the replacement program to reach completion reduced him to dependence upon land planes alone in the battle of October, and to employing the remnants of his once formidable carrier fleet as bait.

The air and naval engagements of June 19 and 20 demonstrated that American carrier planes, assisted by the improved antiaircraft defenses of the fleet, could protect their own carriers, their surface ships, and the amphibious forces from the combined assault of all the land and carrier planes the Japanese could concentrate in the Marianas. Furthermore, American carrier planes practically annihilated the attacking aircraft in an area where the enemy possessed a number of airfields, and during an amphibious landing where the location of the American task forces was known and the advantage of carrier mobility was lost.

The strategical consequences of the capture of the Marianas were far reaching. Naval and air bases within 1,500 miles of the enemy's home islands were obtained. Spruance's fleet was now within easy striking distance of the Inland Sea. Also, the Army's very long-range bombers obtained a suitable and convenient base from which they could strike at Japanese industry and strategical areas. Enemy factories, land transports, strategic cities, all now felt the weight of air force bombs. The Japanese home islands had been bombed previously from United States Army air bases in China, but these bases had been subject to capture by Japanese ground troops. The new insular bases, on the other hand, could be attacked only by enemy aircraft. The great damage done to Japan by the very long-range bombers would alone have justified the cost of taking Saipan and of the subsequent seizure of Iwo.

SEA POWER AND AMPHIBIOUS WAR

Normandy Invasion, June 6

Practically every shore battle in the Pacific took place in easy range of ship's artillery. In contrast, the landing in Normandy on June 6 was a vast over-Channel invasion of Hitler's fortress Europe, followed by a continental war. The Royal Navy was the preponderant partner in the Anglo-American naval team that supported the landing, but the American contribution alone included 37,000 men for the landing craft, 22,000 in the amphibious bases in England, and 15,000 aboard the combat ships. The heavy guns of the battleships *Arkansas, Texas,* and *Nevada* which fought in English waters in 1917–18, the modern cruisers *Tuscaloosa* and *Quincy,* and many destroyers assisted British battleships, cruisers, and destroyers in blasting the way for the ground troops to enter the European citadel. Before the invasion a projected attack on the amphibious force during its crossing of the Channel, by U-boats that Doenitz had concentrated in German-held Channel ports, was neutralized by an Anglo-American air and naval offensive.

The Normandy landing had many of the features of the amphibious landings in the Pacific, and a few peculiar to itself. The final overwater hop covered a scant 100 miles compared with the vastly greater jumps in the Pacific. Eisenhower's invasion had been preceded by the prolonged air war between the Luftwaffe and the Anglo-American air forces, practically all land based, in which Allied airmen had been given every opportunity to compel the Germans to surrender by air attacks alone. They did not surrender. But the Normandy invasion was possible only when the Allied airmen had enough strength to dominate the skies over the Channel and the beachheads, and then prevent all German attempts to use ground troop reserves to mount a counterattack that would throw the invaders back into the Channel. The airmen thus performed the same service for the Normandy landing that carrier pilots did for the amphibious attacks across the Pacific.

A D-Day feature peculiar to the invasion of Normandy was the construction of small boat shelters and artificial harbors. The first was made by sinking a number of block ships that steamed into line at designated points, blew their bottoms out, and settled into position in 15 feet of water just off the beach, to form a breakwater for the small craft. The artificial harbors, a British conception, were more elaborate. Two were built, one in the British and one in the American sector. The many component parts, secretly constructed in various places in England, were towed to their proper positions by a fleet of tugs directed by Commodore E. J. Moran, U.S.N.R. Hollow concrete caissons, each mounting antiaircraft batteries, were sunk in designated positions to form the "posts" to which were secured various other caissons; together they formed the breakwaters of the artificial harbors. Inside the harbors, floating pierheads were constructed at which large, deep draft ships could dock to discharge heavy equipment, while sunken causeways and roadbeds on pontoons connected pier and beach.

A contingent of American Seabees built these harbors, and all were completed in the remarkably short period from June 7 to June 11. From landing craft and steamers men, munitions, and supplies poured ashore in a steady stream. Munitions and supplies were piled in dumps. The troops would enlarge and connect the bridgeheads.

A severe Channel gale that lasted from the 18th to the 22d damaged the whole construction so severely that the American harbor had to be abandoned altogether; the British was rehabilitated, partly with material salvaged from the American. Before the gale, however, enough men and supplies had been put ashore so that Cherbourg could be taken by the 27th. Thereafter General Eisenhower had at least one good port at his command.

Assuming that until a port could be captured troops and supplies could be landed only on the open beaches, Field Marshal von Rundstedt and his staff underestimated the size of the forces the Allies had put ashore. So they retained the Seventh Army in Normandy and ordered repeated counterattacks to drive the invaders into the sea; and, for fear the landing in Normandy was a diversion, held another army near the Calais-Dunkirk area to resist a possible attack on that region.

SEA POWER AND AMPHIBIOUS WAR 243

Bradley broke through with the First Army at Avranches, Patton exploited the break with the Third Army and soon encircled and rapidly destroyed the German Seventh Army, which was pinned down by the American First and the British Second Army. By August 1 Eisenhower began the advance that caused the German debacle the following spring. As soon as the Allied armies were advancing ashore, the battle for France became a land campaign. And after a division of American battleships had assisted in the capture of Brest the Allied navies resumed their old tasks of maintaining trans-Atlantic sea communications.

In the middle of August American land, sea, and air forces under Vice-Admiral Hewitt landed in southern France. Lieutenant General Patch commanded the land forces and advanced along the valley of the Rhone to join with the right of Patton's army near the Rhine. Admiral Hewitt, veteran commander of the landings in Africa, Sicily, and Italy, had little difficulty in escorting and supporting this last opposed landing in Europe. After Toulon and Marseilles were occupied, late in August, 1944, the naval part in the Mediterranean was limited to forwarding and protecting supplies and giving tactical fire support in the Adriatic and Tyrrhenian Seas to the American Army as it fought its way through one strong fortified position after another from Rome to the Alps.

The unqualified success of Eisenhower's invasion of Normandy drew a tribute from Stalin for its massive conception, its gigantic scale, and masterly execution. But Allied sea power almost simultaneously achieved another massive landing on Saipan. The month of June, 1944, witnessed, in fact, an exhibition of sea power not seen since 1762 when, under plans inspired by the first Pitt, British amphibious forces captured Havana in the Caribbean and Manila in the western Pacific within three months. Eisenhower and Cunningham stormed Hitler's European fortress in the same June week that Admiral Spruance and General Howland Smith broke into Hirohito's inner defenses. The sound of Anglo-American naval guns supporting the landing in Normandy had scarcely died away when the battleships, cruisers, and destroyers of Spruance's Fifth Fleet opened fire on Japanese defenses on Saipan, preparing the way for American soldiers and marines to take the Marianas.

XIII

Reconquest of the Western Pacific

Japanese Preparations for Final Defense of the Philippines and Formosa

JAPAN'S strategical situation continued to deteriorate throughout the summer of 1944, and the loss of the last of the Marianas group by early August meant that the Empire's inner line of defense had been breached. After the defeat of the Japanese Fleet in the air-naval engagement in June Admiral Toyoda faced the same tactical problem that had confronted Admiral Koga in November, 1943: his carrier pilots had been annihilated. In addition the fleet had lost three carriers and the remaining five or six were in need of repairs. In an effort to silence influential critics of the government, Tojo was replaced by Koiso as Premier. And Admiral Nagano, who had been Chief of Naval Staff, was "pushed upstairs" as principal naval adviser to the Emperor, for even the docile and patriotic Japanese citizens had begun to ask, "What is the navy doing?"

Toyoda claimed that he was not influenced by public opinion, but that he and the Imperial General Staff were convinced of the wisdom of the general plan, namely, to risk the fleet for the defense of Formosa and the Philippines. The army, finally realizing that the Empire was imperiled, during the summer transferred the bulk of its combat air force from China to Luzon.

Toyoda gave another reason for the effort to defend the Philippines at all costs: he was convinced that fuel for the fleet could not be obtained from the East Indies unless the Philippines were held, and without fuel the fleet was useless, so he prepared to risk the entire navy to hold the Formosa-Philippines-East Indies line. This was the mental atmosphere in the Japanese High Command as Toyoda de-

RECONQUEST OF THE WEST PACIFIC

ployed the fleet and the navy's land-based air forces to resist a further American advance.

Admirals Toyoda, Ozawa, Kurita, and Fukudome have given many reasons for using their surface navy in a final desperate effort to hold the Philippines. They have omitted the most compelling. After the capture of the Marianas, the annihilation of the carrier planes, and the heavy losses inflicted on army and navy land-based planes, the Japanese Fleet was at the mercy of the United States Navy even when in the Inland Sea itself. Escorted by Lee's battle line, Mitscher and McCain could, and subsequently did, sink Japanese battleships, carriers, and cruisers as easily in port as at sea.

The enemy's tactical plan was substantially the same as that which had failed in the June battle, namely, to depend primarily upon a combination of carrier and land-based planes to destroy or at least to neutralize the American covering fleet, and to employ the battleships, cruisers, and destroyers to follow the hoped-for defeat of the American Fleet with the destruction of the amphibious forces.

To prepare the naval forces to defend the Philippines and Formosa, Toyoda ordered Kurita, with the Second Fleet and a destroyer squadron from Ozawa's Third (Air) Fleet, to the Singapore-Lingga area to rehearse for an attack on the expected American invasion in the Philippines. Naval crews were exercised in the use of star shells, radar fire control, and antiaircraft defense, in preparation for night battles and to attack enemy vessels at anchor. Kurita's fleet would have prepared in the Inland Sea but sufficient fuel was not available there, and American submarines had reduced the number of tankers to such an extent that bunker oil could not be shipped from the East Indies. Ozawa, detained in the Inland Sea to supervise the completion of repairs on the carriers and to train a new group of carrier pilots, hoped the pilots would finish their training in October so that he could join Kurita in the southern area, and thus be poised for a concentrated attack to repel any further American invasion.

American Preparations for Battle and Preliminary Strikes

While Toyoda attempted to prepare for another battle, Admiral Spruance occupied Guam and Tinian, and on August 26 turned over the ships of the Fifth Fleet to Halsey and returned to Pearl Harbor with his staff to prepare for the seizure of Iwo Jima and Okinawa.

Halsey had relinquished command of the south Pacific to Newton on June 15, and while Spruance occupied the Marianas, Halsey and his staff in Pearl Harbor were preparing plans to support the invasion of the western Carolines. When Spruance returned to Pearl Harbor the task forces of his fleet reported to Admiral Halsey and became the Third Fleet. Thereafter the two admirals alternated in command of the bulk of American naval forces in the Pacific. While one carried out one campaign, the other prepared the plan for the next. Both admirals were under the operational control of Admiral Nimitz, who directed naval operations in the Pacific in accordance with the strategic directives of the Joint Chiefs of Staff.

By using the terms Third and Fifth Fleets, Nimitz possibly confused the enemy's intelligence personnel into visualizing two fleets. The two fleets were composed of the same ships, but Nimitz, by pushing the Mobile Base Force up to the combat zone, made it possible for the ships to fight almost continuously, and to the enemy it may have seemed as if one fleet were resting while the other fought. Only very badly damaged ships were withdrawn as far as Pearl Harbor. Practically continuous sea and combat service placed a severe physical strain on American personnel, but it kept an unremitting pressure on the Japanese Navy, and placed a greater strain on the enemy, thus hastening the end of the war.

Admiral Nimitz and General MacArthur were already on the move. In late July and August the general had occupied the western extremity of New Guinea. In September, under cover of air strikes by Admiral Halsey that ranged from Iwo Jima in the north to Mindanao and the western Carolines in the south, forces from the central Pacific success-

RECONQUEST OF THE WEST PACIFIC 247

fully invaded Peleliu and Angaur, thus gaining control of the Palau Islands, and occupied Ulithi Atoll practically without opposition. In the middle of September MacArthur seized Morotai Island, isolating large Japanese garrisons in the Halmahera Islands. Local Allied air and naval forces blockaded a steadily growing number of by-passed ground troops and harassed them with systematic air strikes.

The technique of American amphibious forces was constantly improving. The capture of Peleliu took place just ten months after Tarawa, with physical conditions that made attack even more difficult. The outlying reef was a greater obstacle, the terrain ashore more favorable for defense, the Japanese garrison larger, the shore fortifications more skillfully sited, of greater strength, and employing such modern devices as land mines and booby traps. Yet Peleliu was taken with less loss of life than Tarawa.

A contributory cause of the American successes during August, September, and early October was the preoccupation of the Imperial Staff with preparations for the defense of Formosa and the Philippines. The entire combat navy and the bulk of the army's air force were being trained or deployed for the expected American attack upon one of these areas. Other factors had also contributed to the success of the amphibious operations, one of the most important undoubtedly being the system of command. An admiral commanded an amphibious force while the troops were embarked, during the landing, and until they were firmly established in their immediate and principal objectives along the shore. When the commander of ground troops, a marine or army general, believed he could maintain his position ashore, the command of troops passed to him.

No American landing in World War II was repulsed, but if that had occurred, the responsibility of evacuating the troops would have belonged to the naval commander, and he would have retained or resumed command. This rule, which in application proved a practical one, kept officers of "paramount capability" in command at each stage of the operations—admirals at sea, and generals—marine or army—ashore. There was not permanent "unity of command," as is sometimes believed. Throughout the Pacific campaigns the command in amphibious operations passed back and forth to that branch of the service most competent to command. Nimitz was in operational control of the central Pacific and MacArthur in the southwest Pacific, but admirals never exercised tactical command over soldiers ashore nor generals over sailors afloat.

The occupation of the western Caroline and Morotai Islands not only isolated large Japanese garrisons but gave the American forces additional naval and air bases. Ulithi enclosed a spacious and secure anchorage with several easy entrances. And Mobile Base Squadron Ten was speedily advanced to this point so that Ulithi became a supply and repair base for the fleet. In the new conquests, airfields were soon in operation, from which land-based planes could strike at the Philippines. Above all, however, the massive air blows of Halsey's Third Fleet dominated the campaign for the Philippines, just as the fast carriers of Spruance's Fifth Fleet had been the deciding factor in the fate of the Marianas.

After supporting the landings in the western Carolines, Halsey began air strikes at Mindanao and the Visayan Islands in the central Philippines in the first part of September. During the attacks on Leyte and Samar, September 11 to 13, little air opposition was encountered and few airfields noted. An American naval flier forced down near Leyte ascertained from friendly natives that enemy garrisons in the island were negligible, whereupon Halsey recommended, MacArthur agreed to, and the Joint Chiefs of Staff approved a plan to abandon the proposed capture of Yap and put forward the date of MacArthur's advance on Leyte.

After attacking Mindanao Halsey made the first air strikes on Luzon, in the Manila area, on September 20–21. He destroyed 150 ships, exclusive of small sailing craft in the Bay, and then smashed practically all enemy planes available at the time on Luzon, an estimated total of 900. More important, he demonstrated that it was possible to keep the carrier force within easy striking distance of the widespread net of 100 Japanese airfields that dotted Luzon

RECONQUEST OF THE WEST PACIFIC 249

like a checkerboard. On September 24 he launched a strike against Coron Bay, a fine harbor in the Culion Islands southwest of Manila, and followed it by a final blow at the Visayan Islands, including Leyte, before returning to base for refueling preparatory to striking at Okinawa and Formosa.

The heavy losses Halsey inflicted on enemy planes and shipping reduced the ability of the enemy to continue the war, but the primary task given Halsey by Nimitz in the operation orders for September was to "utilize every opportunity which might be presented or created to destroy major portions of the enemy fleet." This directive accords with American naval tradition and strategic theory, that the enemy fleet is the primary objective. The reason is plain. When the enemy fleet and carrier planes are destroyed, control of the sea and the air over strategic areas is assured, and other objectives can be secured with little difficulty. In the October operations Halsey's directive included the following: "In case opportunity for destruction of major portions of the enemy fleet offers or can be created, such destruction becomes the primary task [of all Pacific Ocean Area forces]." The operations of Halsey beginning October 10 and continuing through the month will be easier to follow if his directive is remembered.

Naval history shows that an attempt to land an army on a hostile shore frequently brings on a fleet engagement. The weaker fleet is encouraged to take risks influenced by fear of the consequences of a successful enemy invasion and also by the hope of gaining a tactical advantage while the hostile fleet is handicapped by protecting its amphibious forces.

Attack on Formosa, October 12–16

The date for landing on Leyte had been advanced two months, from December 20 to October 20. Halsey, after giving his personnel a brief rest and filling his ships with fuel and ammunition, struck Okinawa on October 10, and then steamed down to hit Formosa on the 12th. All four air task groups participated.

While American forces were occupying the western Carolines and making air strikes on Formosa and the Philippines, Kurita continued exercising the Second Fleet and Ozawa training his carrier pilots in the Inland Sea. At Toyoda's headquarters in Tokyo there was none of the optimism that had prevailed prior to the battle in June. Captain Omae, Chief of Staff for Admiral Ozawa, explaining the Japanese plan, stated that if the "navy did nothing the Philippines would be lost, so we did our best." Toyoda called the decision to attack "a gamble." The gloom deepened when Halsey attacked Formosa from October 12 to 16. One Japanese naval aviator said the battle of the Philippines was won by Halsey in his air strikes over Formosa. When asked his opinion of this statement, Ozawa said it "was a little strong," but agreed that the weakness of Japanese air forces was the decisive factor.

In September Admiral Fukudome, Commander of the Second Air Fleet, had established his headquarters in Formosa, brought in a large part of his air force, and been given command of all army planes on the island, about 200. Formosa and the adjoining Pescadores Islands had 28 widely dispersed and well-equipped airfields; the antiaircraft batteries were strong and well manned. It was estimated that there were 700 planes on Formosa and the Pescadores and their proximity to Japan insured a steady flow of replacements. In spite of the destruction of planes by earlier American attacks, Fukudome admits having 600 planes when he launched counterattacks on the nights of October 15 and 16.

Halsey had four task groups in Task Force 38, commanded by Mitscher, who had commanded the carrier task force for Spruance in the June battle. The task groups were designated 38.1, 38.2, 38.3, and 38.4. In addition to 9 large and 8 small carriers, a covering force of five fast battleships, 14 cruisers, and 58 destroyers was present under Admiral Lee. Halsey was aboard the battleship *New Jersey,* Mitscher, the *Lexington,* and this formidable team, which had worked over Okinawa on October 10, struck Formosa on the 12th. Although Fukudome expected the attack, the first wave of fighters took off from the 17 carriers unopposed, but met

RECONQUEST OF THE WEST PACIFIC 251

strong resistance as they neared their targets. During succeeding strikes enemy opposition weakened.

Fukudome used the largest part of his force in day counterattacks. He admits the results were disappointing. But he thought the attacks made just after dusk by 300 planes from Kyushu, landing on Formosa after the assault, were considerably better. It was these after-dusk attacks that furnished the slim basis for the greatly exaggerated claims made public in Japan that Halsey's fleet had been destroyed. And these night attacks were formidable. Against any other carrier force they might well have been disastrous, but they barely penetrated the American defenses.

On the 13th the cruiser *Canberra* was torpedoed and on the 14th the *Houston*. When the question arose on the 13th whether to sink the *Canberra* or tow her out, Halsey decided to tow in the hope that the enemy surface fleet might attempt to intervene and thus "create an opportunity to destroy a portion of the fleet." The tone of Japanese broadcasts indicated that Tokyo had overestimated the damage inflicted by their planes, which may have assisted Halsey's ruse. In any event the Japanese Fifth Fleet, recently recalled from the Kuriles, Vice-Admiral Shima commanding, was despatched to destroy the "remnants" of Halsey's fleet on the night of the 14th. Commander K. Mori of Shima's staff admits that when they found that Halsey's force was "very strong" they retreated hastily to Amami-o-Shima.[1]

Admiral Fukudome had made an all-out effort to destroy Task Force 38 by air attacks. Admiral Toyoda had assisted by sending 150 carrier planes and pilots from Ozawa's fleet to aid the land planes on Formosa, repeating the mistake made by Koga in November, 1943. They could not change the decision over Formosa and the loss of the carrier pilots had an important influence on the approaching naval engagement.

Between October 12 and 16 Task Force 38 had engaged nearly 1,000 air-borne enemy aircraft. Except for the air

1. Soon afterward the Japanese Fifth Fleet was to be ordered to join Kurita's Second Fleet and assist in attacking Kinkaid's amphibious forces in Leyte Gulf.

action on June 19, this was the heaviest series of air attacks yet launched against American naval forces. As Halsey slowly withdrew, towing two crippled cruisers, the over-all score was the destruction of 600 enemy planes and 26 ships, most of them small, and a substantial reduction of the air facilities on Formosa, at a cost of 90 American planes and 64 aviation personnel.

Admiral Ozawa had made an oral report to Admiral Toyoda after the battle of June 19–20, but states he was not consulted about the plan to defend the Philippines. Undoubtedly Toyoda and his staff made the decision, and apparently without much consultation with Admirals Kurita and Ozawa, who were to be responsible for carrying it out. Kurita testifies that he "received orders and directives" from Admiral Toyoda. After leaving the Inland Sea, in July, Kurita did not see Ozawa, but Ozawa's staff went to Lingga and conferred with Kurita's staff in the middle of August.

The original plan contemplated that Ozawa would proceed with the carrier force to the southern area as soon as the training of his pilots was completed, take command of both forces and make a concentrated attack on the American forces when invasion occurred. When Toyoda sent carrier planes to Formosa without consulting Ozawa, the latter thought Toyoda "had sacrificed the carriers to reënforce Formosa." It was evident that the training of the new carrier pilots could not be completed in time for Ozawa's forces to join Kurita before the expected invasion. Ozawa therefore asked Toyoda to take Kurita's force directly under his command, to which Toyoda agreed.

Pre-Invasion Strikes against the Philippines

After his attacks on Formosa Halsey stood south. Opportunity was taken to refuel and replenish his carrier groups, and on October 17 he took up the attacks on the Philippines where he had left off in September, this time coördinating his strikes with the landing operations themselves. Particular attention was given the Visayan group, especially Leyte and Samar, where the landings were made. By October 19 little enemy air resistance was encountered, and when

RECONQUEST OF THE WEST PACIFIC 253

the landings took place in the area of Leyte on the 20th, enemy air opposition was negligible. American strikes against enemy shipping were very destructive to tankers and other fleet auxiliaries, particularly in the Manila area.

Landings on Leyte

General MacArthur was in operational command of the landings on Leyte. Lieutenant General Krueger commanded the ground troops comprising the Sixth Army. Vice-Admiral Kinkaid commanded the naval operations, and had been ordered to "transport, protect, land, and support elements of the Sixth Army in order to assist in the seizure, occupation, and development of the Leyte area." Under Kinkaid, Rear Admiral Barbey commanded the northern attack group and Vice-Admiral Wilkinson the southern attack group. Admiral Halsey, who as we have seen, had been operating since September to soften the defenses of the Philippines and isolate the airfields, continued to pound enemy airfields and to prevent air or surface interference with the landing operations. Kinkaid's Seventh Fleet had been reënforced by Nimitz until its combat ships alone totaled 6 older battleships, 11 cruisers, 18 escort carriers, 86 destroyers, and 25 destroyer escorts, and had ample strength to give direct support to Krueger's landing.

The amphibious forces assembled in the Admiralty Islands and Hollandia, New Guinea, were escorted and landed October 17–18 by Kinkaid on the Dinagat, Suluan, and Homonhon Islands that command the approaches to Leyte Gulf. Mine-sweeping and underwater demolition parties began operations on the 17th and surface bombardments of Leyte Island took place on the 18th.

The Imperial Staff had expected an attack at about this time, but army members had believed Mindanao would be the landing place. Toyoda heard' of the Leyte landing on the 17th. Proceeding on his decision to defend the Philippines at all costs, he ordered Admiral Kurita to move up with the Second Fleet from Singapore to attack the American forces according to their plan, and Admiral Shima with the Fifth Fleet from the Pescadores, Formosa, to reënforce Kurita.

Ozawa's Third (Air) Fleet was without trained pilots, but Toyoda decided to resist the invasion with every ship at his disposal and made a quick decision to use Ozawa's fleet as a "lure." According to Captain Omae, Toyoda's decision was made "on the spur of the moment," when news of the landing was received and he, was finally forced to face the fact that carrier pilots could not be provided for all the carriers. Ozawa received his instructions over the telephone. He stated afterward that he had no confidence in the plan of "being used as a lure," but accepted the orders to sacrifice his fleet in an effort to assist Kurita in an all-out attack on the American landing force.

Toyoda was employing the entire surface fleet to attack the transports. The more difficult tasks of neutralizing or destroying Halsey's Fifth Fleet that was covering the landing was given to Admiral Fukudome, who commanded the Second Air Fleet and the remnants of the First Air Fleet. And, despite continuous attacks by Task Force 38 on Fukudome's air forces and on Formosa and Luzon, Fukudome flew into Manila on October 22, and on the 23d some 450 planes from Formosa landed on the adjacent airfields. They attempted to attack Halsey's carriers en route, but were prevented by bad weather. Planes from the First and Second Air Fleets struck at Halsey's carriers on the 24th, 25th, and 26th, as will be seen, while about 200 army planes on Luzon, commanded by General Tominaga, attacked Krueger's army in direct support of General Yamashita's ground troops.

By October 22 the Japanese naval and air forces were either on station or en route to make a last ditch defense of the Philippines. Toyoda commanded the sea and naval air forces from his headquarters in Japan, and General Yamashita commanded the army ground and air forces and was forwarding ground and air reënforcements to Leyte. According to Omae, Toyoda only "gave orders to attack and return." But Toyoda did intervene at least once very decisively, as will be related. Krueger's army was ashore in five places on Leyte by the 22d; his advance had met little opposition except from the Japanese Army air attacks.

Summary of the Battle for Leyte Gulf

The opposing naval forces were poised for three separate naval actions which took place almost simultaneously and have been designated collectively as the battle for Leyte Gulf. But the battle for the Philippines had been in progress since Halsey's air strikes in September, and to get the full picture of the triphibious operations that culminated on October 25, the whole battle panorama must be borne in mind.

While the ground action proceeded, the three naval engagements were getting underway: the battle of Surigao Strait, the battle off Samar, and the battle off Cape Engaño. It is not a coincidence that all three actions reached their height on the 25th, for as will be seen it was Toyoda's plan that the three Japanese forces would coördinate in a "devastating attack" on the Americans on that day.

The three separate, simultaneous engagements will be summarized to show the courses followed by the Japanese forces involved, after which the more important activities of all the forces on each succeeding day will be described.

Admiral Nishimura with a detachment of the Second Fleet, followed by Admiral Shima with a small force known as the Fifth Fleet, comprised what will be referred to as the Southern Group. They steamed from the Sulu Sea into Surigao Strait, and there fought and were almost annihilated in the battle of Surigao Strait.

Admiral Kurita's heavy combat force, headed by five battleships, comprised the Second Fleet. They are designated as the Central Group because, coming up from the south, they assumed a central position, steamed through the Sibuyan Sea into San Bernardino Strait, being heavily attacked meanwhile. Proceeding through the Strait, they moved southward off the east coast of Samar, where the battle was fought. Kurita's heavy units eventually retired with American planes in pursuit, although not before they had battered the lightly armed escort carriers and destroyers which had been giving direct support to the Leyte landings.

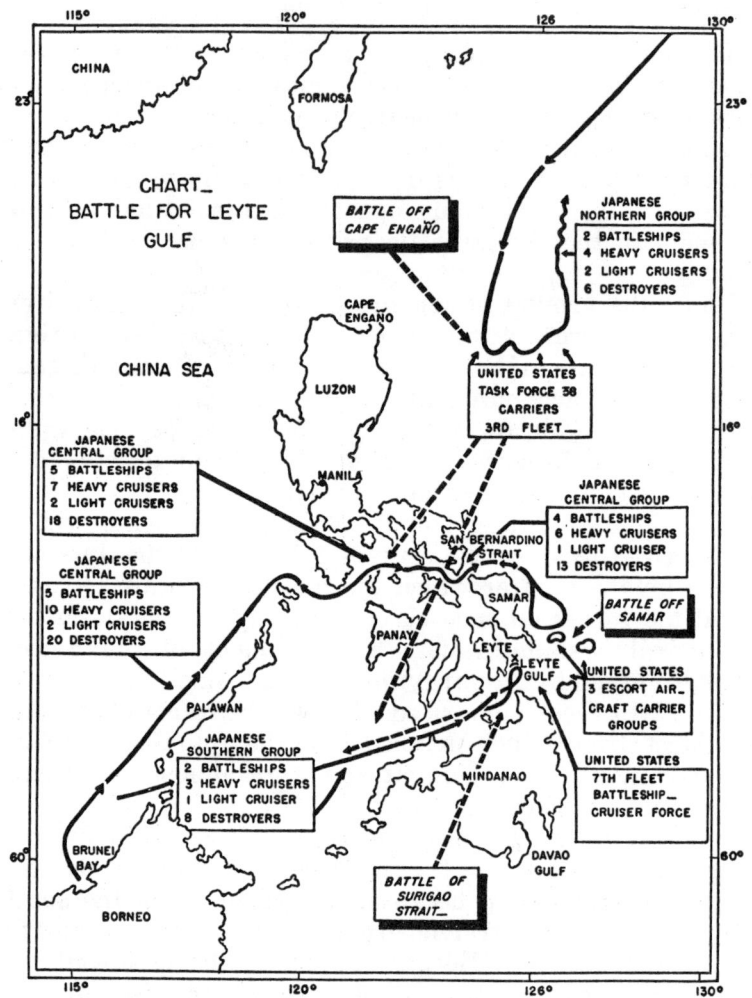

THE BATTLE FOR LEYTE GULF

RECONQUEST OF THE WEST PACIFIC

Ozawa's Third Fleet, called the Northern Group, moved down from Japan proper, was sighted as it approached Luzon from Formosa, and was then met and decisively defeated by one of Halsey's task groups, under Vice-Admiral Mitscher off the northeastern tip of Luzon. This was the battle off Cape Engaño, so named for the nearest point of land.

Events of October 20

Admiral Ozawa's carrier fleet, whose mission was the last to be determined, left for the battle first, departing from the Inland Sea on October 20, with four carriers, the *Zuikaku,* the *Chitose,* the *Chiyoda,* and the *Zuiho,* and two hybrid battleship-carriers, *Hyuga* and the *Ise,* each with flight decks aft and 14-inch guns forward. These were all that were available of the once-powerful Air Arm of the Imperial Navy. The carriers had only about 90 poorly trained pilots, the battleship-carriers none. With them went two light cruisers and six destroyers, and their mission, as we have seen, was to "be a lure, a sacrifice to assist Kurita in a final gamble," not to defeat the American Fleet but simply to attack the landing force which, if it had been defeated, could have been replaced in a comparatively short time. The desperate condition of Japan is revealed in the fantastic plans its navy made for this attack.

Events of October 22

On October 22 the Japanese admirals and captains of Kurita's Second Fleet had a last conference and drank a few toasts to the Emperor in Brunei Bay, North Borneo. At 10 A.M. Kurita got under way for Leyte Gulf via Sibuyan Sea and San Bernardino Strait, with the bulk of the Second Fleet: 5 battleships, including the *Yamato* and the *Musashi,* pride of the Japanese Navy, carrying the only 18-inch guns afloat, 10 heavy cruisers, 2 light cruisers, and 14 destroyers. At 3 P.M. Admiral Nishimura left with the remainder of the Second Fleet, the battleships *Yamashiro* and *Fuso,* the heavy cruiser *Mogami,* and three destroyers. He would be joined en route by Admiral Shima with the Fifth Fleet, who had arrived from Formosa at Coron Bay for refueling. Nishimura and Shima had been ordered by Toyoda to open the attack on the American amphibious forces in Leyte Gulf at 6.30 A.M. on October 25; Kurita's larger force would follow two hours later in an annihilating attack on the American transports. For this particular task Kurita had been rehearsing the Second Fleet since July 22. In view of their decisive defeat it would be easy to underestimate the potential menace of the Japanese forces.

Events of October 23

On Luzon Fukudome, without consulting Admiral Toyoda, authorized Onishi to use the few remaining pilots of the First Air Fleet to initiate the "Kamikaze" attacks on the 23d, in a desperate effort to clear the seas for Kurita's advance. This was the first organized Kamikaze attack.

On Leyte Krueger was making satisfactory progress ashore, while Kinkaid gave direct artillery and air support with his massive force of battleships, cruisers, escort carriers, and destroyers. The local airfields had not been captured, and the reaction of the enemy's army planes was vigorous.

Admiral Kinkaid had deployed submarines of the Seventh Fleet in various strategic positions to obtain information of the movements of Japanese forces, and to attack as opportunity presented. Just as in the June campaign for Saipan, American submarines struck the first blow at the enemy surface fleet. The *Darter* sighted Kurita's force (the Central Group) in Palawan Passage at 2 A.M. on the 23d, and between 6 and 7 A.M., with the *Dace,* delivered a combined attack that sank two heavy cruisers, the *Atago,* Kurita's flagship, and the *Maya,* and disabled still another, the *Takao.*

Kurita's material loss was three heavy cruisers and the use of a destroyer which escorted the disabled *Takao* back to Brunei. Furthermore, one half of Kurita's communication staff went down on the *Atago.* And when Kurita and the remainder of his staff shifted to the battleship *Yamato,* he had difficulty controlling his fleet and maintaining radio contact with Toyoda, Ozawa, and Fukudome. Captain Omae testifies that Kurita did not receive three important messages from Ozawa, and attributes the failure of Kurita's attack on the 25th to defective communications.[2] Kinkaid's submarines, *Dace* and *Darter,* like Lockwood's *Albacore* and *Cavalla* in the battle of the Philippine Sea, sank the enemy flagship at the opening of the campaign, discommoding the admiral and his staff and contributing largely to the American victory.

Events of October 24

The loss of three heavy cruisers before he was fairly on his way to Leyte Gulf, and the necessity of shifting to the *Yamato,* could not have encouraged Kurita. Re-forming his fleet, he continued, and by forenoon of the 24th the Central Group was in the Sibuyan Sea steaming for San Bernardino Strait. The Southern Group, Nishimura leading, was in the Sulu Sea, heading for Surigao Strait; Shima was astern of Nishimura, ready to follow up the attack. Ozawa (Northern Group) was off the northeast coast of Luzon, heading south. In the forenoon he launched about 80 planes, all he had except a small fighter patrol, and en route to landing fields in Luzon they attacked Halsey's northernmost task group (38.3).

As Kurita steamed through the Sibuyan Sea, Admiral Fukudome used planes of the Second Air Fleet on Luzon in heavy attacks on Halsey's carrier forces. But in spite of these Halsey's carriers made six organized air strikes against Kurita's group. Kurita reports that the pilots concentrated on the battleships and that his cruisers and destroyers, therefore, suffered less. His flagship, the *Yamato,* was hit three times by bombs and her speed reduced. All other battleships were hit but were able to continue in formation, except the *Musashi,* which received 21 torpedo hits and 40 bombs, and sank while being escorted to Manila. After receiving several bomb hits the heavy cruiser *Myoko* left the formation, accompanied by one destroyer.

2. Captain Omae, a well-trained staff officer, obviously possessed a highly developed critical instinct. While he is well informed and generally frank, these judgments seem oversimplified.

About 4 P.M. Kurita turned west and, according to his statement, reported to Toyoda that he was retiring temporarily to evade air attacks and would return to the action later. In his statement concerning the incident Toyoda did not mention a message from Kurita, simply testifying that when Kurita started to turn back he sent him an order of this general tenor: "Advance, counting on divine assistance." Commander Otani, operations officer on Kurita's staff, was positive that Toyoda's message to advance was received before he knew of Kurita's temporary retirement. In any event, the message was sent, received, and executed. Toyoda afterward testified that he intended Kurita to "advance even though the fleet be completely lost." On June 20, when Ozawa had been preparing to renew the attack on Spruance's force off Saipan, Toyoda had intervened to order the fleet to break off the engagement. On this occasion he was convinced that if the Philippines were lost, fuel could not be obtained and the fleet would be useless without it; therefore it was foolish to save the fleet at the expense of the Philippines.

Halsey's Task Group 38.3 was about 150 miles east of Manila. It was located by Fukudome's planes about dawn on the 24th, and before it could launch its major strikes had to beat off three heavy attacks from Luzon and from some of the 80 carrier planes that Ozawa was sending ashore. The presence of carrier-type planes caused Admiral Halsey to order Rear Admiral Sherman, group commander, to launch a search northeastward. This Sherman did as soon as he had beaten off the Japanese planes.[3] At about 5 P.M. Ozawa's force, variously estimated at a total of 17 to 24 ships, including battleships, carriers, cruisers, and destroyers, was sighted and reported to Halsey.

While Kurita was proceeding toward San Bernardino Strait, Nishimura was steaming for Surigao Strait, and for some reason had increased speed so that he would arrive in Leyte Gulf before dawn, ahead of schedule. On the 24th Nishimura's force was struck only once by a "search-strike"

---

3. Admiral Sherman had destroyed Ozawa's carrier planes off Rabaul and disabled Kurita's cruisers in Rabaul Harbor in November, 1943.

plane group from Halsey's forces. The battleship *Fuso* and a destroyer were damaged, but the force was otherwise unhurt. As Nishimura increased speed, Shima's fleet, after leaving Coron Bay, also increased speed in order to arrive at Surigao Strait an hour earlier than planned. His fleet was not attacked during the 24th as he passed through the Sulu Sea.

In the early afternoon of the 24th both Kinkaid and Halsey knew the approximate position and strength of Kurita's and Nishimura's forces which were heading for San Bernardino and Surigao Straits, respectively, and apparently attempting to converge on Leyte Gulf. Kinkaid assumed from a message from Halsey to Nimitz that Halsey would leave a task force of fast battleships to oppose Kurita if he came around from San Bernardino Strait, although, as we shall see, Halsey did not do so. On this assumption, however, Kinkaid concentrated his forces to intercept and defeat Nishimura's force coming through Surigao Strait.

In the late afternoon both Halsey and Kinkaid learned of the approach of Ozawa's force from the north. For the first time both had a complete picture of Ozawa's, Kurita's, and Nishimura's forces. The last two were near enough to reach Leyte Gulf with their surface ships, and any planes on Ozawa's carriers could strike simultaneously at dawn. Neither Halsey nor Kinkaid knew that Ozawa's carriers were without planes, simply phantom ships.

Halsey knew Kinkaid had ample force to beat off any attack from Nishimura's southern force. He knew that in spite of heavy air strikes Kurita with the Central Group could debouch from San Bernardino Strait and attack the ships in Leyte Gulf. But he thought Kurita's force had been too heavily damaged to win a decision, while the northern carrier force was a fresh and powerful threat.

Halsey could divide the Third Fleet, taking the carriers to attack Ozawa's fresh force coming down from the north, and leaving the battleships to attack Kurita if he continued through the Strait, but exposed to a combined land-based air and surface ship attack. This course he rejected, for it imperiled the whole battle line.

Or he could keep his fleet concentrated, await the exit of Kurita's fleet from San Bernardino, and annihilate it. But this would leave the carrier fleet free to launch air strikes at Kinkaid's Seventh Fleet and the amphibious force still in Leyte Gulf. It must be remembered that Halsey did not know that what planes Ozawa's fleet possessed had already flown ashore. In view of the information he had he decided to proceed with all his forces to attack Ozawa in order to prevent Ozawa's planes from striking at either Kinkaid's forces or his own fleet, as well as to create for himself a chance to destroy a major portion of the Japanese Fleet. This has been described as the most important American decision during the battle.

In the early evening of the 24th Kinkaid received an information copy of Halsey's radio orders to the Third Fleet. Kinkaid had committed the combat units of the Seventh Fleet under Admiral Oldendorf to the defense of Surigao Strait, but still assuming Halsey had left a force of battleships to block the exit of the Japanese from San Bernardino Strait, he did not change the disposition of his escort carriers giving direct air support to Krueger's ground troops on Leyte.

In the afternoon Oldendorf disposed his forces as follows: the battle line *West Virginia, Maryland, Mississippi, Tennessee, California,* and *Pennsylvania* maintained position across the entrance to Leyte Gulf from Surigao Strait; down the Strait about 14,000 yards were the cruisers and destroyers in two groups, one on each side of the Strait. The destroyers patrolled across the Strait. Still farther down were 39 motor torpedo boats acting as pickets.

Events of October 25

Nishimura steamed doggedly into this fatal trap, followed by Shima in the Fifth Fleet. Only one destroyer of Nishimura's force, the *Shigure,* survived the combined torpedo and gun attack of Oldendorf's force. Shima, with equal resolution, followed until 5 A.M. of the 25th, when he withdrew. On the 25th surviving ships of the Fifth Fleet were attacked by aircraft but sustained little additional damage.

Admiral Shima reached Coron Bay with his flagship, the *Nachi,* and the *Ashigara,* both damaged, and two destroyers; he had lost one third of his cruisers and half his destroyers.

Just as the remnants of Nishimura's and Shima's forces abandoned their effort to reach Kinkaid's transports in Leyte Gulf, Halsey's carrier planes made their first strike on Ozawa's carriers off Cape Engaño, Luzon. The Third Fleet had steamed full speed during the night to reach a position to launch the attack on the enemy carriers at dawn on the 25th. Ozawa testifies that the first and second air attacks were the heaviest; he transferred to the cruiser *Oyodo* after the first attack. Four carriers, including the flagship *Zuikaku,* were eventually sunk.

While the first air strikes on Ozawa were being made Halsey began receiving requests for assistance from Kinkaid, who, as will be related, was under attack by Kurita's still-powerful Second Fleet. Just before 9 A.M. Halsey ordered Task Group 38.1 which was refueling east of San Bernardino, to proceed at best speed toward the Straits. About 11 A.M. Halsey, having sunk or routed Ozawa's carrier force so its planes could not attack Kinkaid's transports, sent Rear Admiral Du Bose with a force of cruisers and destroyers to pursue the fleeing enemy, and himself proceeded toward San Bernardino with Task Force 34 (fast battleships) and Task Group 38.2 (Carriers), at full speed.

As a result of Halsey's concentrating upon Ozawa and Kinkaid upon Nishimura, only Kinkaid's escort carriers and a few destroyers stood between Kurita and Leyte Gulf as this heavy force steamed through San Bernardino Strait at midnight, the 24th–25th, and moved down the east coast of Samar Island. But in judging Kurita's actions during the battle that followed it should be remembered that he had received no information from Ozawa, did not know the disposition of the American forces, and the heavy air attacks he had suffered on the 24th were ample reason for expecting equally severe ones on the next day.

About 7 A.M. Kurita opened fire on the American escort carriers and made the first of three ineffectual destroyer attacks. He was promptly counterattacked by American carrier planes and destroyers through a smoke screen which he and his Chief of Staff testify was very effective. Occasional rain squalls further obscured the scene, so that Kurita and his staff caught only blurred glimpses of the American ships. Kurita also states that his battleships could not overhaul the American carriers because of the necessity of using evasive tactics to avoid American plane and destroyer attacks.

Kurita's heavy force presented an undenied menace. American commanders noted, however, that the Japanese destroyer captains did not show their previous skill and daring, which was not surprising, for at this stage of the war almost half the enemy's total of 180 destroyers had been sunk. Nor was the enemy's gunfire very effective, for only three American escort carriers were damaged by gunfire, the *Fanshaw Bay*, the *Kalinin Bay*, and the *Gambier Bay*. The latter lost speed and was sunk by point-blank fire of two or three heavy cruisers. Three destroyers, the *Hoel*, the *Johnston*, and the *S. B. Roberts*, were sunk by enemy gunfire but only after pushing home their torpedo attacks through the smoke screen.

About 9 A.M., when the American situation appeared critical, the Japanese suddenly began to withdraw. Kurita, in testifying, explained his withdrawal. During the air and torpedo attacks, the heavy cruisers *Kumano*, *Suzuya*, *Chokai*, and *Chikuma* were all damaged severely, and he thought the lull in the air attacks which came about 8.30 presaged a larger air attack to follow. His fleet formation was ragged due to ships pursuing the carriers at different speeds and using evasive tactics to avoid air and torpedo attacks. So at 9 he decided to re-form his force into an antiaircraft formation. After the fleet was in the new formation, Kurita spent two or three hours assessing the damage to his ships and then decided that "under the heavy air attack" that he anticipated, if he entered Leyte Gulf, his force "would not be effective." So, after a staff conference he decided to "go north and join Admiral Ozawa." The decision to "join Admiral Ozawa" was soon abandoned for he frankly admitted he "wanted to be at San Bernardino Strait at sunset to get as far west as possible during the night."

Captain Omae explains that three messages sent by Ozawa were not received by either Toyoda or Kurita, and as we have said he attributes the "lack of success of the entire operation" to the failure of communications. This is plainly an excuse, for Omae previously stated that in Tokyo when Toyoda made the plan to defend the Philippines it was recognized that it offered little hope of success and Toyoda himself called it a "gamble."

The escort carriers and destroyers saved themselves and the transports by very effective air and destroyer attacks on Kurita's already weakened force. Kurita reported that the air attacks, though small in number, were "very aggressive and skillful, and the coördination [of fighters and bombers] very impressive."

Retirement of Remnants of the Japanese Fleet

During Kurita's retreat through the Sibuyan Sea on the 26th his ships were attacked by American planes and the light cruiser *Noshiro* was destroyed. The remainder, the only surviving remnants of the Second Fleet, returned to Brunei, refueled, and shortly afterward proceeded to the Inland Sea where they joined with the fragments of Ozawa's fleet late in November.

Toyoda did not criticize Kurita's retirement. Omae said Kurita "should have been braver and gone on to Leyte." Unquestionably he might have inflicted severe losses on Kinkaid's ships in Leyte Gulf. But he could not have interrupted the landing. Krueger was already ashore. Other supply ships and transports could have been forwarded from Ulithi or Morotai. Kurita barely escaped Halsey's hot pursuit by his rapid retreat. He could not have lingered east of San Bernardino Strait and escaped total destruction. It would not have been a bad exchange for the Americans, to lose some half empty transports, supply ships, and perhaps a few escort carriers from which most of the personnel could have been rescued, in order to destroy Kurita's four battleships and three or four heavy cruisers, whose survivors would have drowned.

Toyoda's loose reasoning had led him to attach undue importance to the occupation of the Philippines. A few bases in the central Philippines assisted ships and planes in cutting off fuel supplies from the East Indies, but the carrier

DESTRUCTION OF JAPANESE FLEET IN BATTLE FOR LEYTE GULF, OCTOBER 23–26, 1944

COMPOSITION

FLEETS ENGAGED	Battle-ships	Car-riers	Heavy Cruisers	Light Cruisers	De-stroyers
Second Fleet—Admiral Kurita	5	—	10	2	20
Second Fleet—Admiral Nishimura (Detachment of Kurita's fleet)	2	—	1	—	4
Fifth Fleet—Admiral Shima	—	—	2	1	4
Third Fleet—Admiral Ozawa	2	4	—	2	6
TOTALS	9	4	13	5	34
SHIPS LOST—OCTOBER 23d to 26th	3	4	6	2	8
SHIPS REMAINING (Many damaged)	6	0	7	3	26
DISPOSITION OF REMAINING SHIPS					
To Japan (Ozawa)	2	—	—	1	5
To Philippines (Shima)*	—	—	2	1	4
To Philippines and Borneo (Kurita)*	4	—	5	1	17

* Most of these returned to the Inland Sea in November.

RECONQUEST OF THE WEST PACIFIC

planes, surface ships, and submarines were already denying fuel to the Japanese Fleet. Ground troops in the Philippines could not stop a single tanker proceeding from Borneo to Japan. And if after taking Leyte and Mindoro the Philippines had been by-passed, as positions in north and south Bougainville had been in 1943, Japan's fuel supply would still have been cut by American submarines and carrier planes.

The landing on Leyte nerved Admiral Toyoda to risk the fleet in one decisive engagement. Preceding and during the battles of Surigao Strait, Cape Engaño, and Samar, the entire Japanese Fleet that Toyoda had been able to assemble was decisively defeated and its remnants dispersed. After October 26 the Combined Fleet ceased to exist as an organized command.

Fate of Remnants of Japanese Fleet

It is convenient to anticipate the final fate of the battleships, carriers, and heavy cruisers that remained as remnants of the homogeneous, balanced, and well-trained Imperial Fleet that had overrun the western (and threatened the central) Pacific in the three winter months of 1941–42. Of six remaining battleships, the *Ise* and the *Hyuga* reached home ports uninjured. The *Yamato*, the *Nagato*, the *Haruna*, and the *Kongo*, after temporary repairs in Singapore and the Philippines, headed for Japan. The *Kongo* was sunk and the *Haruna* badly damaged by submarines off Foochow. The *Nagato*, the *Yamato*, and the crippled *Haruna* finally joined the *Ise* and the *Hyuga;* eventually the *Nagato* was badly damaged and the other four were sunk by American carrier planes.

Only the helpless *Nagato* remained to surrender and to serve later as a target ship at Bikini Atoll. Except for her sister ship, the *Mutsu*, which had been sunk in Hiroshima in June, 1943, from an accidental explosion, the entire battle line of Japan had been destroyed by the planes, submarines, and surface ships of the United States Navy.

Seven heavy cruisers survived the October battles but did no further harm. The *Nachi* was sunk by American planes November 5 in Manila Bay. The *Myoko,* the *Haguro,* the *Takao,* and the *Ashigara* reached Singapore badly damaged. The *Takao* and the *Myoko* were never able to leave that harbor. The *Ashigara* and the *Haguro* were sunk by British ships off Singapore and Peñang attempting to carry supplies to beleaguered garrisons. The *Aoba* and the *Tone* were sunk with the battleships by American aircraft in Kure in July, 1945.

All four Japanese carriers participating in the October battles were sunk. Nine other carriers built or building remained. They were useless without carrier pilots but all except one were soon sunk or disabled. In November the submarine *Queenfish* sank the *Jinyo* in the Yellow Sea, and the *Archerfish* demolished the *Shinano* on her trial trip off Kobe. In December the *Junyo* was heavily damaged by another submarine. Carrier planes sank the *Kaiyo* and heavily damaged the *Ryuho* in March, 1945, and in July practically completed the annihilation of the enemy carrier force by heavily damaging the *Amagi* and the *Katsuragi* in Kure. All that remained of 21 carriers and five escort carriers was the obsolete training carrier *Hosho* and the completed but not commissioned *Kasagi,* whose camouflage enabled her to escape detection at Sasebo.

Operation of American Submarines in the Pacific

The end of 1944 is also a convenient time to compare the results of the operations of American submarines in the Pacific as an arm of a superior fleet with the German U-boats in the Atlantic, which could be assisted only by the Luftwaffe. By 1945 it had become very difficult for American submarines to find sufficient Japanese target ships, although they cruised inside the Inland Sea and in Tsushima Strait along the vital line of communication with Manchuria.

American submarines, operating as an arm of the surface fleet, steadily increased in effectiveness as commerce destroyers until they exhausted Japanese targets. Although the U-boats increased in numbers and their crews in experience, and had a constantly increasing number of target ships, the number of sinkings steadily decreased, whereas

American submarines sank over a million more tons of shipping in 1944 than in 1943. Even if American submarines and crews should be adjudged superior, those of the Germans were extremely efficient, and the relative efficiency of personnel and craft will not explain the disparity. The U-boats fought almost single handed and against Anglo-American antisubmarine devices. American submarines fought as a part of the American fleets in the Pacific, which absorbed so much of the time and energy of the Japanese Navy that it could not take the comprehensive antisubmarine measures that the Allies used to combat U-boats in the Atlantic.

RELATIVE MERCHANT SHIPPING LOSSES
DUE TO SUBMARINE ACTION

(In dead weight tons)

Year	Japanese Losses	Anglo-American Losses
1942	580,390	8,245,000
1943	1,341,968	3,611,000
1944	2,387,780	1,422,000
1945	469,872	458,000

The significance of this comparison is that the submarine, which France first hailed as the destroyer of the surface fleet and the doom of sea power, proved, as torpedo boats and destroyers had already proved, to be a natural partner of the surface ship.

The Japanese employed their submarines exclusively against American combat ships and with considerable success in the first part of the war. Japanese submarines assisted in the destruction of two large carriers and sank several cruisers and destroyers. In the invasion of the Philippines and the Solomons campaign Japanese submarines were very effective as scouts, but in the latter part of the war American countermeasures rendered them less effective, while in 1944 American submarines as an arm of the steadily increasing fleet reached their pinnacle of success.

In addition to sinking 4,750,000 tons of Japanese merchant ships, American submarines sank 37 per cent of all enemy combat ships lost during the war, including some damaged by aircraft or surface ships. Among their victims were 1 battleship, 8 carriers, 12 cruisers, 43 destroyers, 23 submarines, and 60 escort vessels. The aggressiveness of United States submarines is shown by their sinkings of destroyers and escort vessels—the ships that traditionally prey on submarines. Wherever possible American underseas craft assaulted their attackers. In addition to their attacks on enemy ships, submarines did the distant scouting for the surface fleet and in the two major battles of the western Pacific, as related, made the first contacts with the enemy. They supplied equipment and maintained communications with friendly forces operating behind Japanese lines. And in the final phase of the war they became the life-saving service for American aviators forced to land in enemy waters, rescuing more than 500 airmen who otherwise would have perished or fallen into enemy hands.

Credit for achievements of our submarines could not be given during the war without adding to the perils of the personnel. Even since V-J Day the public has been told very little, but within the Navy the importance and the contribution of this branch of the service is known and appreciated. Forty-six American submarines did not return from their combat patrols; in grim official language they were "presumed lost due to enemy action."

Formation of Kamikaze Corps

As the year 1944 drew to a close, it was evident that the beaten and dispersed Japanese Fleet would have little or no further influence on the course of the war. American submarines, assisted by aircraft, had practically annihilated the merchant marine; American carrier pilots had destroyed not only the enemy carrier pilots but also the bulk of the land pilots. During 1945 the Japanese Imperial General Staff had only Kamikaze pilots and ground troops to interpose between the home islands and the juggernaut advance of the American amphibious forces. Suicide attacks by Japa-

RECONQUEST OF THE WEST PACIFIC

nese planes comprised the only serious opposition faced by the American surface fleet during that year.

The Kamikaze Corps was not organized "on the spur of the moment." During earlier air battles American and Japanese pilots whose planes had been hopelessly disabled attempted and several times succeeded in crash-diving into an enemy ship. And there were a few not fully authenticated reports that individual pilots of both nations, with planes in perfect condition, had deliberately crash-dived into hostile ships.

Until the air battles over Saipan and Guam, the Japanese leaders, while realizing they might not be able to replace their carrier pilots in time, were convinced they could still depend upon their ample supply of land-based pilots. But these air battles convinced the Japanese Air Force commanders that their land pilots were not sufficiently experienced to cope with American carrier pilots. The superiority of these Americans over the Japanese operating from airfields ashore compelled the Japanese Army and Navy to resort to Kamikaze tactics. And after considerable discussion Japanese officers decided that only by deliberately crash-diving American ships could they hope to oppose the fast carrier force successfully. Very wisely, Toyoda delayed formal organization until it was demanded by the pilots themselves, but after the remnants of the First Air Fleet flew to Luzon from Guam in July, the question of a Kamikaze Corps was under continuous consideration. Vice-Admiral Onishi not only encouraged discussion but established a nucleus organization in September.

According to Captain Inoguchi, Onishi's Chief of Staff, on October 15 Rear Admiral Arima, Commander of the 26th Air Squadron, dove into an aircraft carrier, and crystallized a desire among the pilots to emulate his example which could no longer be resisted. On October 19 Admiral Onishi formally organized the corps in his air fleet. When the airmen on Luzon learned that Kurita had been ordered to destroy the American forces landing in Leyte at any cost, they insisted that aviators immediately be given the same privilege. Toyoda yielded to this apparently spontaneous demand

and, thanks to Onishi's preliminary organization, the first large Kamikaze attacks were made on October 25 against Kinkaid's escort carriers off Leyte a few hours after Kurita abandoned the attack. Thus, on the day that the Combined Fleet ceased to exist as a fighting unit, the Kamikaze Corps took up the task of resisting the American advance.

The Kamikaze was based upon the devotion of the armed forces to the Emperor. Skilled or unskilled, all pilots took a short course of religious and military training in which the doctrines of Shintoism were stressed. The accompanying ceremonies included investitures suggestive of medieval chivalry, when a young squire first assumed the obligations of knighthood. When candidates for the corps emerged from their final retreat, their ardor for the Emperor and their country had been inflamed and they were altogether willing to sacrifice themselves in a fiery dive onto an American ship.

Although verging upon the mystical, the organization was practical and well adapted to the defense against amphibious operations during which American ships were compelled to remain in easy range of enemy planes for weeks, even months, supporting the landings and the ground troops ashore. After the Kamikaze organization was established only inexperienced pilots were employed to crash-dive. The experienced pilots were assembled in scouting groups and when necessary located the American ships, sometimes accompanying the Kamikaze planes to the vicinity of the target ships. The Kamikaze usually operated in groups of five, flying at about 18,000 feet until they were picked up by American radar. They then dove to 80 or 90 feet altitude for the final approach. They maneuvered to attack from astern and endeavored to hit a carrier at the forward elevator.

According to Lieutenant General Kawabe, the army was compelled for lack of materials to stop building bombers in 1944, and thereafter built only fighters. The navy Kamikaze employed fighter and scouting planes until the supply was exhausted; after that they used trainer planes. As early as the summer of 1944 the army as well as the navy was running short of trained pilots. Accordingly, soon after Onishi

RECONQUEST OF THE WEST PACIFIC 273

organized the naval Kamikaze, Lieutenant General Tominaga, commanding the Fourth Air Army in Luzon, formed a similar corps in that service.

Suicide crash-dive attacks in the Philippines caused the immediate reorganization of the American Carrier Task Force into three groups, to increase the antiaircraft defenses and the proportion of fighter planes on the carriers. Throughout November and December these Kamikaze attacks continued against the carriers giving air support to Krueger's ground troops.

The waters of the Philippine Archipelago offered an ideal setting for the Kamikaze pilots. The Mindoro Expeditionary Force, for example, which moved from Leyte through the Mindanao and Sulu Seas, landed on Mindoro on December 15 and established air facilities there, was subjected to Kamikaze attack en route. The day before the force left Leyte Task Force 38 maintained an "air blanket," that is, a continuous fighter patrol, over the 90 airfields (10 had been abandoned) in Luzon. While the force passed through the Sulu Sea Kinkaid's escort carriers provided direct air cover, and MacArthur's land-based planes furnished fighter cover at dusk each day in the Mindanao Sea. Yet in spite of the continuous Japanese air losses and the combined air escort given the Mindoro expedition, the *Nashville,* flagship of the attack group, and several destroyers were hit by suicide planes. The otherwise safe transit of this expedition indicated the increasing effectiveness of carrier planes against the Kamikaze Corps.

In spite of Kamikaze warfare enemy air resistance in the Philippines was sharply reduced by the end of December, and the Japanese situation there deteriorated during the end of 1944 and the first part of 1945. Allied airfields were rapidly constructed on Mindoro, and heavy air losses forced the Japanese to abandon their efforts to reënforce the Second Air Fleet on Luzon. Commander Yamaguchi, Operations Officer on the Staff of the Second Air Fleet, testifies that only 50 fighters and 20 bombers were left on Luzon by the end of December, all employed as Kamikaze.

The air and sea blockade of the Philippines permitted

General Yamashita to bring into Luzon only one fifth of the troops which he held within easy forwarding distance, and General Kawabe, Deputy Chief of the Army Bureau of Aeronautics, admits that practically all the army planes sent to Luzon between September, 1944, and January, 1945, were destroyed. Many of the planes which the enemy did have on Luzon in late December were not in operation for lack of engine parts. Not only was production in Japan faltering but the Japanese found it almost impossible, in spite of their Kamikaze tactics, to ship planes or aviation parts into Luzon on account of attacks on shipping by American ships, submarines, and carrier planes. Nevertheless Kamikaze attacks from Clark and Nichols Fields on American battleships and cruisers in Lingayen Bay, January 7–8, inflicted considerable damage. And on January 12 a number of Kamikaze planes flew in from Formosa and made another attack.

The Kamikaze attacks represented the last attempt of a doomed nation to stave off the irresistible American advance. The Japanese used them with dogged persistence during the Iwo Jima and Okinawa campaigns, and up until the surrender of Japan. Fanatical and strategically fruitless as they were, neither the fierce courage of their pilots nor the menace they temporarily constituted to American ships and crews should be forgotten.

XIV

Sea Power and Surrender

Later Phases of the Philippines and East Indies Campaigns

AFTER the decisive naval battle for Leyte Gulf General Krueger's troops occupied Samar without difficulty and fought their way inland on Leyte against Japanese air and ground opposition. But heavy rains soon made progress more difficult and delayed establishment of army aircraft ashore. By the end of October General Yamashita was reënforcing Ormoc Peninsula on Leyte and had succeeded in slowing the advance of Krueger's troops. Enemy ground and air resistance continued throughout November and the first half of December. The continued inability of MacArthur's air force to establish itself ashore compelled Halsey's Third Fleet to delay its program of air attacks on Japan, scheduled for the middle of November.

The occupation of Mindoro offered a base on the China Sea to attack enemy shipping and airfields to support the landing on Lingayen Gulf on January 9, 1945. During the Lingayen landing the Third Fleet was assigned to what was becoming its routine task of covering the landing by preliminary air strikes; these hit Formosa, Nansei Shoto, and Luzon itself during a six-day period before the landing. The Seventh Fleet, still augmented with reënforcements from the central Pacific, Vice-Admiral Kinkaid commanding, escorted the combined forces to land and support Krueger's Sixth Army. The same forces under the same commanders had seized Leyte. These were seasoned veterans and the operations moved practically on schedule. Halsey's air strikes relieved them of enemy air opposition during the landing itself, but during the approach extensive air attacks, mainly Kamikaze, sank the escort carrier *Ommaney Bay* and three fast mine sweepers, besides inflicting considerable damage to the upper works of several heavier ships.

Once landed on Luzon, the troops pressed southward over the same roads used by General Wainwright's troops in December, 1941. The scene was different. American troops followed closely on the heels of the Japanese and were soon beyond range of ships' artillery. But it was necessary to retain a large number of combat ships in Lingayen Gulf to cover the landing of reënforcements and supplies.

On January 29 Rear Admiral Struble landed the 11th Army Corps northwest of Subic Bay, unopposed. In a rapid advance Subic was reached by noon, and on the 30th Fort Grande at the entrance of the Bay was taken. Rear Admiral Fechteler landed another assault force 15 miles south of Manila Bay, and on February 13 Rear Admiral Berkey, with cruisers and destroyers, bombarded Corregidor and swept the enemy mine fields. By February 16, 1945, American troops returned to Corregidor. In less than six weeks Manila was practically surrounded and the Bay was in American possession, but the unnecessary conquest of Luzon was a longer and more costly operation.

At the end of February Rear Admiral Riggs landed troops in the Palawan Islands, providing additional air and naval bases from which American forces could operate against Japanese traffic to the Netherlands East Indies. In March, April, and May landings were made in the southern Philippines and Borneo. These furnished more bases and deprived the Japanese of oil fields, but as the enemy had no fleet to use oil and their tankers, at heavy cost, could supply sufficient aviation gasoline from Singapore, the loss of the oil fields did them no appreciable harm. However, their acquisition provided another and nearer source of fuel oil for the American forces.

The strategy was questionable, the tactics superb. The use of amphibious forces in these campaigns became a commonplace. The Seventh Fleet and the Sixth Army could mount an amphibious attack on short notice. In their constantly improved landing craft the soldiers could form for combat and rush a beachhead faster than ground troops ashore could march.

The Third Fleet, after maintaining a continuous air pa-

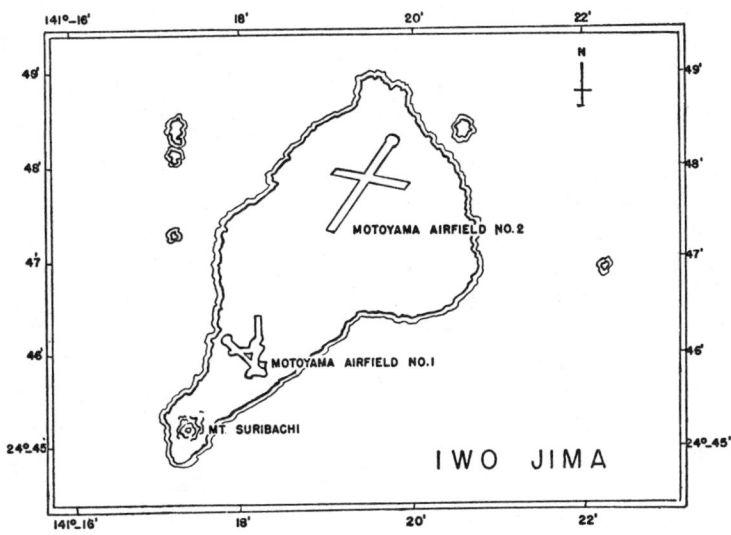

trol over enemy airfields on Luzon to assist MacArthur's forces, made a deep penetration into the South China Sea, with air strikes on Camranh and Saïgon, sinking 14 and damaging 31 enemy ships on January 12. On January 15 Formosa was again struck, and strikes on Amoy, Swatow, Hong Kong, and Hainan Island followed. Japanese shipping, almost destroyed by submarines, faced annihilation from the air, for remnants of the Japanese air forces in that area dared not come within 20 miles of the fast carriers.

The Struggle for Iwo Jima

In the north the situation was different. As early as November Japanese planes on Iwo Jima had begun to be a serious nuisance to Army B-29's operating from Saipan and Tinian. Iwo's catacombs protected the planes from air attacks, and well-trained ground crews quickly repaired crater damage inflicted on airfields by ships and planes.

The execution of plans made for the capture of Iwo Jima was delayed by the necessity of furnishing air support for the Philippines campaign, but on February 19 the Fourth and Fifth Marine Divisions landed on the southeast coast of the formidable little island which is but five miles long and less than two miles wide.

Admiral Spruance, commanding the Fifth Fleet, had taken over from Admiral Halsey. With him was Vice-Admiral Turner commanding the amphibious forces. Lieutenant General Howland Smith commanded the expeditionary forces. The same High Command had taken Saipan, Tinian, and Guam.

For seven months Iwo had been subjected to air attacks and surface bombardments. From December until the landing their frequency and intensity had increased. Vice-Admiral Mitscher conducted the preliminary air strikes, while Rear Admirals Badger and A. E. Smith alternated in surface bombardments. Three days preceding the landing an intensive bombardment by ships of the Fifth Fleet and strikes by carrier and Army shore-based planes reduced the enemy's power to oppose the landing. But heavy resistance was encountered as soon as the advance landing began. Nevertheless the Marines went forward inch by inch in spite of the fire of artillery, rockets, and mortars concentrated on the beaches.

The Japanese troops ashore approximated 20,000. The tiny island was a labyrinth of interlocking caves, pill boxes, and blockhouses. On the southwestern tip was the extinct volcano Suribachi, whose guns, coördinated with batteries in the northern area, covered the sea approaches, the landing beaches, and the successive Marine positions as they cleaned out one cave after another.

There was no room for maneuver on the islet, no easy way to take Iwo. But every day of the campaign exposed the surface ships to Kamikaze attacks, and it was therefore necessary to take the island as quickly as possible. By the end of D-Day the Marines had crossed the island and isolated the garrison at Mount Suribachi. Early the next day they threw back the inevitable counterattack, and during the day captured Motoyama Airfield Number One. On the night of February 21–22 the Marines proved their superiority in night tactics by repulsing renewed counterattacks. On February 23 Motoyama Airfield Number Two was taken. Fanatical resistance from enemy troops in caves and pill boxes, made it necessary to land the entire Third Division. But within a week the three divisions, led by their tanks, had taken over half the island. On February 28 observation and spotting planes were operating from captured airfields, the Marines were firmly established on high ground, and the capture of Iwo was assured. On March 3 a B-29 made an emergency landing on Airfield Number One. Thus even before the Marines had completed their occupation of Iwo, the island had begun to serve as a haven for injured bombers returning to their bases in the Marianas. By March 16, 25 days after landing, all organized resistance ceased.

Enemy dead were estimated at over 20,000. Casualties among American Marines totaled 20,200, of whom 4,300 were killed in action. Iwo was purchased dearly. But possession of its airfields reduced the time American ships were exposed to Kamikaze attacks and cut naval casualties and air personnel losses. Within three months from the time the first crippled B-29 crash-landed there, 852 Superforts with crews of 9,361 men, who might otherwise have fallen into the ocean, had made emergency landings on Iwo Jima.

The 21st Bomber Command acknowledged its indebtedness to the Navy and Marines, stating that possession of Iwo provided fighter escort for the bombers, increased the possible bomb tonnage per plane, reduced by half the dangerous return trip from Japan, and decreased the number of bombers that failed to reach their target due to poor navigation, weather conditions, or battle damage. It was the ability of the various services to coöperate, even to subordinate the interests of one service to the over-all goal when necessary, that welded American forces into the irresistible combat team that dominated the western Pacific.

Proper emphasis should be given to the work done by the

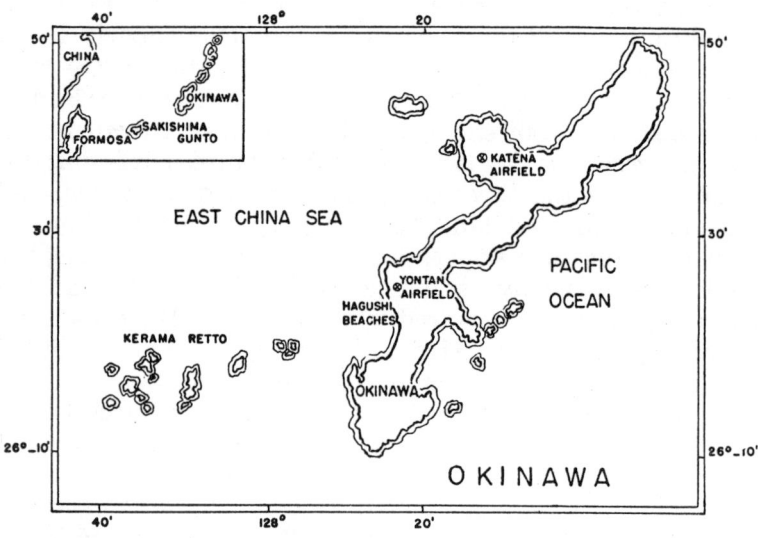

Army Air Force in the Pacific. Beginning at the battle of Midway, Army bombers took part in the campaigns that conquered the central and western Pacific. Halsey's forces in the Solomons at all times included a substantial contingent of Army air forces, and General Millard Harmon, the air commander, was a member of Nimitz' High Command. General MacArthur coördinated the air operations of his Strategic Air Force with the air operations of Nimitz' fleet. When the Palawan Islands were occupied, for example, MacArthur's airmen continued to coördinate their operations in the China Sea with those of the carrier forces, thus assisting in cutting Japanese communications to Malaya and the East Indies.

The Capture of Okinawa

Before the capture of Iwo was complete the fast carrier forces under Admirals Mitscher and Lee were bombarding

SEA POWER AND SURRENDER

Okinawa preparatory to invasion. It needed softening, being defended by 120,000 troops, including natives serving with the combat troops. In easy forwarding distance were 60,000 troops in the Nansei Islands; still more were available in Formosa and Nagasaki, each about 350 miles distant. The native population furnished a practically inexhaustible supply of labor.

Admiral Spruance was in command. Vice-Admiral Turner commanded the Joint Expeditionary Force; Lieutenant General Buckner, U.S.A., who had been in command in Alaska, the ground troops; Vice-Admiral Rawlings, R.N., the British Carrier Force, which had recently reported to Admiral Nimitz for duty; and Rear Admiral Beary the Supply Group (tankers and cargo vessels), while Commodore Carter, with Service Squadron Ten, again furnished repair, supply, and service vessels of all kinds. Rear Admiral Blandy had the Amphibious Support Force (escort carriers, mine sweepers, underwater demolition teams, gunboats, and special gunnery ships), and Rear Admiral Deyo commanded the battleships and other gunnery vessels, except for Admiral Lee's fast battleships. The total force aggregated 548,000 Army, Navy, and Marine personnel, with 320 combatant and 1,140 auxiliary vessels.

As usual, the mine sweepers were in front; protected by the battleships of the fast carrier force, they swept for eight days preceding the landings, clearing the entire shore line of mines. The preliminary assault on Kerama Retto, small islands due west of South Okinawa, began on March 25 and by the 31st they were occupied, harbors were netted, and a seaplane base was established. This small anchorage also furnished a vitally important repair base, for Kamikaze planes were damaging more and more ships.

Okinawa itself was bombarded intermittently for seven days prior to the landing on April 1. The assault waves in amphibious vehicles landed over the Hagushi beaches on schedule at 8.30 A.M., and four hours later had captured both Yontan and Katena Airfields with light losses. Before dark 50,000 of Buckner's Tenth Army were ashore, with a beachhead two or two and a half miles in depth. The landing on

Normandy had been a prodigious feat; 21,000 troops were put ashore in the first 12 hours. At Okinawa Buckner poured over twice as many troops onto the beach in the same length of time, a fact that bears witness to the indefatigable efforts of the Army and Navy to improve amphibious methods, weapons, and tactics. Within four days the central section of Okinawa, the Yontan-Katena area, was in American hands. It then became apparent that the Japanese general had concentrated his troops in the southern part of the island, with the defenses—mainly blockhouses, pill boxes, and caves—organized in depth.

On May 7, while the Third Fleet was combating planes off Okinawa and General Buckner was meeting increased resistance ashore, Grand Admiral Karl Doenitz, who had succeeded Hitler as head of the Reich, surrendered unconditionally.

The collapse of Germany had no immediate effect on the tactical situation on Okinawa. The Japanese fought as savagely; it required 52 days to gain four miles and 36 days to advance the last ten miles against their desperate resistance. The German surrender did, however, have important political and strategical effects on the campaign in the western Pacific. It added to the depression felt among the Japanese people and encouraged responsible officials and the Emperor to make efforts for peace. Strategically it made available additional ships, planes, and troops for the war against Japan. The Joint Chiefs of Staff began a gigantic movement of American land, sea, and air forces to the western Pacific.

Since the landings in France, the Navy in the Atlantic had continued its successful fight against the new tactics and devices of the U-boats. After the surrender of Germany, naval components joined the Army in enforcing the terms of the Armistice. But the primary naval concern was to concentrate its forces in the Pacific; the Atlantic Fleet and its air force now redoubled their efforts to forward reënforcements to the Far East.

Only three days before the surrender of Okinawa, which came on June 21, General Buckner was killed directing

SEA POWER AND SURRENDER

operations from his forward command post. Lieutenant General Geiger, U.S.M.C., succeeded to command until enemy resistance was overcome. General Stilwell, U.S.A., then relieved Geiger and began preparations for the invasion of Japan.

For almost three months Spruance's Fifth Fleet had remained in support of Buckner's army ashore. The fleet had destroyed 2,336 enemy planes, while losing 557 of their own. During that time approximately 250 ships, from battleships and carriers to destroyers and landing craft, had been struck by air attacks, by far the greatest number of which were Kamikaze. Thirty-four destroyers or smaller ships were sunk. Serving on outpost duty, they were sacrificed to break up incoming formations and to warn larger ships of approaching suicide planes.

During this period the Fifth Fleet thus displayed its ability to operate continuously with bearable losses in approximately the same ocean area, with the enemy aware of its position and regularly delivering suicide attacks.

During much of this same period the British Fast Carrier Force under Vice-Admiral Rawlings had assisted in air-support operations around Okinawa, neutralizing enemy installations on Sakishima Gunto, southwest of the largest island.

Captain Fuchida of the Japanese Air Force staff reports that during the Okinawa campaign 550 navy and 350 army planes were used in suicide attacks, of which it was estimated 200 crashed their targets. This is one instance in which the Japanese underestimated their successes. They made about 250 hits with 900 planes, mainly Kamikaze. Twenty-eight per cent of hits is a high average. Fortunately most of the larger ships were not seriously damaged.

The Kamikaze forced Admiral Mitscher to shift flagships twice. In return, however, on April 7 his planes intercepted and sank the *Yamato,* the 18-inch gun battleship that had escaped on October 26 after being hit four times. The light cruiser *Yahagi* and four destroyers that accompanied the *Yamato* were also sunk. When Admiral Toyoda ordered Rear Admiral Ito to attack the American forces off Okinawa,

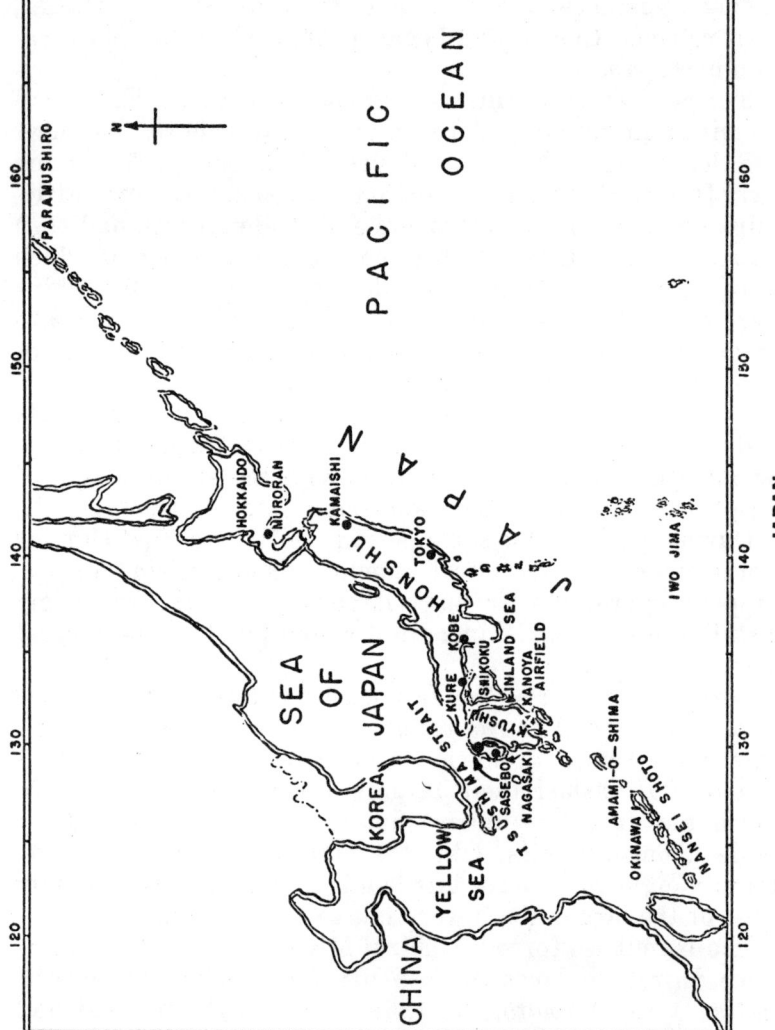

SEA POWER AND SURRENDER

he knew he was sending the *Yamato* and her companion vessels to their doom, but he also knew that retaining men-of-war in Japan would only postpone their destruction.

The Japanese Air Force reacted vigorously; while American planes sank the *Yamato*, the Kamikaze renewed their attacks and badly damaged the carrier *Hancock*.

Japan Facing Unconditional Surrender

Throughout the invasion of Okinawa, to prevent Japanese planes from reaching the island and to prepare for the invasion of Japan proper, the fast carrier force repeatedly attacked the airfields in Kyushu. On April 17 fighter sweeps shot down 17 air-borne planes and 54 on the ground. (Japanese officers state that many "planes" reported destroyed on the ground were decoys.) On May 24 Mitscher launched a "clean-up" fighter sweep over southern Honshu but no enemy planes were encountered except over the Kanoya Airfield on Kyushu. Eighty-four aircraft were destroyed, with a loss of three United States planes.

On May 28 Vice-Admiral Mitscher turned over the fast carriers to Vice-Admiral McCain. After the final bombardment of two islands east of Okinawa, the task force proceeded on June 10 to Leyte Gulf to replenish ammunition and supplies.

With the capture of Okinawa and Iwo Jima the Navy could either starve the Japanese people or support an invasion of Japan. The fleet had been sunk or driven into protected harbors, Japanese land and carrier planes had been destroyed except for 5,000 flown by inexperienced pilots who were compelled to use suicide tactics. The merchant marine faced annihilation, while American submarines patrolled Tsushima Straits and the Inland Sea and cut the last life line of Japan to Manchuria.

Shortly after the capture of Okinawa Admiral Spruance turned over command to Admiral Halsey and returned to Pearl Harbor to plan the next campaign. After a refit in the new base on Leyte Gulf Halsey, commanding the largest fleet ever assembled, proceeded to a convenient launching area 170 miles southeast of Tokyo. Making no attempt to conceal the location of his fleet, on July 10 he launched his planes against airfields and industrial plants in the Tokyo area. Extensive damage was done to industrial establishments and 72 planes were destroyed on the ground. Little air opposition was encountered, probably because the Japanese were husbanding their planes to use in suicide attacks on the expected invasion force.

Moving north, Halsey on the 14th and 15th struck northern Honshu and southern Hokkaido, dealing a serious blow to water transportation between the two islands by sinking five and damaging four railway ferries. Simultaneously Rear Admiral J. F. Shafroth, with fast American battleships and a division of British battleships, bombarded the cities of Kamaishi and Muroran, practically destroying their steel mills and oil refineries. On July 17 Anglo-American forces again bombarded Japan, the battleships firing 2,000 tons of shells into the coastal area northeast of Tokyo. On the 18th Anglo-American air strikes heavily damaged the *Nagato,* while on July 24–25 the battleships *Haruna, Hyuga,* and *Ise,* the carrier *Katsuragi,* and the heavy cruisers *Aoba* and *Tone* were heavily damaged at Kure. On the 28th McCain's carrier planes returned and sank the *Haruna,* the *Ise,* the *Hyuga,* the *Tone* and the *Aoba.* Halsey and McCain thus put the finishing touch on the battles of June and October, 1944.

Army airmen paralleled the carrier planes and their heavy bomb loads increased the devastation. The 20th Air Force, operating from the Marianas, began increasing its attacks on Japan, and on July 27 added to the psychological effect by warning 11 cities that they would be destroyed in the near future. On July 29, six of the 11 were heavily bombed.

A year before, with the loss of the Marianas, the Japanese Naval Staff had known defeat was inevitable. As Admiral Nagano said, "Hell was on us." Admiral Toyoda had then been driven to sacrifice the fleet in a futile effort to hold the Philippines, and the Cabinet, headed by General Tojo, had resigned. The new Premier, Koiso, appointed Admiral Yonai, who had opposed the tripartite agreement with Germany and Italy, new Deputy Premier and Navy Minister.

Yonai testified that he knew the conquest of the Marianas had meant the doom of Japan.

In April, 1945, just before the German surrender, Admiral Suzuki became Premier, and Admiral Toyoda was raised to Chief of the Naval General Staff. Toyoda confirmed Yonai's view of the hopelessness of the situation; after the war he stated that early in May, 1945, probably after the German surrender, members of the Supreme War Guidance Council (the Premier, Navy Minister, War Minister, Foreign Minister, and Navy and Army Chiefs of Staff) discussed ways of making peace. In June other members of the government were included in the discussions and at a meeting held in the Emperor's presence a report was made on the desirability of asking the Russian Government to mediate.

From this point the Emperor, according to Admiral Toyoda, took the lead. On June 26 he called the Supreme Council into his presence and said it was necessary to "consider the possibility of bringing the war to a conclusion." The Ministers replied that they fully concurred with the imperial view. On July 10, the day Halsey's planes hit Tokyo, the Emperor summoned the Foreign Minister to ask if a special ambassador should not be sent to Moscow without delay. The Japanese Ambassador to Moscow on July 13 asked the Russian Government to intervene "with a view to bringing peace." The Russians replied on August 8 by breaking off diplomatic relations.

Evidence given by Japanese officials indicates that by the end of July responsible officers in both army and navy realized the war was lost. According to Lieutenant General Kawabe, however, the army was in favor of continuing the war in order to compel an Allied invasion, during which the army hoped to inflict such heavy losses on the invading forces that the American people would compel their government to abandon its demand for unconditional surrender and grant more favorable terms. Kawabe asserts that members of the Navy General Staff were willing to have navy personnel fight ashore if necessary. Toyoda said that up to the end the men at the front were all "raring to go." And, according to his testimony, he was convinced that the dropping of the atomic bomb and the entry of Russia into the war "enabled us [the Cabinet] to bring the war to a termination without creating too great chaos in Japan."

While the government considered ways to end the war, the Imperial Staff concentrated its land forces and the remnants of air and naval forces to resist the expected invasion of the home islands. The ground troops were deployed and a comparatively small group of army planes was reserved in tactical support. But the Japanese still hoped to repulse the amphibious forces as they disembarked. The army and navy each mustered about 2,500 planes, practically all manned by Kamikaze pilots. The planes were pooled. Three thousand were stationed on Honshu, the most important island, 1,000 of them in the Tokyo area; another 1,000 were on Kyushu, the island nearest Okinawa, 400 on Shikoku, and 600 on Hokkaido. These groups were all in easy supporting distance of one another and the Imperial Staff had resolved to employ them all in a final effort to repulse the American invaders. Japanese submarines, concentrated in or near home waters, had developed their own suicide tactics in which their motor torpedo boats and midget submarines would participate.

The British and United States Governments adhered to their demand for unconditional surrender, and the almost continuous attacks of Halsey's Third Fleet and the Army's 20th Air Force paved the way for an invasion by the amphibious forces which Fleet Admiral King and General of the Army MacArthur assembled meanwhile in operating bases that extended from the West Coast of the United States and Australasia to Okinawa and Iwo Jima.

The land, sea, and air forces operating under Nimitz and MacArthur had met and overcome all forms of attack the Japanese could deliver. Iwo Jima and Okinawa had improved the defenses against Kamikaze. If the number of hits made by suicide pilots and the damage done at Okinawa are taken as a standard, the United States Navy could have supported an invasion. And the successful landings by the Army and Marines from the Solomons, Africa, Italy, Normandy, and

SEA POWER AND SURRENDER

the Marshalls across the Pacific is sufficient evidence that they could have successfully invaded Japan.

The Marines had six divisions, the Army practically unlimited troops available. Fleet Admiral King had furnished Fleet Admiral Nimitz and Admiral Kinkaid with 90 per cent of the total combat Navy, including 23 battleships, 90 aircraft carriers, 52 cruisers, 323 destroyers, 298 submarines, 323 escort vessels, 15,000 planes, and the necessary auxiliary vessels, transports, and landing craft. There was no weak link in the chain. Veteran sailors, soldiers, and marines were led by competent officers, whose flag officers were directed by the Joint Chiefs of Staff.

Unquestionably Nimitz and MacArthur could have invaded Japan and dictated peace in Tokyo. But any believer in Mahan's thesis of sea power will question the necessity of landing in that heavily populated insular Empire. It would have been far easier to starve and bomb the overcrowded islands into submission. Submarines, surface ships, and aviation with advanced bases in the Marianas, Okinawa, and Iwo Jima could have forced the Japanese people and their government to surrender unconditionally or starve. The entry of Russia and the atomic bomb may have helped the Emperor and the government to persuade their people to surrender. But even fanatical leaders and fervently patriotic people are helpless when food gives out. And to gradual starvation the Superforts of the Army and the carrier planes and guns of the Navy were rapidly adding physical devastation. It is no reflection on the endurance, courage, and patriotism of the Japanese people to assert that they must very shortly have surrendered unconditionally, even if there had been no atomic bombs and no Russian intervention.

XV

New Weapons and World Relations

THE atomic bombs that were dropped on Hiroshima and Nagasaki may well change the entire course of the development of armaments. But the bombs were dropped by planes based on islands that had been captured by amphibious forces supported by the Pacific Fleet. Clearly at this point it would be going too far to say that surface fleets were obsolete and sea power useless.

And as we have seen, similar assertions in the past have always proved to be wrong. The country is being urged on the one hand to discard the weapons that actually won World War II and to concentrate its energies on the new weapons, and on the other, to share the knowledge of the atomic bomb with other countries and to trust to international agreements to control its use. The United Nations, conceivably, may at some future time work out a disarmament plan or system of international control that will work and not be subject to veto. But that consummation is obviously a matter of the future. Today the United States Navy must be prepared to deal with a military problem in a real world of armaments and planes and ships and the possibility of sudden unilateral action. All we shall attempt here is to survey the situation as it is, and on the basis of actual historical experience to look into the future for a short space.

The production and use of atomic bombs and other new weapons has already profoundly influenced the construction of ships and planes. Methods of controlling the sea will certainly be modified, and the influence of sea power may increase in some directions and diminish in others. National policies of the United States will also be affected, and as these policies should determine future naval planning it is logical to consider first the impact of the new weapons on

NEW WEAPONS AND WORLD RELATIONS 291

international relations before anticipating the changes they will impose upon plans of the United States Navy.

Since the bow and arrow first made their appearance every improvement in weapons has first been denounced as the destroyer of civilization and later hailed as the harbinger of universal peace. This paradoxical argument has contended that the new or improved weapon will make war so frightful that nations will keep the peace. Nevertheless wars have recurred. The new weapons have been added to arsenals, but, even so, many old ones have been modified and retained. Wars have become more complicated, but it is questionable if the horrors of absolute or total war have increased and it is clear that the theory that war can be made so terrible that all nations will remain at peace has no historical foundation. Obviously, the United States cannot depend on the increasing destructiveness of weapons to insure peace.

On the contrary, history indicates that, until human nature changes, conflicting national policies will cause international rivalries, and that, unless diplomacy and negotiation reconcile resulting antagonisms, war will follow. Experience has shown that energetic, ambitious, perhaps predatory national leaders will resort to war regardless of its dangers to the nation and the hardships it imposes upon the people. This willingness of some nations to go to war was formally recognized in the charter of the United Nations; and the Security Council was not only authorized but required to take all measures necessary to prevent or suppress war. In other words, the only sure preventive of war that the charter members of the United Nations could devise was another war.

Americans should bear these facts in mind and should also remember that outlawing the atomic bomb will give no protection whatever against guided missiles armed with biological and other weapons, and that future scientific developments will be immediately utilized to increase the effectiveness of armed strength. Thus prohibition of armaments, to be effective, must include those still in the experimental stage, on the drawing boards, and those that are certain to emerge in the future. Attempting to end war by controlling armaments and by degrees of disarmament is attacking a symptom, not the causes. Control of armaments, reduction of arms, and partial disarmament may be necessary preliminaries to establishing an international organization to enforce peace but of themselves they do not eliminate the causes of war.

Assuming that good faith existed among all nations, there would still be numerous administrative obstacles to disarmament. Regulation of armaments must precede even a partial disarmament. An international inspection commission would be necessary because potential aggressors would not hesitate at deception, and in a matter vital to national security no government could trust the word of any but its own officials. A thorough inspection of every laboratory, factory, arsenal, and shipyard would be imperative, but an international commission going about the world peering into all establishments capable of making old and perhaps new weapons would not only be likely to arouse resentment and suspicion but would have extreme difficulty in accomplishing its purpose, should any nation choose to manufacture arms in secrecy. Armaments are hard to distinguish from peaceful implements, and still harder to balance against one another. Certain weapons will be more useful to one nation than another; for example, control of the sea, essential to one nation, may have less value to another. Manifestly, outlawing the atomic bomb is only one step toward regulation, reduction, and, finally, perhaps total abolishment of all arms.

These formidable obstructions to disarmament exist and cannot be ignored. There is no short cut to a warless world, and the only hope of eventual success is by a gradual approach to a hitherto insoluble problem. Specifically, this country should not again attempt to lead the world to disarmament by example or permit another aggressor nation the first blow. It should keep its military establishment strong until other nations disarm too and the future of the United States can safely be entrusted to some sort of international order. Otherwise the United States will be unable to influence the future of civilization and will be exposed to the first predatory nation that can manufacture enough atomic bombs and long-range planes to support a surprise attack.

The advantage which Japan gained by being permitted to strike the first blow in 1941 added months of hard fighting to the war and increased unnecessarily the loss of American lives. To await attack in the atomic age might well be fatal. Obviously accurate information of potential attacks is essential, but there must also be a firm national resolve to anticipate a probable enemy blow with a heavier one. Time may not permit a debate in Congress during a period of strained relations. In peacetimes the President should be empowered to order the armed forces to strike the first blow in an emergency, and they should be maintained in readiness to do so. Under the Constitution and in accord with policies approved by Congress the President is responsible for the conduct of foreign affairs; his personal day-to-day decisions may involve the nation in war. A further extension of presidential powers, if necessary by Constitutional amendment, is a wry necessity in the atomic age and with safeguards would not of itself increase the risk of war, whereas a surprise attack could indeed jeopardize the country. If the enemy was victorious he would prescribe the form of government. It would be of little service to preserve the Constitution and lose the war.

With the general approval of public opinion Congress has already authorized the President to contribute a contingent of American forces to assist in preventing or suppressing war whenever the Security Council of the United Nations decides that the peace or security of the world is threatened. The states and Congress should specifically give the President equal authority to employ the armed forces to protect the United States whenever there is positive evidence that *its* safety is endangered. If the President can be authorized to employ the Armed Forces, without consulting Congress, to preserve or restore peace in any part of the world, surely he can be empowered to use them, under similar circumstances, to protect the United States.

By being the first to produce the atomic bomb this country

has gained time to consider all the effects of the bomb upon national policies. The people of the United States should not be stampeded into precipitate or ill-advised measures. For example they should scrutinize the assertion that modern wars are more terrible than were wars of ancient times. Modern weapons carry farther and strike faster. Civilians of many nations were in the combat zones of World War II; in the next great war practically every city would be exposed to attack. But the populations of all defeated nations have eventually found themselves at the mercy of the victor. In the many wars between the despotisms of Asia Minor and even in those occurring between the sister republics of Greece, the victors usually destroyed the cities and enslaved the population. Rome razed Carthage. In recent years Hitler and Japanese commanders showed no mercy to defeated enemies. Nations that lay down their arms have always been and probably always will be at the disposition of the foe. The cultural inheritance of the victor, his philosophy, his mores, even his whims, not the weapons he has employed, decide the fate of the vanquished.

The Navy Department is aware of the consequences of a national defeat and also of the terrific effect of atomic bombs on cities and harbors. It is doing its utmost to strengthen its ships and protect the nation, but its plans must fall within the pattern of national policy which will in turn be determined by public opinion. The Navy is basing a great many of its technical changes upon the results of the experimental bombings at Bikini Atoll conducted by Vice-Admiral W. H. P. Blandy. Admiral Blandy reported, and Senator Hatch, chairman of the President's Civilian Board substantially concurred, that the bomb which exploded in the air damaged more ships than have ever before been damaged by a single explosion, although it should be borne in mind that at Bikini the ships were placed much closer together than they would normally be allowed to be, even in peacetime, at sea or in port. All vessels within one mile of the explosion point were either sunk or damaged. Two battleships and a heavy cruiser suffered little damage to their hulls but their superstructures were badly wrecked. Within the area of extensive blast damage, the crews would have been exposed to deadly doses of radioactivity. Numerous fires were started on ships, in one case two miles distant. The underwater explosion hurled aloft masses of radioactive water that drenched many ships and after four days it was still unsafe to spend much time aboard a contaminated ship.

The scientific data obtained at Bikini are proving very valuable both for ship design and industrial developments. Further, the board has announced its conclusion that "Only by further large-scale research and development can the United States retain its present position of scientific leadership. This must be done in the interest of national safety." Few will challenge this conclusion; the United States could have defeated Japan eventually without using the bomb, but if Germany had produced it, victory would certainly have been much more difficult, perhaps impossible, for the Allies.

So far as its funds permit the Navy will continue its own research and maintain close contact with scientific developments in the Army, universities, industry, and scientific societies. Rear Admiral H. G. Bowen, former Chief of the Bureau of Engineering and until recently Director of the Naval Research Laboratory, reported that the Navy's program included the development of a system of propulsion for ships, submarines, and planes by nuclear energy, further improvement of nuclear weapons and the vehicles to launch and carry them, and a thorough exploration of all means of defense against nuclear weapons. Just as the Navy formerly attempted to produce armor that would resist enemy projectiles and projectiles that would pierce enemy armor, today it is seeking means to increase the effectiveness of nuclear weapons and at the same time developing means of defense against them.

Attention of the public has been almost exclusively concentrated upon the destructive effects of the atomic bomb. According to Bowen the adaptation of nuclear energy to ship propulsion will be as revolutionary as the transition from sails to steam. Heat obtained by atomic fission will generate steam to drive turbines or reciprocating engines, thus eliminating boilers, auxiliaries, and thousands of tons of fuel. The weight saved can be used to strengthen the structure of the ship's hull and add more armor. Economy of fuel will no longer be necessary; turbines can be designed solely for maximum speed which will be further increased by a new underwater shape for the hull. What is still more important for future naval operations, ships powered by atomic energy can remain at sea almost indefinitely, inasmuch as the Navy has also developed an antifouling paint which makes drydocking comparatively unimportant except for underwater injury. The length of a cruise will be determined by the amount of rations that can be carried for the crew, and methods of preserving and packaging foods become constantly more efficient. Vice-Admiral E. L. Cochrane, Chief of the Bureau of Ships, predicts that within five years warships propelled by atomic energy may be operating at sea. Eventually destroyers and submarines as well as larger ships will be propelled by nuclear energy.

Perhaps the greatest danger to ships from the atomic bomb would result from an underwater explosion in a landlocked harbor. Ships will expose themselves to this danger only when absolutely imperative and it is hard to imagine circumstances that would compel the concentration of the greater part of a fleet in one enclosed harbor. In the future a method of decontaminating a harbor may be discovered; in the meantime ships will be much safer at sea. The next greatest danger to a fleet results from the bomb's enormously enlarged cone of destruction. With the atomic bomb it is not necessary to make a direct or near hit. Even at high altitudes a plane can drop a bomb within half a mile of the target. The best defense is a still wider deployment of the fleets and task forces. Planes with ordinary bombs compelled fleets to enlarge their formations greatly during the last war; atomic bombs will merely force still further dispersion. Improved methods of interfleet communication will enable flag officers to control their forces over greater areas. Likewise, considering the matter from the offensive point of view, as guided missiles replace guns as the primary weapon on ships, commanders of widely deployed fleets can concen-

NEW WEAPONS AND WORLD RELATIONS

trate on enemy ships or ports at greater ranges and as efficiently as if concentrated in a compact formation.

The amphibious landings of the last war in the Pacific will be difficult, perhaps impossible, against an enemy possessing atomic bombs. No longer can a vast collection of ships lie within easy range of an enemy island for several weeks to support operations ashore. This may be advantageous to the United States which today possesses sufficient strategic bases to meet forseeable needs. A future enemy attempting to capture these bases would be compelled to expose his ships to American bombs.

In addition to strengthening its ships against bomb injury the Navy is converting the new battleships *Kentucky* and *Hawaii* into guided missile or rocket ships. When the new ships are completed their principal offensive equipment will be tubes for launching rockets or guided missiles. The 16-inch batteries that so long dominated the battle line are passing from the scene. Admiral Cochrane reports that the rapid improvement in guided missiles justifies the change. Plans are being made to equip submarines to carry and launch the atomic bomb. Thus the cycle would be complete, because surface ships and planes can already carry and launch atomic bombs or guided missiles carrying biological or other deadly weapons. Future American ships that are exposed to new weapons can strike back with the same and even more efficient weapons as long as American science and industry maintain their world leadership. Like all previous discoveries, nuclear energy that can be employed to destroy ships can also be used to protect them. And the Army Air Corps reports that the air force is planning to employ nuclear energy to power planes.

It will be easier for fleets with high mobility, and the weapons to strike back, to defend themselves from atomic bombs than for cities whose location is fixed and well known. However, citizens of the United States should not be subjected to the exaggerated descriptions of their helplessness that appear in some periodicals. Most of the push-button weapons only exist in the mind of a possible inventor; only a few have reached the laboratory or drawing board. And in fact the only nation that could launch a full-scale atomic bomb attack today is the United States. There is every reason to believe that before any enemy is able to launch a similar attack, means of defense will be greatly increased.

Americans should not be appalled by imaginary invasions of the United States by paratroopers flying over the North Pole. It would be a senseless waste of men and material to attempt such an attack. Nor can any form of winged- or guided-missile attack be launched against continental United States now or in the immediate future. The air route over the north polar regions from New York to London is 3,420 miles; to Paris the distance is somewhat greater; to Moscow 4,620 miles. The distance by air from Yakutsk, Siberia, to Fairbanks, Alaska, is 2,460 miles, from Fairbanks to Seattle 1,540 miles.[1] The extreme range of German V-bombs was 200 miles, and they have not been greatly improved either in range or accuracy. The best information indicates that no nation except the United States has produced an atomic bomb. Under these circumstances there is no immediate threat of an atomic attack upon this country. And only a nation possessing thousands of very long-range transport planes could land on this continent a force of paratroopers that would be formidable. As for the future, both the Army and Navy are aware of the possibilities and as is well known are conducting experiments in countermeasures.

Of course improvements are being made in all weapons by other nations as well as the United States, and as has already been emphasized, it is essential that American science and industry maintain their present lead. This continuous advance in science will be necessary even if the United Nations outlaws the atomic bomb and other new weapons. The use of poison gas was prohibited by most of the nations during the last war and it was not employed. Nevertheless the Chemical Warfare Service was obliged to maintain not only means of defense but also of offense; undoubtedly only the knowledge that Britain and the United States were prepared to use a more effective poison gas deterred Hitler from using it.

1. Distances in statute miles from *The Fortune Atlas*.

Both the Army and Navy are making every possible effort to improve the defenses against air attacks on American cities. Planes from ships and advance bases will intercept as many hostile planes or missiles as possible. Certainly great improvement in methods of interception will come during the next few years. Efficiency of antiaircraft gun laying and fire control is likewise being increased. Fire control centers for the defense of cities as well as fleets will embody the latest designs in electronics, while proximity fuses will guide projectiles toward bomb-carrying planes or flying missiles while they are still far beyond the range of human vision. And as they approach an American city they will fly through an increasing number of barrages of controlled antiaircraft missiles whose fragmentation has been greatly extended. Means of resistance will be strengthened in almost exact proportion to the possible injury. It is already known that shelters provided with sufficient thickness of cement will protect inhabitants of cities from the blast effect of atomic bombs; there need not be the great loss of life that occurred in Nagasaki and Hiroshima. And in all probability the damage to American buildings would not be as extensive as to those of Japan.

During World War I weapons of defense dominated most of the fighting ashore; during World War II weapons of offense did. The trend seen in World War II may be halted or even reversed. Offense and defense are never absolute, and neither is the term "protection." There will never be a perfect defense of the United States against every weapon that future enemies might employ. American forces could never guarantee to intercept every plane or guided missile bearing an atomic bomb to this continent. But if the United States maintains a preponderant navy and air force its citizens can be given the best protection available if the funds are provided and the government is alert to possible perils. And it is inexact to say that there is no defense against the atomic bomb today.

Unquestionably atomic bombs, like submarines and aircraft, add to the difficulties of controlling the sea and using it in time of war. And a nation without a navy but with enough atomic bombs can make the use of the sea very dangerous and can deny adjacent waters to even the most powerful fleet. But certainly the nation with the most powerful fleet and its own supply of atomic bombs will have the advantage. There will probably be times when all the ships in the world will be denied certain sea areas because of bombs, but even in the sailing era, no single nation was ever able to control all the oceans and the connecting seas. The United States, however, thanks to its geographical position, its powers of production, and its proved capacity to fight on the sea, has the best opportunity of retaining and using sea power.

Not until the oceans cease to be the highways of the world will sea power lose its influence. And in addition to its previous value it has the present superlative merit of keeping all possible enemies at a distance from the continental United States and affording its cities, towns, and hamlets the utmost protection possible in the present uneasy world, without maintaining a huge conscript army.

Index

AANDALSNAES, 47
ABDA Command, 123, 129
Adak, 138, 140
Admiralty Islands, 222, 228, 230, 253
Adriatic, 57, 243
AGO Plan, 234–235
Ainsworth, R.A., 205–206
Air Forces, 20–22
Aitape, 231
Akagi, disabled, 148
Albania, 61, 70
Albion, Prof. G., x
Aleutians, 82, 110, 137–138, 146, 153, 181, 207, 209, 212, 215
Alexander, Czar, 74
Alexandria, 55, 57, 60, 72
Algiers, 170–171, 174–176
Amagai, Capt., 147
Amami-o-Shima, 251
Amboina, 127
Amchitka, 207
Amoy, 277
Amphibious operations, 216–221, 247–248
Andaman Islands, 130
Angaur, 247
Antigua, 65
Antwerp, 50, 66, 214
Aobi, Capt., 148, 155
Aoki, Capt., 146
Aparri, 120
Arima, R.A., 271
Arnold, Gen. H. H., 79
Arras, 51
Arzeu, Algeria, 175–176
Aslito Field, 234
Asquith, Prime Minister, 7–8
Attu, 138, 140, 180, 182, 207–212
Atwood, Lt. C. C. (W), x
Auchinleck, Gen. Sir Claude, 72
Ault, Comdr. W. B., 132, 136
Austerlitz, 33
Australasia, 215, 288
Australia, 122, 127, 129, 131, 137, 155, 180, 184
Aviation, 3, 20–21, 27
Avranches, 243

BADGER, R.A., O. C., 278
Bahamas, 65
Bairoko Harbor, 206
Balfour, Prime Minister A., 6
Bali, 128; — Strait, 129
Balikpapan, 106, 123
Balkans, 73–76
Baltic Sea, 48, 73
Barbey, R.A., D. E., 216, 230–231, 253
Bard, Undersecretary Navy R., 78
Bataan, 122, 125–126, 130, 132
Batavia, 129
Batjan, 229
Bawean Island, 128
Beachy Head, 3
Beary, V.A., D. B., 281
Beck, 63
Bengal, Bay of, 112, 130, 156–157
Bergen, 46
Berkey, R.A., R. S., 276
Bermuda, 65
Bessarabia, 31, 59
Biak Island, 229, 231–232
Bikini Atoll, 40, 267, 294–295
Binford, Comdr., 129
Biscay, Bay of, 7, 159–161
Bismarck, Archipelago, 181, 205, 215, 222; by-passed, 230
Bismarck, sinking of, 39–40
Blakey, Maj. G. A., 149
Blandy, Adm. W. H. P., 281, 294
Blida Airfield, 176
Blind Cove, Kiska, 210
Blomberg, von, 63
Borneo, 122, 266, 276
Bougainville, 224–226, 230, 266
Boulogne, 52, 66
Bowen, R.A., H. G., 295
Bradley, Gen. O. N., 243
Brest, 39–40, 66–67, 124, 159, 243
Brett, Lt. Gen., 123
British Guiana, 65; — Isles, 36; — Malaya, 77, 105, 108; — New Guinea, 112
Brown, Gen. A. E., 210–211
——— V.A., W., 131–132
Brunei Bay, 257–258, 265

Buckmaster, Capt., 152
Buckner, Gen. S. B., 281–282
Buin, 197
Buka, 225
Burke, Capt. A. A., 225
Burma, 130, 155; — Road, 24
Byrnes, Hon. J. F., 84 n.

CAIRO, 62
Calais, 52, 66, 242
Callaghan, R.A., M. W., 198
Campbell-Bannerman, Sir H., 6–7
Camranh Bay, 277
Canal Zone, 161
Canning, 9
Canton, 119
Caribbean Sea, 161, 215, 219, 243
Caroline Islands, 222, 227, 229–231, 246, 248
Carpender, V.A., A. S., 184
Carter, Com. W. R., 220, 281
Carthage, 294
Casablanca, 170–175
Castlereagh, 9
Cavite, 106, 116, 119, 144; — Navy Yard, 119
Celebes, 122, 227
Chamberlain, Sir N., 36
Cherbourg, 242
Chesapeake Bay, 171, 215
Chiang Kai-shek, 24–25, 78
Chichagof, Kiska, 210–211
Chichi Jima, 233
China, 77; — Sea, 280
Choiseul Island, 191, 224
Christmas Island, 130
Chuikov, Marshal, 177
Chungking, 24, 130
Churchill, Winston, 25, 33, 42, 50, 52, 55, 59, 61, 69, 74, 77, 123, 125, 168
Clark Field, Luzon, 117
Cochrane, V.A., 296
Colomb, Adm., 4
Colombo, 126, 129–130
Commerce, British, attack and defense of, 33, 64–68
Consett, R.A., 12 n.
Coral Sea, 132, 138, 140–141, 149, 154–155, 180; battle, 134–137
Corap, Gen., 50–51
Coron Bay, 249, 258, 261, 263
Corregidor, 122, 137, 276
Crace, R.A., J. G., 134

Cresswell, Col., 188
Crete, 62, 71–72, 75
Crutchley, R.A., V. A., 186
Culion Islands, 249
Cunningham, Adm. Sir Andrew, 60–70, 171, 176, 212, 243
Curzon, Lord, 31
Cyprus, 71

DAKAR, 56, 92, 177
Dardanelles, 57, 90, 214
Darlan, Adm. J., 54, 176
Davao, 106, 116, 120, 228
Decatur, Stephen, 166
de Gaulle, Gen., 55, 75
De Weerd, H. A., 168 n.
De Witt, Lt. Gen., 210
Deyo, R.A., M. L., 281
Dinagat Island, 253
Disraeli, 6
Dodecanese Islands, 61
Doenitz, Grand Adm., ix, 31–32, 63, 66–70, 73–74, 160, 162–165, 168, 172, 241, 282
Doma Cove, 200, 201
Doolittle, Gen. J. H., 138
Doorman, R.A., 126–128
Dover, 63, 65; — Straits, 76, 124
Du Bose, R.A., 263
Dunkirk, 52–53, 57, 66, 242
Dutch Army; Navy, 49
Dutch (Netherlands) East Indies, 108, 112, 123, 276
Dutch Harbor, 140–142, 146, 150, 156
Dyle River, 50

EASTERN ISLAND, 138–139
Eastern Solomons, battle, 188–191
East Indies, 82–83, 105, 130, 139, 157, 227–228, 244, 266, 280
Edwards, Adm. R. S., 80, 87
Egypt, 59–62, 71–72, 177
Eisenhower, Gen. D. D., 162, 170–171, 176–177, 212, 215, 241–243
El Agheila, 62, 72
El Alamein, 177
Ellice Islands, 131, 229
Empress Augusta Bay, 225, 230; landing, battle, 224
Engaño, Cape, 267; battle, 255–257
English, R.A., R. H., 141, 184
English Channel, 124

INDEX 303

Eniwetok, 92, 207, 220–222, 229–230, 233
Esperance, Cape, 187, 197, 200, 202, 263; battle, 191–192
Espiritu Santo, 197–198, 202

FAIRBANKS, ALASKA, 298
Faroe Islands, 54
Fechteler, R.A., W., 230–232, 276
Fedala, 172, 174
Fife, V.A., James, 184
Fiji Islands, 122, 131, 184–185, 197
Finland, 44; Gulf of —, 43
Finschafen, 222
Firth of Forth, 35
Fitch, V.A., A. W., 132, 134–137
Fleming, Capt., U.S.M.C., 151, 157
Fletcher, V.A., F. J., 81, 132, 134–135, 137, 141–142, 145, 150, 155, 157, 184–185, 189
Florida Island, 185, 201
Flushing, 66
Foch, Ferdinand, 42
Ford Island, 111
Formosa, 19, 113, 117, 120, 244–245, 253, 254, 257–258, 275, 277, 281; air battles, 249–252
Forrestal, Sec'y Navy J. F., ix, 78, 80, 85–87, 89, 93, 163
Fort Grande, 276
Franco, Gen. F., 170, 176
Frederick the Great, 112
Fritsch, von, 63
Fuchida, Capt. M., 228, 283
Fukudome, V.A., S., 82–83, 206, 228, 245, 250–251, 254, 258–259
Funafuti, 229
Furlong, R.A., W. R., 137

GALLIPOLI, 90
Gamelin, Marshall G., 31, 41–42, 49, 51
Gatch, R.A., T. L., 195
Gates, Undersec'y Navy, A. L., 78
Geiger, Lt. Gen. R. S., 283
Gela, 212
Genoa, 57
Gensoul, Adm., 55
German Navy, 8–9, 31, 57, 81
Ghormley, V.A., R. L., 178, 184, 189–190, 193
Gibraltar, 56; Straits of —, 7, 31, 56–57, 60, 168

Giffen, R.A., C. H., 210
Gilbert Islands, 125, 180, 183–184, 207, 221–222, 225–226, 229
Gladstone, W. E., 6
Glassford, V.A., W. A., 106, 116, 119, 123, 129
Gloucester, Cape, 92
Goering, H., 40, 65
Goltz, Lt. Gen. von der, 43
Good Hope, Cape of, 7, 168, 177
Gort, Lord, 42, 52
Goto, R.A., 191–192
Graf Spee, loss of, 37–38
Graziani, Marshal R., 61–62
Greece, 10, 59, 61–62, 68, 70–71, 73, 75, 294
Greenland, 69; — Strait, 39
Grey, Sir Edward, 7–8
Guadalcanal, 142, 159, 180, 183–184, 186, 188–191, 193, 195–196, 203–204, 207, 214–215, 221; battle, Oct. 25–26, 194; — Nov. 12–15, 197–202
Guam, 92, 98, 100, 107–109, 112, 233, 235–238, 246, 271, 278
Guantánamo, 161
Gulf of Mexico, 161

HAGUSHI, 281
Haig, Lord, 42
Hainan Island, 277
Haiti, 91
Halifax, 161
Halmahera Islands, 247
Halsey, Adm. W. F., 79, 81, 89, 125, 158, 178, 193, 196–197, 201–202, 204–207, 215–216, 220, 222, 224, 230, 246, 248–253, 261–263, 278, 285–286
Hamburg, 66
Harmon, Gen. M., 280
Harstad, 47
Hart, Adm. T. C., 106, 116–120, 122–123, 126
Harwood, Com. H., 37
Hashimoto, Comdr., 211
Hatch, Sen. C., 294
Havana, 243
Hawaiian Islands, 116, 122, 156–157, 215–216, 220
Heffernan, Capt. J. B., x
Helfrich, Adm., R.N.N., 126–129
Heligoland Bight, 10

Henderson Field, 185
Hensel, Ass't Sec'y Navy S., 85
Herbert, Adm., 3
Hewitt, Adm. H. K., 81, 89–90, 171, 173, 175–176, 212–213, 215–216, 243
Hickam Airfield, 111
High Commands, Anglo-French, 41–43, 50; Japanese, 25–26, 131; opposing, 77
Hiroshima, 267, 290, 299
Hitler, 22, 24, 30–32, 40–44, 49–51, 54, 56, 59, 63–65, 70, 73–76, 81, 162, 168, 170, 213, 282, 294, 298
Hitokappu Bay, 110
Hokkaido, 286, 288
Holcomb, Gen. T. J., 92
Holland, R.A., 39
Holland, 49, 65, 123
Hollandia, New Guinea, 231–232, 253
Holtz Bay, 210–211
Homma, Gen., 132
Homonhon Island, Leyte Gulf, 253
Hong Kong, 24, 119, 277
Honolulu, 28, 111, 140
Honshu, 285–286, 288
Hoover, Pres. H., 24
Hore-Belisha, 42
Horne, Adm. F. J., ix, 80–81, 87–88
Hosogaya, Adm., 140, 153–154, 207, 209, 211
House, Col., 18
Hull, Sec'y State C., 25, 108
Humboldt Bay, 231
Huon Peninsula, New Guinea, 230

ICELAND, 54, 69, 106, 160
Ilu River, 188
Indispensable Strait, 201
Indo-China, 77, 106, 118
Ingersoll, Adm. R. E., 81, 89
Inland Sea, 109, 130, 140, 235, 239–240, 245, 250, 257, 265, 268, 285
Inoguchi, Capt. R., 271
Inoue, V.A., 132, 134, 186, 190, 192
Iran, 57, 75
Iraq, 57, 75
Ireland, 63
Iseley, Prof. J. A., x
Italy, 162, 171, 215, 243, 288, invaded, 213
Ito, R.A., 283
Iwo Jima, 86, 92, 100, 233, 240, 246, 277–280, 285, 288, 298

JACOBS, V.A., R., 80
Jamaica, 65
Japanese strategic plan, 107–110; attack on Pearl Harbor, 108–112; occupy "southern resources area," 112–130; raid Bay of Bengal, 130
Java, 122–123, 125–127, 129–130; — Sea, campaign, 125–129
Jellicoe, Adm., 10–11
Jodl, Col. Gen. Alfred, 63
Joffre, Field Marshal, 42
Johnson, Adm. A. W., 15
Jolo, 120, 122
Jombard Passage, 134
Jones, John Paul, 166
Jutland, 35; battle, 10

KAKUDA, R.A., 235–236, 238
Kamaishi, 286
Kamikaze Corps, 90, 100, 153, 270–274
Kaneoke Bay Air Station, 111
Karelian Peninsula, 43
Kasserine Pass, 177
Katena Airfield, 281–282
Kato, Adm. Baron, 19
Kattegat, 46
Kavieng, 187
Kawabe, Lt. Gen. T., 272, 274, 287
Kelly, R.A., M., 173
Kerama Retto, 281
Key West, 161
Kijima, Capt., 192
King, Adm. E. J., ix, 78–82, 87–88, 90, 93, 122, 125, 131, 140–141, 154, 157–163, 170, 177–178, 180, 184, 187, 201, 288–289
Kinkaid, Adm. T. C., 81, 134, 141, 189, 193–195, 198, 202, 209–210, 212, 220, 253, 258, 261, 263, 272, 275, 289
Kirk, R.A., A. 90
Kirkuk, 72
Kiska, 138, 140, 180, 182, 207, 209; evacuated, 211; reoccupied, 212
Kitchener, Field Marshal, 9
Kleist, Gen., 51
Knox, Sec'y Navy F., ix, 78, 93
Kobe, 268
Koga, Adm., 83, 183–184, 205, 207, 222, 224–229, 232–233, 244, 251
Koiso, Prime Minister, 244, 286
Koli Point, 196
Komandorski Islands, 212; battle, 209–210

INDEX

Kondo, Adm., 112–130, 138–139, 142, 193
Korea, 115
Korima Bay, Biak Island, 229
Kota Bahru, 118, 119
Kra Peninsula, 117
Kristiansand, 46
Kronstadt, 43
Krueger, Gen. W., 231, 253, 258, 265
Kukum, 188
Kula Gulf, 205
Kunming, 24
Kure Island, 112, 138–139, 268, 286
Kuriles, 110, 207, 212, 251
Kurita, R.A., 139, 150–151, 224–226, 238, 245, 250, 252–255, 257–265, 271–272
Kusaka, Adm., 192, 197, 206
Kwajalein, 216, 226, 233
Kyushu, 158, 251, 285, 288

LAGUNA DE BAY, 106
Lamon Bay, 120
Landrum, Maj. Gen., 211
Lands End, 39
Lashio, 24, 130
Latvia, 43
Leahy, Adm. W. D., 56, 79, 170
Lee, V.A., W. A., 198, 201, 245, 250, 280–281
Lend-Lease Act, 69
Lengo Channel, 198, 202
Lenin, 43
Leningrad, 43, 75
Leopold, King, 51
Les Andalouses, Algeria, 175–176
Leyte, 216, 220, 248–249, 252–255, 262, 265–266, 271–272; — Gulf, 275, 285; battle for, summary, 255–257; details, 257–267
Libya, 57, 60, 62, 72
Licata, 212–213
Liddell Hart, B. H., 42
Lingayen Gulf, 120, 274–276
Lingga, Malaya, 245, 252
Lithuania, 43
Lloyd George, 9, 42
Loch Swilly, 35
Lockwood, V.A., C. A., 184, 233, 236
Lofoten Island, 47
Lorient, France, 163
Louisiade Islands, 134
Louvain, 50
Low countries, invasion, 49–50

Luetjens, Adm., 38–40
Luftwaffe, repulsed, 65–66
Lunga Point, 187; — River, 188; — Ridge, 194
Luxembourg, 51
Luzon, 79, 113, 115–116, 120, 122, 125–126, 244, 248, 254, 257–258, 260, 271–277

MACARTHUR, GEN. D., 89, 106–107, 116, 120, 122, 137, 184, 197–198, 205, 215–216, 220, 222, 229–231, 246–248, 253, 280, 288
McCain, V.A., J. S., 79, 81, 89, 184, 245, 285–286
McClusky, Capt. C. W., 147
McMorris, R.A., 209–210
Madras, 130
Magicienne Bay, 234
Maginot Line, 41, 49–50, 76
Magnetic mines, 36
Mahan, R.A., A. T., vii n., viii, 1–2, 14, 15
Majuro, 226, 233
Makin, 225–226
Malaya, 82–83, 107, 112, 116–118, 124, 130, 139, 157, 159, 227, 280
Malta, 59–60, 70
Manchuria, 25, 268, 285; invaded, 23
Manila, 28, 106, 117–118, 120, 122, 231, 243, 248–249, 253–254, 260, 276; — Bay, 106, 119, 268, 276
Marcus Island, 125, 139, 230
Marianas, 79, 90, 97, 217, 222, 227, 229–230, 232–233, 235, 238, 240, 243–246, 248, 279, 286, 289
Marquesas Islands, 122
Marrakeech, 174
Marseilles, 243
Marshall, Gen. G. C., 79–80, 91, 107, 180, 207
Marshall Islands, 92, 125, 139, 141, 183–184, 216, 220–222, 225–226, 229, 233, 289
Martinique, 22, 92
Massacre Bay, 210–211
Matanikau River, 196
Mediterranean, 57, 59, 60–63, 69–70, 72, 76, 79, 105, 117, 124, 168, 170, 177, 216, 243
Mehdia, 172, 174
Merrill, R.A., A. S., 205, 224–225
Mesopotamia, 10, 90

306 SEA POWER IN WORLD WAR II

Messina, 213
Meuse, 50–51
Mexico, 91
Midway, 82, 108, 110, 112, 122, 130, 137–138, 140–141, 180–181, 184, 188, 193, 207, 280; battle, 142–158
Mikawa, Adm., 186–187
Mindanao, 122, 222, 232, 246, 248, 253, 273
Mindoro, 266, 275
Ministry of Economic Warfare, 11
Mitscher, Adm. M., 79, 81, 89–90, 212, 230–231, 239, 245, 250, 257, 278, 280, 283, 285
Mobile Base Force, 246
Moffett, Adm. W. A., 15
Molotov, 59
Moltke, 220
Montgomery, Gen., 170, 177, 213
Moosbrugger, Comdr. F., 206
Moran, Com. E. J., 242
Mori, Comdr. K., 251
Morison, Capt. S. E., x
Morocco, 170–174, 177
Moratai Island, 247–248, 265
Moscow, 43, 75, 298
Mosul, 72
Motoyama Airfields, 279
Mount Suribachi, 279
Munda, 204–205
Murmansk, 43, 178
Muroran, 286
Murphy, Robert, 170
Murray, Capt. G. D., 141
Muselier, V.A., E. H. D., 55
Mussolini, 44, 57, 61, 68, 70, 73

NAGANO, ADM. O., 82, 97, 157–158, 244, 286
Nagasaki, 281, 290, 299
Nagumo, V.A., 110, 112, 138–140, 142, 155–156, 193, 195
Namsos, 47
Namur, 50, 92, 226
Nansei Islands, 275, 281
Naples, occupied, 213
Napoleon, 1, 9, 33, 74–75
Napoleonic Wars, 73
Narvik, 45–47, 53
Nassau Bay, New Guinea, 131, 205
Navy Dept., organization, 87–104; Marine Corps, 90–92; Coast Guard, 92–93; Personnel, 93–97; Aeronautics,

96–99; Yards and Docks, 97–98; Medicine and Surgery, 98–99; Ordnance, 99–101; Naval Reserves, 101–104
Nelson, D. M., 84, 87
———, Adm. Horatio, 76
New Britain, 112
New Caledonia Islands, 122, 131, 180, 184
Newfoundland, 65, 68
New Georgia Island, 191–192, 204–206, 212
New Guinea, 131, 134, 184, 205, 215, 222, 227–228, 230–231, 233
New Hebrides, 131, 180
New Ireland, 112, 187
New London, 95
Newport, 94
Newton, V.A., J. H., 230, 246
New York, 298
New Zealand, 180, 184–185, 224
Nicaragua, 91
Nichols Field, 117
Nimitz, Adm. C. W., ix, 81–82, 88–90, 98, 122, 125, 131, 137–138, 140–142, 145, 154–155, 158, 178, 215, 220, 222, 229, 236, 246, 248–249, 253, 261, 281, 288–289
Nishimura, V.A., S., 255, 257–263
Noble, R.A., 231–232
Nogi, Field Marshal, 182
Nomura, R.A., 139, 196
Norfolk, 94–95, 161
Normandy, 90, 243, 282, 288; invasion, 241–242
North Africa, 74, 76, 87, 215
North Cape, 57
North Sea, 7, 10
Norway, 35, 40, 46–47, 49, 63, 65, 75, 159
Noumea, 131, 184
Noyes, R.A., L. S., 184

OAHU, 91, 110, 112, 138, 142, 149, 156
Office of Procurement and Material, 85
Ohara, Capt., 146, 148
Okinawa, 86, 90, 92, 98, 100, 153, 239, 246, 249, 281–283, 289
Okochi, V.A., 228
Okuiya, Comdr., 193
Oldendorf, V.A., J. B., 262
Omae, Capt., 197, 200–201, 204, 250, 254, 258, 265

INDEX

Omori, V.A., S., 224
Onishi, V.A., T., 258, 271
Oran, Algeria, 55, 170, 174–175
Orkney Islands, 35
Ormoc Peninsula, 275
Oslo, 46
Otani, Capt. T., 260
Ozawa, V.A., T., 206, 224–226, 235–239, 245, 250–252, 258–260, 262–264

PALAU, 120, 122, 222, 226–228, 232, 235, 247
Palawan Islands, 258, 276, 280
Palembang, 127
Palestine, 10
Pallisier, R.A., R.N., 129
Panama Canal, 28
Paramishiro, 211
Paris, 56, 298
Parker, Capt., R. C., x
Patch, Gen. A. M., 202, 243
Patton, Lt. Gen. G. S., Jr., 171–172, 174–175, 177, 212–213, 243
Patterson, Sec'y War R. P., 86
Paulus, Gen. von, 177
Pearl Harbor, 28, 77, 83, 93–94, 96, 105–112, 116, 122, 137, 139, 155, 157, 160, 184, 193, 220, 246, 285
Peleliu, 92, 100, 247
Penang Island, 118–119, 130, 268
Peronne, 51
Pershing, Gen. J. J., 56
Persian Gulf, 178
Pescadores Islands, 250, 253
Pétain, Marshal, 49, 54, 56, 170
Phillips, Adm. Sir T., 50, 117–119
Philippines, 19, 25, 77, 82–83, 97, 105–108, 112, 115–116, 122–123, 139–140, 157, 159, 184, 222, 227, 229, 233, 245–248, 250–253, 255, 260, 265–266, 269, 273, 276, 286
Philippine Archipelago, 215, 273; —— Sea, 259; battle, 234–240
Pierse, Air Chief Marshal, Sir R., 123
Pitt, W. (Lord Chatham), 243
Pitt, W., 33, 76
Point Cruz, 196
Point Judith, R.I., 168
Poland, 41, 63, 65
Pooten, Lt. Gen. H., 123
Port Arthur, 83, 154, 183
Port Darwin, 122, 127, 144
Port Lyautey, 172–174

Port Moresby, 132, 134, 137, 158, 197
Portsmouth, 64
Portugal, 48
Potomac River, 91
Pound, Adm. Sir Dudley, 50
Prien, Lt. Comdr. G., 35
Prince of Wales and *Repulse* sunk, 117–118
Pruth River, 31
Purnell, R.A., W. R., 106
Pyrenees, 47, 57

QUANTICO, 91
Quonset, 98

RABAUL, 130–131, 134–135, 158, 184, 186–190, 197, 204, 206, 222, 224–227, 230
Raeder, Grand Adm., 32, 67, 117, 162
Rainbow Plan, 105–106, 117
Ramsay, V.A., B., R.N., 53
Rangoon, 24–25, 130
Rawlings, V.A., H. B., R.N., 281–283
Recife, Brazil, 161
Rendova Island, 200
Reynaud, Premier, 49–54
Rhine, 41, 243
Rhone, 243
Ribbentrop, von, 160
Riggs, R.A., R. S., 276
Robinson, Capt. A. G., 126
—— Adm. S. M., 85, 87
Rockwell, R.A., F., 106, 122, 210
Roi, 92, 226
Rome, 243, 294
Rommel, Field Marshal E., 51, 62, 72, 177
Rooks, Capt. A. H., 129
Roosevelt, Pres. F. D., 41, 24, 54, 56, 65, 77–78, 111, 123, 168
Roosevelt, Pres. T., 18
Rosebery, 6–7
Rostov, 75
Rota, 233
Rotterdam, 49
Rozhestvenski, Adm., 183
Rumania, 73–74
Rundstedt, Field Marshal von, 51, 242
Russell Islands, 204
Russia, 70, 72–76

SADOWA, 220
Safi, 172–174
Saigon, 115, 277

St. Cloud, Algeria, 175
St. George, Cape, battle, 225
St. Helena, 9
St. Lucia, 65
St. Matthias, 222, 230
Saipan, 92, 98, 100, 140, 216–217, 220, 227–228, 233–236, 238–240, 243, 260, 271, 277–278
Sakishima Gunto, 283
Salerno, 213
Salisbury, 6
Salonika, 90
Samar, 216, 248, 252, 263, 267, 275; battle off, 255
Samoan Islands, 122, 131, 184
San Bernardino Strait. 236, 255, 257, 259–263, 265
San Diego, 91, 94
Sand Island, 138–139
Santa Cruz, battle, 193–195
Santo Domingo, 91
Sasebo, 268
Savo Island, 192; battle, 186–187
Scapa Flow, 35
Scheer, Adm., 10
Schoolcraft, Lt. R. W., x
Scoglitti, 212
Scott, R.A., N., 191, 198
Seaborne trade, attack and defense of, 33–34
Sea, control of, 9; British-French, 1914, 9; British, threatened by U-boats, 10–11; Allied, decisive factor in World War I, 12
Sea Lark Channel, 185, 188
Sea Power, air power, land power, compared, defined, 14–17; British exercise of, 7, challenged, 7–9, effect of new weapons upon, 4–5, Napoleon's respect for, 9, struggle for, 16–18, triumph of, 76
Seattle, 298
Sebou River, 172–173
Sedan, 51
Sekino, Comdr., 137
Shafroth, R.A., J. F., 286
Shanghai, 24
Sherman, V.A., F. C., 136, 224–225, 260
Shibata, Capt., 115
Shikoku, 288
Shima, V.A., K., 251, 253, 255, 257–259, 262–263

Shortland Island, 197, 205, 224, 230
Shugg, Roger, W., 168 n.
Sibuyan Sea, 255, 257, 259, 265
Sicily, 57, 60, 70, 162, 168, 171, 175, 177, 212–213, 215–216, 243
Sidi Barrani, 61–62
Sidi Ferruch, Algeria, 175
Singapore, 19, 113, 115, 117–119, 124–126, 130, 226, 245, 253, 268, 276
Sinkiang, 25
Skagerrak, 43
Smith, R.A., A. E., 278
—— Gen. Howland, 226, 233–234, 243, 278
—— Col. T., 74
—— R.A., W. W., 141
Soenda Straits, 128
Soerabaja, Java, 116, 119, 122–123, 126–128, 228
Soji, Adm., 151
Solomon Islands, 82, 98, 130, 132, 134, 155, 157–158, 178, 180–183, 191, 196, 204–207, 209, 215–216, 220, 222, 224, 227, 232, 269, 280, 288
Somerville, V.A., Sir James, 55, 60
Somme, 54
Sonokawa, Capt., 115, 118
South China Sea, 106, 115, 277
Spaatz, Gen., 212
Spain, 57
Spanish Morocco, 170
Speer, Armament Minister, 162
Spruance, Adm. R. A., ix, 79, 81, 89–90, 125, 141–142, 145–146, 150–152, 155, 157, 184, 207, 215–216, 220–221, 225–226, 229–230, 233, 235–236, 239, 243, 246, 250, 278, 281, 285
Stalin, 25, 43, 59, 70, 74–75, 78, 243
Stalingrad, 177
Stark, Adm. H. R., 107
Stilwell, Gen. J. W., 130, 283
Stimson, Sec'y War H. L., 24, 78
Strassburg, 41
Struble, R.A., A. D., 276
Subic Bay, 106, 119, 276
Submarines, effectiveness, 2; proposed abolition, 20; American, German, Japanese, compared, 268–270
Sulu Sea, 255, 259, 261, 273
Suluan Island, Leyte Gulf, 253
Sumatra, 127, 130
Surcouf, Algeria, 175
Suribachi, 278

INDEX 309

Surigao Strait, 260–262, 266; battle, 255
Suva, 184
Suzuki, Adm., 287
Swatow, 277
Sweden, 45
Sweeney, Col. W. C., 142, 144–145
Switzerland, 47–48
Syria, 50–57, 62, 76

TAFT, PRES. W. H., 18
Takahashi, V.A., 123, 128, 138–139
Takata, R.A., 155
Talbot, Comdr. P. H., 123
Tanah Meroh Bay, 231
Tanaka, R.A., 189, 202
Tandjoeng Priok, 126, 128
Taranto, 108; battle, 61
Tarawa, 92, 216, 225–226, 247
Tassafaronga, battle, 202–203
Tawi Tawi, Philippines, 229, 236
Tennant, Capt., 53
Thames River, 64
Thursfield, R.A., H. G., ix
Tjilatjap, 126–128
Tinian, 92, 98, 100, 233, 236, 246, 277–278
Tinker, Gen. C. L., 157
Tobruk, 72
Togo, Adm. H., 4, 83, 154, 182–183
Tojo, Gen., 111, 244, 286
Tokuno, Lt. Comdr., 199
Tokyo, 81, 88, 108, 111, 138, 184, 207, 226–227, 250–251, 265, 285–288
Tominaga, Lt. Gen., 254, 273
Toulon, 56, 243
Tourville, Adm., 4
Toyama, Capt., 142
Toyami, Capt., 202
Toyoda, Adm. S., 83, 228–229, 232, 235, 239–240, 244–246, 250–254, 258, 260, 265–266, 267, 271, 283, 286, 287
Trafalgar, 33
Treasury Island, landing, 224
Treaties, Naval Limitations (Washington Conference), 1921–22, 18–19, 23; Russo-German, 73
Trinidad, 65, 161
Trincomalee, 130
Tripoli, 168, 170
Trippe, J., 166
Trondheim, 46
Truk, 206–207, 222, 225–226

Truscott, Gen., 173
Tsukahara, V.A., 113, 115, 117–120, 126
Tsushima Strait, 268, 285
Tulagi, 132, 134, 185–186, 200
Tunis, 170, 176
Tunisia, 168, 170–171, 177
Turkey, 48, 59, 75
Turnbull, Capt. A. D., x
Turner, V.A., R. K., 81, 184, 186, 216, 278, 281
Tyrrhenian Sea, 243

U-BOATS, 10, 64, 81, 90, 159; increase, 32, 162; wolf-pack tactics, 67–69
Ugaki, R.A., 150
Ukraine, 70
Ulithi Atoll, 247–248, 265
United Kingdom, invasion proposed, abandoned, 63–67
U.S. Chiefs of Staff, joint, 79

VANDERGRIFT, GEN. A. A., U.S.M.C., ix, 178, 185, 187–188, 191, 197, 201–202, 216, 224
Van Mook, Gov. Gen., 126, 129
Vela, 205
Vella Lavella, 206
Vichy, 56, 62, 79
Vigan, 120
Visayan Islands, 248–249, 252
Vladivostok, 109, 117

WAINWRIGHT, GEN. J., 120
Wakde Island, 231
Wake Island, 92, 107–109, 112–113, 125, 152, 180, 230
War Production Board, 84
War Trade Agreements, 45–46, 48
Washington, 40, 69, 77, 79, 108, 126, 222
Watanabe, Capt., 138, 140, 150, 153
Wavell, Gen. Sir A. P., 60, 62, 72, 123, 126
Wehrmacht, 51, 59, 63–64, 70–71, 74–75
Weichold, V.A., ix, 32
Weneker, Adm. P. H., 81
Weygand, 49, 51
Wilhelm, Kaiser, 81, 162
Wilhelmina, Queen, 49
Wilkes, Capt., 122

Wilkinson, V.A., T. S., 224, 253
Wilson, Pres. W., 11, 18
—— V.A., R., 80
Woleai Island, 229
Woodlark Islands, 205
Wright, R.A., 202

YAKUTSK, SIBERIA, 298
Yamaguchi, Comdr., 273
Yamaguichi, Capt., 146
Yamamoto, Adm. I., 82–83, 107–109, 112, 117, 122, 125, 130–131, 137–141, 150–151, 157–158, 181–184, 190, 192–193, 196, 204, 206

Yamashita, Gen., 254, 274–275
Yap, 235, 248
Yarnell, Adm. H. E., 15
Yellow Sea, 268
Yokuni, Lt. Comdr., 199
Yonai, 287
Yontan Airfield, 281–282
Yugoslavia, 59, 70–71, 73

ZAMBOANGA, 229
Zeppelins, in first World War, 20
Zhukov, Gen. G. K., 59